Internationalising Higher Education

In order for Higher Education institutions to compete in today's global market, a different approach has to be adopted which values the contribution that increasing numbers of international students make to the learning community. While insular approaches to Higher Education have been commonplace for some time, diversity is now a universal given, and a fresh approach to curriculum design, delivery, assessment and evaluation is required. This authoritative overview brings together current thinking about internationalisation and academic pedagogy in Higher Education, and explores how developing good practice for international students is good practice for all students.

Challenging the notion that the international student is a problem student, this book proposes that the international student lies at the heart of the university as a source of cultural capital and international diversity, enriching the learning experience, enhancing staff experience, and building a more powerful learning community. Using real examples from universities in the UK and elsewhere, *Internationalising Higher Education* provides academic consideration of the key issues of implementation of a cross-cultural strategy. Topics discussed include:

- institutional and organisational perspectives
- ethical dimensions
- visioning and implementing cultural change within an organisation
- quality enhancement issues
- assessment, teaching, learning and student support issues for home and international students
- the process of inducting, welcoming and guidance for students
- enhancing employability
- fostering engagement of students and staff within the wider community.

Illustrated by case studies and vignettes from the US, Europe, Canada,

Australasia and South-East Asia, this practical book considers the key issues for practitioners, staff and educational developers and managers in Higher Education. It is essential reading for anyone wanting to broaden their approaches to learning and teaching in the HE/FE environment, to encompass the fast-growing global imperative.

Elspeth Jones is International Dean at Leeds Metropolitan University. She has extensive experience of learning, assessment and cross-cultural issues working with students and teachers from many nationalities and backgrounds.

Sally Brown is Pro-Vice-Chancellor (Assessment, Learning and Teaching) and Professor of Higher Education Diversity in Teaching and Learning at Leeds Metropolitan University. Her best known books include *Assessing Learners in Higher Education* (with Peter Knight), *Lecturing: A practical guide* (with Phil Race), *Assessing Skills and Practice* (with Ruth Pickford), and *Towards Inclusive Learning in Higher Education* (with Mike Adams).

Internationalising Higher Education

Edited by Elspeth Jones and Sally Brown

Routledge
Taylor & Francis Group

LONDON AND NEW YORK

First published 2007
by Routledge
2 Park Square, Milton Park, Abingdon, Oxon OX14 4RN

Simultaneously published in the USA and Canada
by Routledge
270 Madison Ave, New York, NY 10016

*Routledge is an imprint of the Taylor & Francis Group, an informa
business*

© 2007 selection and editorial matter, Elspeth Jones and Sally Brown;
individual contributions, the contributors

Typeset in Times New Roman by
RefineCatch Limited, Bungay, Suffolk
Printed and bound in Great Britain by
TJ International Ltd, Padstow, Cornwall

British Library Cataloguing in Publication Data
A catalogue record for this book is available from the British Library

Library of Congress Cataloging-in-Publication Data
Internationalizing higher education : enhancing teaching, learning and
    curriculum / edited by Sally Brown and Elspeth Jones.
    p. cm.
    Includes bibliographical references and index.
    1. International education. 2. Education and globalization.
3. Universities and colleges – Curricula. 4. Educational tests and
measurements. I. Brown, Sally, 1950 Feb. 1– II. Jones, Elspeth, 1956–
    LC1090.I5797 2007
    378′.016–dc22
    2006102521

ISBN10: 0–415–41989–1 (hbk)
ISBN10: 0–415–41990–5 (pbk)
ISBN10: 0–203–94596–4 (ebk)

ISBN13: 978–0–415–41989–5 (hbk)
ISBN13: 978–0–415–41990–1 (pbk)
ISBN13: 978–0–203–94596–4 (ebk)

We would like to dedicate this book to Steve and Joel Smith and Phil Race for their support, patience and cross-cultural capability. We also wish to thank Deb Chapman for tireless and meticulous editorial support and all those who continue to promote internationalisation at Leeds Met.

Contents

Figures and tables

Figures

Tables

Notes on contributors

Jo Appleton is a Senior Lecturer in ELT at Leeds Metropolitan University. She is the Course Leader for the International Foundation Studies Programme and International Teacher Fellow. She has many years' experience as an ELT teacher in different countries but more recently she has been involved in teaching on the MA in Materials Development and in materials writing projects for China, Singapore, Ethiopia and Estonia. As a Leeds Met International Teaching Fellow she is working to raise the profile of internationalisation in the University, including embedding global perspectives across the curriculum and consolidating international exchange partnerships.

Tim Birtwistle is the Head of Leeds Law School and also Professor of the Law and Policy of Higher Education and Jean Monnet Chair in European Legal Studies at Leeds Metropolitan University. Tim is a former President of the European Association of Higher Education; he is currently a UK Bologna Promoter and ECTS/DS Counsellor; he was formerly a Socrates Promoter. He sits on the UK Socrates and Erasmus Council. He is on the International Advisory Board for Stetson College of Law (the US Higher Education Law and Policy Conference) and an invited participant at the European Network of Higher Education Ombudsmen. He is a visiting professor at Normandie Business School, the Hochschule Bremen and VLECKO Brussels.

Julie Brett has undertaken various academic library roles since graduating from the University of Wales, including at the School Curriculum Development Council and King's College London. In 1993 she joined the library service at Leeds Metropolitan University, two years later becoming manager of the Euro Info Centre and European Documentation Centre. She is now responsible for the library European and off-campus services team. She additonally works as Senior Learning Adviser for the Leslie Silver International Faculty, with responsibility for communicating and supporting academic colleagues at faculty level. She also has oversight of the internationalisation strategy for the library, working to ensure that the service continues to develop and improve the University's performance.

Sally Brown is Pro-Vice-Chancellor with responsibility for Assessment, Learning and Teaching and Professor of Higher Education Diversity in Teaching and Learning at Leeds Metropolitan University. She is widely published: her best-known books include *Assessing Learners in HE* (with Peter Knight) (1994), *Strategies for Diversifying Assessment* (with Graham Gibbs and Chris Rust) (1994), *Assessment Matters in HE* (edited with Angela Glasner) (1999). More recently she has written, *inter alia, Lecturing: A Practical Guide* (with Phil Race) (Routledge, 2002) and *Assessing Skills and Practice* (with Ruth Pickford) (Routledge, 2006) and has edited (with Mike Adams) *Towards Inclusive Learning in Higher Education* (Routledge, 2006).

Jude Carroll is Deputy Director of ASKe, a Centre for Excellence in Learning and Teaching based at Oxford Brookes University, UK. ASKe, founded in 2005, is designed to enhance students' understanding of assessment and assessment standards. In addition, she works as an educational developer within Oxford Brookes as well as nationally and internationally. Her professional interests include deterring student plagiarism and enhancing academics' teaching skills. She is the author of *A Handbook for Deterring Plagiarism in Higher Education* (2002) and, with Dr Janette Ryan, *Teaching International Students: Improving Learning for All* (2005).

Glauco De Vita is a Reader in International Business Economics and a University Teacher Fellow at Oxford Brookes University Business School. His research interests also include the internationalisation of business education and culturally inclusive pedagogies. He has published widely in these areas in journals such as *Studies in Higher Education, Journal of Further and Higher Education, Assessment and Evaluation in Higher Education, Teaching in Higher Education, Active Learning in Higher Education*, the *International Journal of Management Education* and *Innovations in Education and Teaching International*. He has taught international students and run teaching and learning development workshops at universities and colleges in several countries, including the UK, Italy, Turkey, India, Malaysia and Hong Kong.

Vicky Harris is currently Associate Dean, International Partnerships at Leeds Metropolitan University. Previously, as Head of the School of Tourism, Hospitality and Events, she was closely involved in developing the School's international profile through student recruitment, curriculum consultancy and partnership development primarily in South-East Asia. For a number of years she has been closely involved in various quality enhancement initiatives within the University and in working on various projects with the Quality Assurance Agency such as Chair of the Benchmarking Group, the Graduate Standards project and as a Subject Reviewer.

Stuart Hirst has extensive international educational experience. In 1986/7, he lived and worked in South-East Asia developing the infrastructure of, and teaching at, the Institut Technologi Brunei. In 1994 he was appointed Information Technology Theme Leader to a six-year project to upgrade regional engineering colleges in India. He is currently involved in the REPLIKA project exploring the role and usefulness of a repository of learning objects used in a cross-cultural learning environment (Spain, Denmark and the Czech Republic).

Elspeth Jones is Dean of the Leslie Silver International Faculty at Leeds Metropolitan University. The Faculty delivers a range of academic programmes and is responsible for leading the University's ambitious internationalisation plans including all aspects of the international student experience, from recruitment to alumni relations. With a background in Applied Linguistics and teaching English as a foreign language, she has wide experience of learning, assessment and cross-cultural issues for students from many nationalities and backgrounds. Her output includes *Setting the Agenda for Languages in Higher Education* (edited with David Head, Mike Kelly and Teresa Tinsley) (CILT, 2003) and a range of conference papers on values-driven internationalisation.

Gordon Joughin is a Senior Lecturer in the Centre for Educational Development and Interactive Resources at the University of Wollongong, Australia. Prior to this appointment he was Senior Education Development Officer at the Hong Kong Institute of Education and an Affiliated Assistant Professor in the Department of Curriculum and Instruction at the Institute. His research and publications have focused on students' experience of assessment, with a particular emphasis on oral assessment, and the factors involved in developing assessment practices which are congruent with both judging students' performance and promoting their learning. Recent work has focused on Chinese students' experience of assessment and the use of innovative forms of assessment that support learning in Hong Kong universities. He is a co-author of *How Assessment Supports Learning: Learning-oriented Assessment in Action* (Hong Kong University Press, 2006).

Maria Kelo is Senior Officer at the Academic Cooperation Association (ACA). In this role, which she has held since 2003, she is responsible for the acquisition, development and implementation of ACA projects, the planning of ACA conferences and seminars, ACA's public relations and information activities. Recently she was in charge of an extensive study on support for international students in Higher Education, and is the author of the related publication. Maria Kelo is the co-author of *Brain Drain and*

Brain Gain: Migration in the European Union after Enlargement (Kelo and Wächter, 2004) and *The Admission of International Students into Higher Education* (Muche, Kelo and Wächter, 2004), and the co-editor of *EURODATA: Student Mobility in European Higher Education* (ed. Kelo, Teichler and Wächter, 2006).

David Killick spent several years as an itinerant English language teacher in Greece, Morocco and Japan, before returning to the UK to undertake English language teaching and then teacher training. A short posting with the British Council in China was followed by four years as Director of Studies at a well-established English language school in Brighton. Since returning to the UK to take up part-time lecturing in 1991, Leeds Met has provided him with a wide variety of opportunities, from developing the ELT provision from scratch and leading on the development of a research strategy for the School of Languages, to the role he currently enjoys of helping facilitate the implementation of the University's internationalisation strategy in relation to the curriculum and the student experience.

Betty Leask has a national and international research profile in the area of internationalisation of the curriculum, an area in which she regularly researches, publishes and consults. She has a broad range of experience in international education in the areas of teaching, curriculum development, professional development and student services in Higher Education. Her current role as the Dean of Teaching and Learning in the Division of Business at the University of South Australia (UniSA) involves working with academic staff to improve teaching and learning outcomes for all students in all modes of delivery. Details of her publications and further details of her research interests are available from her home page, http://people.unisa.edu.au/betty.leask.

Simon Lee became the Vice-Chancellor of Leeds Metropolitan University on 1 September 2003. He studied as a Brackenbury Scholar at Balliol College, Oxford and then a Harkness Fellow at Yale Law School before becoming a Lecturer in Law at Trinity College, Oxford and then King's College London. He was appointed Professor of Jurisprudence at Queen's University Belfast in January 1989 where he also served as Dean of the Faculty of Law. His work in Northern Ireland was recognised by his appointment as an Emeritus Professor of Queen's when he left in September 1995 to take up the role of Rector and Chief Executive at Liverpool Hope University College. An account of his eight years at Hope has been published by Liverpool University Press: *The Foundation of Hope*, edited by R. J. Elford. Professor Lee has served on a number of government and voluntary sector bodies, such as the Standing Advisory Commission on Human Rights in Northern Ireland, and chaired others, such as the Independent

Monitoring Board for the Liverpool education authority and the board of the Everyman and Playhouse theatres. He is currently on the board of the *Tablet*, the international Catholic weekly paper. He is the author of several books, from *Law and Morals* (Oxford University Press, 1986) through to *Uneasy Ethics* (Pimlico, Random House, 2003).

Dawn Leggott spent one year as an English language teacher in Germany and ten years in Spain, before returning to the UK to specialise in teaching Academic English to international students. She is currently the Course Leader of the International PreMasters programme and the in-sessional Academic English course at Leeds Metropolitan University, in addition to being Spanish Placements Tutor. She is a Principal Lecturer and International Teacher Fellow, and her recent five-year longitudinal research study into student perceptions of their independent learning and employability skills development on an undergraduate languages and business degree programme demonstrated the extent to which a period of residence abroad helps students to develop vital employability skills and attributes and the importance of making them aware of their development of such skills.

Zoe McClelland graduated from Leeds Metropolitan University in 1996 with a BA (Hons) in Hospitality Business Management and then spent four years working in prestigious hotels at managerial level. She continued her personal and professional development by embarking on an MA in Business at Leeds Business School, moving into academia in 2000 as a Senior Lecturer and Course Leader in Hospitality within the International Faculty of Leeds Metropolitan University. Her responsibilities now include student admissions, induction, teaching on a range of modules and course development and management. She is a member of both the Faculty and the Academic Committee and a mentor within a local school on a volunteering programme.

Dorron Otter is currently the Head of the School of Applied Global Ethics at Leeds Metropolitan University. Born in Birkenhead but with parents having emigrated from India, his early experiences were locally rooted but always in the context of world-wide issues of development and equity. Having studied Politics, Philosophy and Economics at Oxford, Dorron spent a number of years in occupations as diverse as youth and community work in Merseyside, and working in a multi-national financial organisation. Dorron worked for five years as an Economics teacher at Queen Mary's College in Basingstoke. He then wanted to further his interest in global development issues and undertook part-time postgraduate training in International Development at the University of Leeds. Whilst pursuing this, his full-time job was as the first British Petroleum Teacher Fellow responsible for developing Economic Awareness across the curriculum at the University of Durham. In 1990 he came to Leeds Business School, working in the Economics department. He has developed a number of economics courses which explore different economic perspectives but his main interests lie in the area of the political economy of international development.

Elizabeth Phizackerley-Sugden graduated from Leeds Metropolitan University with a BA (Hons) in Business Management. She spent the year from July 2003, which overlapped with the end of her degree, as a sabbatical officer for the Student Union before her current role as Student Liaison Officer. She has represented students at the highest level within the University so has a good understanding of how everything works and how it can affect students. She now works within the University structure supporting students during their studies at Leeds Met.

Simon Robinson is Professor of Applied and Professional Ethics, Leeds Metropolitan University, Associate Director, Ethics Centre of Excellence, and Visiting Fellow in Theology, University of Leeds. He was educated at Oxford and Edinburgh Universities and then entered psychiatric social work before being ordained into the Church of England priesthood in 1978. After spells in the Durham diocese, he entered university chaplaincy at Heriot-Watt University, and the University of Leeds, developing research and teaching in areas of applied ethics and practical theology. In 2004 he joined Leeds Metropolitan University. His ongoing research interests include: religious ethics and care; professional ethics; ethics in Higher Education; spirituality and professional practice; corporate social responsibility; and ethics in a global perspective. His books include: *The Social Responsibility of Business; Ethics in Engineering; Agape, Moral Meaning and Pastoral Counselling; Case Histories in Business Ethics* (ed. with Chris Megone); *Living Wills; Spirituality and Healthcare* (with Kevin Kendrick and Alan Brown); *Ministry amongst Students; Values in Higher Education* (ed. with Clement Katulushi); *Ethics and Employability; The Teaching and Practice of Professional Ethics* (ed. with John Strain). Forthcoming books are on *Spirituality and Sport, Engineering, Business and Professional Ethics*, and *Ethics, Spirituality and Care*.

Jane Stapleford Jane Stapleford is currently Head of the Employability Office and a Teacher Fellow at Leeds Metropolitan University, leading the strategic and operational developments for both graduate employability and personal development planning (PDP) across the University. Jane contributes to national and international conferences on employability, work-related learning and PDP, has created online resources for employability and personal development, and delivers extensive staff development programmes. She has contributed to the Higher Education Academy publication on 'Employability and PDP' and, as a member of the AGCAS Careers Education Benchmarking Steering Group, made a significant contribution to the Careers Education Benchmark Statement. A Chartered Occupational Psychologist with a strong commitment to valuing diversity, Jane has spent many years teaching psychology in FE and HE.

Chapter 1

Introduction

Values, valuing and value in an internationalised Higher Education context

Sally Brown and Elspeth Jones

While the recruitment of international students is nothing new, universities world-wide are increasingly recognising the importance of valuing populations of students who take up Higher Education opportunities outside their home nations. Whereas in the past this has frequently been seen as problematic, as Higher Education institutions (HEIs) get used to competing in a global HE market, a different approach has to be adopted that values the contribution international students make to the learning community as much as being concerned with dealing with the complexities that arise from having a diverse student population. In this volume we bring together the experiences of authors who work with international students in a wide variety of contexts and we draw conclusions about what constitutes best practice.

For many years a neo-colonialist attitude in British Higher Education led to the assumption that an Anglo-centric curriculum and UK-originated teaching approaches were optimum in mainstream Higher Education. This is not just a British issue: other nations experience the same kinds of insular approaches. The time is now ripe for universities and colleges internationally to review how they frame HE curricula and practices. Nowadays, HE in many countries is provided for students who come from an enormous range of cultural backgrounds, not just students who come to study at national universities from abroad, but also students from a diverse range of cultural backgrounds within each nation. Recruitment from outside the home nation is commonplace in many countries, and competition for students is global. Fundamental to the theme of this book is the notion that good practice for internationalisation is good practice for all students.

At the same time, approaches to HE curriculum design, delivery, assessment and evaluation are changing rapidly to take note of new technologies and different perspectives. In a world where global perspectives must be considered in all kinds of contexts, Higher Education can no longer be immune from change and, instead, should be leading it. It is no longer sufficient (if it ever indeed was) for teachers and supporters of learning in Higher Education to assume that the student body can be treated as a homogeneous group, since diversity is now a universal given. Yoni Ryan (2004) suggests that: 'As academics have sought to handle larger numbers of international students, especially from Asia, the presumption that learning styles and cognitive approaches in higher education were homogenous and universal has been severely challenged.'

This book takes a positive and proactive approach to internationalising Higher Education, positing a range of questions about how best to bring in global perspectives to the learning environment and review our means of provision. This is particularly necessary now that widespread e-learning outreach means that students are likely to be studying at a distance in very different learning environments from those in which learning materials are developed and delivered.

To date, recruitment of international students has been seen by many primarily as a source of income generation, a 'cash cow', and often diverse students, once recruited, were problematised by the academy and seen as needy of support in a kind of deficit model. Our approach conversely situates the international student at the heart of the university as a source of cultural capital and intentional diversity, enriching the learning experience both for home students and for one other, expanding staff horizons, building a more powerful learning community and thus deepening the HE experience as a whole.

We provide in this volume a range of responses from a wide variety of authors who address and attempt to resolve some of the dilemmas posed within a rapidly changing environment and argue for an institution-wide approach, strategically implemented, that embodies the values of the institution concerned. This means in practice going well beyond simply changing the content of what we teach to include international perspectives: to a considerable extent this must involve a radical rethinking of all aspects of a university's work. Our book has been arranged in four parts – 'Perspectives on policy and institutional cultures', 'Perspectives on assessment, learning, teaching and student support', 'Perspectives on curriculum enhancement' and 'European perspectives' – before concluding with some thoughts on contextualising international Higher Education.

In Chapter 2, the opening chapter of Part I on 'Perspectives on policy and institutional cultures', Simon Robinson and Simon Lee set the context for the work as a whole by addressing the subject of 'Uneasy global ethics and the university' in a wide-ranging chapter, reflecting on the ethical complexities of a modern university. Many courses and programmes will include discussions of internationally orientated and other ethical dilemmas within their curricula, but this is only part of the story. The authors also explore what an ethically serious university can look like, and how a values-driven approach can underpin the working life of the university as a whole.

The next chapter, Chapter 3, by co-editor Elspeth Jones, shows how this holistic approach can be followed through within an institution. Leeds

Metropolitan University undertook a number of initiatives to support its values-driven approach to internationalisation. These included establishing an International Faculty with responsibility not only for a range of courses and subjects but also for fostering internationalisation across the University. Part of this role is to help deliver the University's international aim in its Corporate Plan, which seeks to ensure that 'an international ethos pervades the University'. A section of the website, established in September 2003 and updated daily, includes reflections, written by staff, students and friends of the University, on international issues. This has had an impact across the whole University, in terms of changing staff and student perspectives and reflecting a fully internationalised community. This chapter considers the particular experience of one HEI and provides evidence of a range of actions that can be implemented in other contexts.

In the final chapter in this part, Chapter 4, 'Globalisation and sustainability: global perspectives and education for sustainable development in Higher Education', Dorron Otter investigates the external factors helping to shape the debate about the role of global perspectives and educational sustainable development in terms of their impact within Higher Education in the UK and explores the relationship between global perspectives and education for sustainable development. He also uses the most recent research to suggest ways in which practitioners might want to implement global perspectives and education for sustainable development in the institutional and curriculum context of Higher Education. He concludes with an optimistic view of the future for education for sustainable development and global perspectives and a challenge to the HE sector to move forward ambitiously.

Part II on 'Perspectives on assessment, learning, teaching and student support' commences with a chapter on assessment, Chapter 5, since this is at the heart of the student learning experience. In 'Assessment and international students: helping clarify puzzling processes', co-authors Sally Brown and Gordon Joughin strive to unpack some of the complexities that both home and international students encounter when being assessed in unfamiliar contexts. Academics, administrators and students all tend to assume that assessment systems, methods and approaches are pretty much universal, whereas in actuality there are significant variations from nation to nation, which can cause substantial problems where students do not understand the local rules of the game and staff make assumptions about student ability and achievement potential based on a variety of misconceptions which are culturally located. As Janette Ryan argues:

> Issues to do with assessment in relation to international students can be complex and frustrating for both sides. Students often feel disadvantaged by the methods used and by their lack of background knowledge, implicitly assumed by lecturers to be in place. Teachers are concerned about maintaining standards and about practical implications, such as the

amount of energy involved in doing things differently for international students.

(Ryan, 2000)

For this reason we argue that a fuller understanding of international assessment systems will have substantial benefits for all concerned.

In Chapter 6 on 'Support and guidance for learning from an international perspective', Jude Carroll and Jo Appleton review students' needs for support and guidance and suggest a variety of approaches to helping students decode and make sense of new academic cultures. They offer a range of alternative tactics, including pre-arrival, post-admissions and ongoing support and guidance, as well as pragmatic advice on enabling students to understand the rules of the new game throughout the life cycle of a learning programme.

There are many facets to internationalisation of Higher Education, including the knowledge, skills and approach of teaching staff and how they use their skills and knowledge to support student learning. It has been common to focus on the characteristics of international students and how institutions can assist them to adapt to the teaching and learning environments they encounter so that they get the most they can out of their experience. In Chapter 7 on 'International teachers and international learning', Betty Leask focuses on international teachers and the characteristics they need to facilitate international learning in international and intercultural settings. She uses as a basis her international qualitative research looking both at how teachers themselves see their roles and at some of the expectations students have of their teachers. She also provides some really useful tasks related to her findings for teachers to try out to ensure that their own practice is international in its approach.

A university or college does not only need excellent strategies and policies; it also needs to assure itself that these are implemented on the ground. Chapter 8, 'Using a quality enhancement audit approach to review provision for international students: a case study', by Harris *et al.*, builds on the work of a team of colleagues who undertook an internal quality enhancement audit of the international student experience at Leeds Metropolitan University in 2006. The methodology, developed by Holmes and Brown in 1998–9, involves asking an internal review team to scrutinise closely published papers and e-documentation and then to talk to staff, students and others about how far principles are evident in practice. The chapter presents the findings from this review and concludes with some recommendations that have wide applicability to HEIs of all kinds.

Part III on 'Perspectives on curriculum enhancement' opens with a chapter by Elspeth Jones and David Killick, Chapter 9, entitled 'Internationalisation of the curriculum', examining a wide-ranging, whole-university approach to transforming the curriculum to provide a truly internationalised approach. The authors argue that tinkering with the taught content is insufficient: what is required is a substantial re-engineering of the curriculum which impacts on the work of every member of staff in the organisation. To support this approach, a cross-cultural capability guidelines document has been produced, which is referred to extensively in this chapter and forms the final appendix of this book. The originators make no claim that this can be universally applied nor that it solves all problems in relation to internationalisation, but offer it here as an instrument that can be customised and adapted to suit other contexts, building as it does on extensive groundwork in a university highly committed to a holistic approach, as exemplified in the approach of Chapter 2 in this volume.

Next in Chapter 10, entitled 'Internationalisation and employability', Dawn Leggott and Jane Stapleford consider how best we can enable students to develop the range of skills they need to enhance their employability on graduation. The term 'employability' is itself contested, and the authors provide some useful pointers here, before outlining the outcomes of a five-year research study of students' perceptions of their employability skills, which can vary substantially depending on their originating contexts.

The following chapter, Chapter 11, 'Internationalisation and engagement with the wider community', by David Killick, reviews the interactions between international students and the communities in which they study. Using a variety of case studies of international practice in community engagement, the author argues that, when purposefully established, such engagement has benefits both for the local community and for the students concerned, especially where there is institution-wide commitment to the internationalisation agenda. He concludes by arguing that strong links between a university and its community that are informed by sound experience and make use of the expertise of staff, students and local stakeholders can significantly impact on both student learning and the life of the community in which the work is located.

Much has been written in recent years on the topic of internationalising Higher Education, but this literature has rarely been brought together in a systematic and helpful way. In Chapter 12, 'Taking stock: an appraisal of the literature on internationalising HE learning', Glauco de Vita provides readers with an overview of relevant work organised in three key thematic groupings: the learning experience of international students; culturally inclusive teaching and assessment practices; and different conceptualisations of curriculum internationalisation. This provides a sound intellectual basis for this book and for subsequent productive work in the field. His approach challenges much conventional wisdom in the field of internationalisation and indeed offers a welcome diverse and contrasting perspective to that found in other chapters in this volume.

In Part IV, we concentrate on European perspectives to internationalising Higher Education. First, in Chapter 13, 'Approaches to services for international students', Maria Kelo takes a European perspective on exploring some of the principles that underpin approaches by Higher Education institutions to providing support to international students. Her work is based on a large-scale study on support for international students in Higher Education undertaken by the Academic Cooperation Association (ACA) between October 2005 and October 2006, looking at good practice in international student support in Australia, Canada, Hungary, the Netherlands, Switzerland, the United Kingdom and to a lesser extent France. This useful review provides those of us working in the field with a valuable synthesis of international approaches.

Next, in Chapter 14, 'European and European Union dimensions to mobility', Tim Birtwistle guides readers through the complex world of European legislation and policy in relation to Higher Education. Following the signing of the Bologna Declaration in June 1999, universities across Europe (for it is a pan-European project) have needed to address a number of relevant internationalisation issues to ensure, for example, transferability of qualifications and mobility for staff and students. Former EU developments such as the Socrates and Erasmus programmes were set up to foster student mobility and de facto create an international learning community, as well as to foster European rather than merely national citizenship. There is a substantial imbalance in take-up of the mobility opportunities. with far fewer UK students taking up the opportunity to study abroad than European students wishing to study in the UK. This has meant that alternative strategies have needed to be adopted to provide virtual mobility for the static majority, giving home students a taste of Europeanisation while studying within Britain. Additionally, there was a commitment by government for all HE students to be provided with the Diploma Supplement on top of their national awards by 2006. Following an outline of the key issues, guidance is provided on what HEIs in Europe need to do in order to address these requirements.

Our final chapter, 'Contextualising international Higher Education', by the editors, draws together twenty key factors in internationalising Higher Education illustrated in this volume that are features of institutions that take international diversity seriously and that adopt a strategic approach to the implementation of cross-cultural approaches.

We conclude in the Appendix with an illustrative example of what such a strategic approach might look like, taken from the editors' own institution, Leeds Metropolitan University, in the form of a cross-cultural capability guidelines document. In the Higher Education community in the global age, sharing of good practice is a necessity, not an option, so we welcome comments and suggestions from readers, both on our own approach and on the ideas expressed within this volume as a whole.

Part I

Perspectives on policy and institutional cultures

Chapter 2

Global ethics on the ascent

Simon Robinson and Simon Lee

Introduction

This chapter, by a Professor of Applied and Professional Ethics and the Vice-Chancellor of Leeds Metropolitan University, sets out an approach to global ethics that permeates the life of our University. It is not our contention that Leeds Met is unique in seeking world-wide horizons or in the study of ethics or in the practice of partnerships. We do, however, think that there might be some wider interest and significance in Leeds Met's thorough-going commitment to the refreshing perspectives that come from the creative combining of these three elements of partnerships, world-wide horizons and ethics.

This might seem surprising to those who, for instance, might have described our part of the university sector as 'secular' or who interpret 'regional' or 'community-based' to mean 'parochial' but we regard Leeds Met as being a university which embraces students of many faiths alongside those of no particular religious belief and which reaches out to serve local communities without stereotyping and ghettoising neighbours. We try to be a bridge between diverse individuals and communities. Leeds Met intends to become the equivalent on this side of the Atlantic of a great American state university system, linking local opportunities for foundation degrees in partner colleges with opportunities for progression to honours degrees and masters at our own campuses. We are going beyond some American precedents by placing a greater emphasis on doing this in a global context. We have students in Hong Kong, Africa and even Antarctica. Far from isolating students in their localities, our university has the potential to bring diaspora communities together with students from the countries of their family origins.

The vision set out by Leeds Met governors is to strive to become 'a world-class regional university, with world-wide horizons, using all our talents to the full'. Inaugural lectures and publications by Leeds Met staff indicate that there is a running stream of ethical thought and action flowing through this commitment to world-wide horizons.

The University's educational, cultural and sporting partnerships reflect the same attitude, and student volunteering is increasingly happening abroad.

Research, including our own into such matters as 'uneasy ethics', is of course committed to global ethical concerns. War and peace are now very much on the curriculum as well as being explored in books such as *Cyberwar, Netwar and the Revolution in Military Affairs*, edited by four of our colleagues, Edward Halpin, Philippa Trevorrow, David Webb and Steve Wright (2006). We have attracted researchers and teachers of the highest quality in such international spheres as responsible and sustainable tourism, with a focus on ethics and the impact of cultural change.

Students from all backgrounds seem increasingly to share some moral intuitions, even if their application of broad concepts to particular contexts will show that their specific conceptions of virtues and values vary. In particular, the student body has an engaging concern with the sustainability of our world environment and with helping the most marginalised human beings in this world. One of our inaugural lectures (Lee, 2003) quoted Onora O'Neill reflecting on this concern for people, but the spirit of this approach applies also to students' concerns for the environment:

> Over the last fifty years boundaries have become more porous. It has happened gradually, selectively and in faltering ways, and has transformed both political and economic life for countless people. For example, most boundaries in Europe stand where they stood at the end of the Second World War, but are unimaginably more porous. Boundaries that were once impervious to capital flows and trade, to cultural and technical influence and above all to movements of people have become highly, if variably, porous. In Western Europe the changes happened incrementally over many years; in Eastern Europe everything stalled for decades but changed rapidly and dramatically after 1990. The changes in boundaries that count for most today are evidently not spatial but qualitative. One consideration that should guide us in making or working towards such qualitative transformations is a recognition of the reality that we constantly act in ways that commit us to seeing those on the far sides of existing boundaries, distant strangers though they be, as having moral standing for us. If we do so, then we shall also have reason to treat distant strangers justly, whether by making the boundaries which exclude them more porous in specific ways or by compensating them for any harms caused by otherwise unjustifiable exclusions.
>
> (O'Neill, 2002)

Given this stance and our emphasis on the inclusion of faith perspectives in our understanding of the university, it might seem natural to adopt Hans Kung's advocacy of a global ethic (Kung, 1991). This is indeed attractive to many students and staff facing difficult ethical decisions involving world-wide horizons.

A background to our global ethics teaching approach

Hans Kung argues strongly for an agreed view of ethics which applies across the world: 'There will be no survival of our globe without a world ethic. No peace among the nations without peace among the religions. No peace among the religions without dialogue and cooperation among the religions and civilizations' (1991: xv).

Globalisation raises so many issues of injustice, from financial and labour markets to ecology and organised crime, that such a global ethics is necessary if the global order is to be managed. Many of these issues rightly are matters of discussion within our curriculum, from Business and Law (see the case study at the end of this chapter) through Health Promotion to Architecture and Environmental Management. As we have seen in recent years of international terrorism, a great deal of the strife in this context comes from the interrelation of different religious groups with politics. Hence, argues Kung, there is a need to develop peace between religions. Such a peace would demand wide-ranging dialogue between religions, cultures and civilisations. The West tends to assume that society is secular and religions are in the minority. Globally it is quite the opposite, with a majority of the world's population being committed to a religious faith.

Leeds Met is a learning community with high participation by students from ethnic minority communities in which the backgrounds of our staff and students include all major world religions and indeed those professing no religious faith. It behoves us therefore to think and talk regularly, individually and collectively, about our roles in the wider community and ethical issues associated with our daily practice.

Kung argues that a global ethic is not a uniform system of ethics but rather 'a necessary minimum of shared ethical values' to which different regions, cultural groups, religions, nations and other interest groups can commit themselves. This involves a continuous process of dialogue which uncovers the shared values already implicit in major ethical principles. The Old Testament commandment 'Thou shalt not kill', for instance, becomes, in positive terms, 'Have respect for life', calling for the safety of all minorities, social and political justice, a culture of non-violence, respect for the environment and universal disarmament. The commandment 'Thou shalt not steal' becomes 'Deal honestly and fairly', standing out against poverty and the cyclical violence which occurs in a society of wealth extremes. Just economic institutions need to be created and sanctioned at the highest levels, suggests Kung, and limitless consumption curbed in the developed countries while the market economy is made socially and ecologically conscious.

Principles and responsibilities that arise from this approach can be affirmed by all persons with ethical convictions, whether religiously grounded or not, who oppose all forms of inhumanity. Such an ethic is aspirational rather than prescriptive, forming the basis of the Declaration of Human Responsibilities (Kung and Schmidt, 1998) as a complement to the UN Declaration of Human Rights. The Human Rights Declaration, itself, can be seen to embody a universal ethic. It is made up of broad rights which are both negative, protecting certain 'goods', such as the right to life, liberty and property, and positive, seeking to enable certain goods, such as care for children and the provision of free education.

Furthermore, while Article 18 suggests a right to change religion, in some countries religion is tightly bound into national identity and there can be religious, cultural and even legal constraints against such change. Equally, rights surrounding freedom of speech or asylum-seekers (some of whom are current or aspiring Leeds Met students) are subject to major questions in practice. What are the limits to freedom of speech on campus as well as in the wider world and how is it possible to deal equitably with all who claim asylum?

General moral principles then seem unexceptionable but when faced by the particular context come up against the difficulty of how to embody such principles in practice. Underlying that difficulty is the phenomenon of moral pluralism, the vast array of different moral beliefs apparent in the world. Even within a single nation in many parts of the West, there has been a gradual breakdown of any meta-narrative, an overarching 'story' that gives shared spiritual or moral meaning (Connor, 1989). This has been replaced by a form of liberal tolerance of a wide diversity of beliefs, principles and practice.

This does not, however, just mean that ethically anything goes. Alongside respect for ethical plurality, there needs to be the balance of a shared ethic that transcends the particular interest of nations and major corporations. Inevitably this is an ethics which is not easily or simplistically applied, requiring careful dialogue around the many different principles, cultural and religious perspectives, ideologies and social expectations that give meaning to any particular situation. The tensions at the heart of such a view make global ethics be 'definition-uneasy'. Staff within the School of Applied Global Ethics are working to develop learning materials that help students collectively work through complex and often conflicting perspectives and ethical dilemmas to achieve better understanding of professional contexts.

As the Leeds Met approach to global ethics within the curriculum matures, we recognise we have much still to do. Our current activities include:

- ensuring that our distinctive freshers' festival for inducting new students fosters mutual understanding and respect between home and international students;
- requiring all programmes undergoing validation or periodic review to address our cross-cultural curriculum guidelines;
- using resources we have won through national bidding processes to support our international staff and student volunteering programmes;

- encouraging staff on international visits to explore pedagogic paradigms in their host communities and in Leeds Met staff development sessions, so we can avoid discontinuities for international students and enhance our own practice;
- supporting international scholars visiting Leeds Met;
- working in interdisciplinary ways to share learning about global ethics across the University and in the wider regional, national and international community.

We welcome contacts from readers who would like to work with us to further expand our horizons and to enhance our international outlook. A case study at the end of this chapter indicates the type of issue which generates student engagement and critical thinking in the spirit of Hans Kung's global ethic and the practical concerns of campaigning groups.

A university, of course, embraces scholarly disputation so it is important to note that our distinguished Visiting Professor of Globalization, Ethics and Islam, Ian Markham, is critical of Kung:

> Hans Kung has suggested that the world religions should converge around a global ethic – an ethical minimum on which we can all agree. Although anything that constructs better relationships between the religions is good, the danger here is that the complexity can be overlooked.
>
> (Markham, 2007)

Professor Markham observes that:

> it is not that all religions agree or disagree with each other, but that certain groups within one religion agree with some groups within another religion and they also disagree with many of their co-religionists as well as other groups in other religions.

He gives examples of his disagreement, from within one of the great faith traditions and as a sympathetic scholar of world faiths: 'In my judgment, the religious traditions have a very poor record on such topics as homosexuality, patriarchy and toleration' (Markham, op. cit.).

It is important for students to hear such voices and to study such disagreements but to do so in a context of university engagement with fundamental ethical issues. Two groups associated with Leeds Met prompted small-scale but vital curriculum experiments in related issues, namely the World Studies Trust Global Teacher Project and the combined ecumenical chaplaincy of the two universities in Leeds. In the good company of the Development Education Association, Anglia Polytechnic (now Anglia Ruskin) University, Bournemouth University, London South Bank University and Middlesex University, Leeds Met was therefore involved in the publication of *Global*

Perspectives in Higher Education. It is our contention, however, that the inter-section of partnerships with ethics and world-wide horizons takes this to a new level by galvanising widespread student and staff interest.

For example, the University supported the attempt by a British army exped-ition in 2006 to climb Everest by the difficult West Ridge route. This attracted interest throughout the University and the wider world, in the latter case primarily owing to Sky television news coverage and the use by the army of the expedition as part of a recruiting campaign. It will be obvious that there will have been concerns within the University as to the ethics of such a partnership with the army. Again, however, as with the Markham critique of Kung, members of a university community can legitimately disagree on such matters without rupturing their common commitment to exploring the rights and wrongs of an approach. The primary ethical debates, however, came about in a surprising way. Just as the expedition was frustrated in its attempt to reach the summit by adverse weather, so the world's media focused on two stories of Everest climbers in distress. Should other mountaineers have gone to their rescue? Discussion among Leeds Met colleagues in England began online as, in the Himalayas, Leeds Met lecturers asked the army expedition for their views. On the return of the climbers, a symposium was held to which another famous climber, Alan Hinkes, the first Briton to climb the world's highest fourteen peaks, was invited. His personal accounts of similar uneasy ethical dilemmas led to an enlightening discussion in the summer of 2006. An ethical case is uneasy if there are moral qualms in pursuing any resolution. Separating or not separating Siamese twins when one seems destined to die and whether or not to cut a rope when death looms through difficulties in mountaineering are classic examples where many people would be left with a sense of moral unease, whichever conclusion they advocate. Students will often find them-selves discussing uneasy dilemmas both within and beyond the curriculum as part of the experience of studying, at least at Leeds Metropolitan University. The Everest example can be pursued through the various streams of daily 200-word reflections on our website that help to foster a cross-University community of practice. Following the seminar with Alan Hinkes and the Everest West Ridge experts, lecturers decided that this running stream of experience and wisdom should flow immediately into the curriculum, so, in the autumn of 2006, 300 students studied a module on Everest Ethics.

These three elements of world-wide horizons, partnerships and ethics continue to refresh our scholarship and our curriculum, while going beyond the boundaries of the curricular and the extra-curricular. What affects us most in the long run in our education is often what we are least aware of at the time it is happening. The ethos of a community, whether a school or a university, is of lasting significance in its students' lives. Its values and its partnerships really matter. Fundamental aspects of Leeds Met's approach, such as working in partnerships and striving to go beyond boundaries, can both raise and help to address uneasy global ethical dilemmas. For it is often the company that you keep and how you keep it which provoke ethical concern. It is relationships, and how we engage the diverse other, both within a university community and beyond, that reveal ethical value. Reflection on value is based in and reinforces the physicality of practice. Where outdoor activities of the university student involve mutual reliance, this reinforces reflection on climbing ethics, which is built around the awareness of inter-dependence in the context of high risk. Hence the excitement of world-wide horizons and partnerships add value and values to the student experience of exploring ethics. In the remainder of this chapter, we summarise our University's journey so far and offer some pointers as to routes which could now be taken in this spirit but we accept that this ethical expedition is only at base camp.

From local origins to a regional university with world-wide horizons

The origins of Leeds Metropolitan University are usually traced to the cre-ation of the Leeds Mechanics' Institute in 1824, followed by a number of colleges (including the Carnegie College for the training of PE teachers) in the nineteenth and early twentieth centuries. The primary intention was to open up educational opportunities for some of the least privileged in local communities. The First World War inevitably affected the colleges greatly and rendered it impossible to think of this country in isolation from the wider world. We know that one of our first Carnegie students in the 1930s was from Australia. Eric Harris, known as the Toowomba Ghost, was one of the greatest rugby league players of all time. We also know that a combined Carnegie and Loughborough team represented Great Britain at a world student games in Stockholm, with Walter Winterbottom (then a Carnegie student, later a Carnegie lecturer and England's first national football team manager, for which service he was knighted) carrying the Union Jack into the stadium. So we know that, before the Second World War, at least some stu-dents were travelling round the world to and from Leeds Met's predecessor colleges. It is not until the colleges became a polytechnic and the polytechnic became a university in the 1990s, however, that the range and the numbers of international students or domestic students on international travel began to seem remarkable.

Nowadays within a student body of more than 50,000, we have some 4,000 students at any one time from well over 100 countries. We have students based in Hong Kong and Tanzania, and many of our home students take up placement opportunities outside the UK. Some courses derive considerable excitement from the mixture of nationalities, such as our executive MBA, with its annual residential week abroad. While these features might be repli-cated in many other universities, there are also some distinctive ways in which Leeds Met highlights our international dimensions.

First, while all of our six faculties have world-wide horizons, one is actually named as an International Faculty: the Leslie Silver International Faculty (Leslie Silver being our former Chancellor, whose family origins were as refugees; he served in the Far East during the Second World War, then created a successful international business in the paint industry and chaired the internationally known Leeds United football club). Second, our website features daily 'International Reflections', as described in Chapter 3. This both enhances and gives high visibility to our international community and orientation. Third, Leeds Met is developing as a university of festivals and partnerships, which immediately engages the wider world, as shown by our facilitation of Northern Ballet's China tour in 2006, our support for the Everest West Ridge 2006 expedition and our status as the only university to name a world sporting cup, rugby league's Carnegie World Club Challenge. Fourth, the focus is explicitly on development and applied global ethics, both within and beyond the curriculum, rather than just on the recruitment of international students who are paying high fees.

What are universities for?

In this section, we aim to relate the evolution and distinctive approach of Leeds Met to wider discussions about the nature of universities and our relationship with uneasy global ethics. Many accounts of the purposes of a university begin with John Henry Newman's mid-nineteenth-century lectures (Newman, 1852). Newman has much to offer Leeds Met and every university today, but his approach to a university for a few middle-class Catholic young men 150 years ago cannot be the last word for a diverse, multi-national university such as ours. John Henry Newman was a Roman Catholic priest who had converted from the Church of England. This conversion meant that, according to the law of the time, he had to give up his work as an Oxford don. He gave in Dublin his series of lectures on the idea of a university in May and November 1852. The texts were published as a book in 1853 and have subsequently been reprinted endlessly, usually with other lectures which were prepared by Newman but were never given in the traditional form. The reason for the lectures was that Newman had been asked by Archbishop Paul Cullen of Armagh (later of Dublin) to establish a Catholic university in Ireland. Although this venture was long in the planning, it proved to be a short-lived failure. Newman's lectures, however, are usually judged to be an enduring success.

Newman was promoting two main ideas. The first was that a proper university should include the queen of the sciences, Theology. He genuinely believed this but it also served to confirm why a Catholic university was needed, in the view of Rome and some of the Irish bishops, even though (indeed because) non-denominational university colleges had just been established in Ireland, such as the forerunner of what is now Queen's University

Belfast. Newman's second point was that a university needs to foster liberal learning, a habit of mind and outlook which creates what he called 'gentlemen'. The gender-specific language reflects the men-only nature of the university which Newman was trying to establish. We could update the rhetoric by reformulating this point as putting collegiality at the centre of university life so that students are encouraged to develop as rounded individuals. Newman also believed strongly in this aim and had good cause to do so, having benefited from a similar experience himself at Oxford.

A century later, Bruce Truscot's *Red Brick University* (1951) took issue with Newman on another point, dismissing his lectures for an 'astonishing' misunderstanding of the meaning or origin of the word 'university'. Truscot explains that the 'medieval Latin word *universitas* meant a corporation, society or community' of any kind and came to refer to Higher Education institutions 'when used in the particular sense of *studium generale*'. Newman and many others, Truscot argued, were wrong to 'talk of universities as if their name indicated that every kind of subject under the sun ought to be studied in them and they were places where knowledge in its most "universal" aspect should be sought'. Their mistake is that 'the universality or generality of *universitas studium generale* relates to admission, not to content'.

The English red-brick universities, such as Birmingham, Liverpool and Manchester, were not to be the last wave of expansion in the UK. They have been followed in the last half-century by colleges of advanced technology such as Bath, Loughborough and Surrey becoming universities, new universities being established in greenfield sites such as Sussex, Warwick and York, the polytechnics becoming universities and now a wider range of former colleges, including several church ones like Newman's intended university, being granted university titles.

It was the 1963 Robbins Report which marked the beginning of this rapid expansion of universities and students in the UK. It had the breadth and depth of vision to refer immediately to a different age and culture in its early reference to Confucius and set out its views clearly on the plurality of aims of Higher Education:

> We begin with instruction in skills suitable to play a part in the general division of labour. We put this first, not because we regard it as the most important, but because we think that it is sometimes ignored or under-valued. Confucius said in the Analects that it was not easy to find a man who had studied for three years without aiming at pay. We deceive ourselves if we claim that more than a small fraction of students in institutions of higher education would be where they are if there were no significance for their future careers in what they hear and read; and it is a mistake to suppose that there is anything discreditable in this. Certainly this was not the attitude of the past: the ancient universities of Europe were founded to promote the training of the clergy, doctors and lawyers:

and though at times there may have been many who attended for the pursuit of pure knowledge or of pleasure, they must surely have been a minority. And it must be recognised in our own times, progress – and particularly the maintenance of a competitive position – depends to a much greater extent than ever before on skills demanding special training. A good general education, valuable though it may be, is frequently less than we need to solve many of our most pressing problems.

Robbins's second objective was: 'that what is taught should be taught in such a way as to promote the general powers of the mind. The aim should be to produce not mere specialists but rather cultivated men and women.'

The third was the 'advancement of learning' for: 'the search for truth is an essential function of institutions of higher education and the process of education is itself most vital when it partakes of the nature of discovery'.

The final objective for Robbins was: 'the transmission of a common culture and common standards of citizenship'.

The Report argued that there were 'at least' these four objectives which were 'essential to any properly balanced system'. It acknowledged that there would be diversity within the university sector:

> The vocational emphasis will be more apparent in some than in others. The advancement of learning will be more prominent at the postgraduate than at the undergraduate stage. The extent of participation in the life and culture of the community will depend on local circumstances. *Our contention is that, although the extent to which each principle is realised in the various types of institution will vary, yet, ideally, there is room for at least a speck of each in all.* The system as a whole must be judged deficient unless it provides adequately for all of them.
>
> (Emphasis added)

In 1997, the UK Dearing Report (the National Committee of Inquiry into Higher Education) also discerned 'four main purposes of higher education'. These were:

- to inspire and enable individuals to develop their capabilities to the highest potential levels throughout life, so that they grow intellectually, are well-equipped for work, can contribute effectively to society and achieve personal fulfilment;
- to increase knowledge and understanding for their own sake and to foster their application to the benefit of the economy and society;
- to serve the needs of an adaptable, sustainable, knowledge-based economy at local, regional and national levels;
- to play a major role in shaping a democratic, civilised, inclusive society.

This is much the same as Robbins. Some think the list is soul-less. The fourth of Dearing's purposes is more sensitive in that, instead of the Robbins rhetoric of transmitting a common culture, it talks of inclusivity, with the implication that we are societies of many cultures. This update could be described as a function of the changing political spirit of the times. Otherwise, the lists are remarkably similar. If anything, the economic basis for Higher Education has become more explicit, with Dearing's first three purposes amounting to variations on the same Confucian theme of learning for earning rather than yearning for learning. Lord Dearing might point to the second phrase about increasing knowledge and understanding 'for their own sake' as evidence to the contrary, but the third purpose makes universities seem like chambers of commerce or the Confederation of British Industry rather than communities of scholars.

Confucius apart, both lists seem to omit international dimensions, yet we believe it is difficult to be a member of the Leeds Met community or of a partner organisation or to look at our website without being caught up in a sense of a university with a commitment to both internationalism and our home region. Both authors of this chapter gave inaugural lectures which offered a sense of these three recurring themes, reflection on the soul of a university, on a world without boundaries and on serving communities.

This is more than paying lip service to the notion that thinking seriously about the wider world and its deepest foundations is important for any university. Leeds Met has established a School of Applied Global Ethics, overcoming some initial scepticism at such an emphasis on world religions, peace studies, conflict resolution and applied global studies. Our university includes students and staff from diverse faith community backgrounds and it is important that we recognise that faith is an important component of individual and collective identities. In a world in which religious beliefs are daily reported as being intertwined with political activities, it is not only theologians, but a wide range of scholars seeking to understand society, communities and the human condition, who need to study religious identities.

This was brought home to us particularly when world-wide interest in our curriculum and community engagement followed the tragic events of 7 July 2005. Two former Leeds Met students were among the London bombers. The two alumni involved were rooted in local Muslim communities in Yorkshire. Our 'widening participation' approach to students' progression through local colleges created opportunities for their higher education but could not in our opinion be reasonably blamed for influencing thereafter, once they attended training schools or camps in Pakistan.

Our immediate institutional reaction was to invite Ian Markham, as a leading scholar of Islam, globalisation and ethics, based in the USA, immediately to visit the University so that all staff had the opportunity to deepen our understanding of the issues. He highlighted the ethnic as well as the religious diversity within Islam, correcting the Western media's preoccupation with Islam in the Middle East and the Indian sub-continent by reflecting, for example, on a significant pacifist Islamic sect in Turkey and the huge numbers of Muslims in Indonesia. There is nobody in the local communities of Dewsbury or Beeston (about which one of our colleagues, Max Farrar, has written in the wake of the 7/7 bombings (Farrar, 2005, 2006)) who thinks that we are unaffected by attitudes in Pakistan, but there equally should be nobody in Leeds Met who thinks that Islam is only to be understood in terms of the Middle or Near East.

Reflecting daily

A unique means by which our university fosters a community of understanding is through our regular reflections, which include not only 'VC Reflects' and International Reflections, but also Assessment, Learning and Teaching, Research, Sporting and Ethical reflections, to which a wide range of students and staff contribute. These brief daily web-based reflections provide opportunities to share perspectives on national and international events, addressing, for example, terrorist attacks and natural disasters such as the Madrid bombs, the Sri Lankan tsunami, the Kashmir earthquake and the Mumbai bombs. They frequently provoke responses from colleagues across the University and enable members of the University community to become aware of mutual concerns that are the modern technological counterpart to Newman's commitment to liberal learning or collegiality. They contribute to a distinctive ethos.

There are other examples of how our colleagues initiate and foster a wide range of international interactions. Individual efforts by staff and students to help in Sri Lanka following the tsunami in 2005 have led to an institutional partnership between Leeds Met and the University of Colombo. Sometimes, unusual partnerships have contributed to local communities' attempts to help those affected by such tragedies. For example, when Bradford City football club was in difficulties in the summer of 2004, Leeds Met stepped in to help it develop a community relations programme. Hundreds of local people with Kashmiri family backgrounds subsequently gathered at the club a year later for a charitable event which raised funds for those struggling with the aftermath of the earthquake. This all helps to create an atmosphere in which more difficult issues can be addressed.

Nor is it the curriculum alone that can measure a university's ethical engagement with major global challenges. The launch of our initiative in 2006 to strengthen our relationships with African communities, Leeds Met Africa, showed, rather, how research, teaching and volunteering come together, with individual pioneers eventually coming to see connections between their independent initiatives.

What is an uneasy global ethical dilemma for a university?

The University has awarded honorary doctorates to Christian, Jewish and Muslim leaders in graduations on either side of 7 July 2005: Bishop David Konstant, the retiring Bishop of Leeds, and the Chief Rabbi, Sir Jonathan Sacks, in 2004, and Sir Iqbal Sacranie, the inaugural general secretary of the British Muslim Council, in 2006. Peter Blackburn, who had been the chief executive of Nestlé UK and Nestlé Europe, was awarded an honorary doctorate in 2005, alongside Professor Rosabeth Moss Kanter of Harvard Business School. Peter Blackburn soon returned to the University to participate in a seminar on business ethics. Some objected even to the invitation, as Nestlé in the UK has been criticised for its promotion of baby milk powder in Africa. A sustained campaign has led many in successive generations of British university students to believe that Nestlé executives have acted immorally. Peter Blackburn begged to differ. He reflected on the excellent reputation Nestlé has in many other countries, for instance on the Continent of Europe, as a model employer. He also explained to students how he came to work for a company which was being subjected to such criticism. He worked his way through to senior positions in Mackintosh, which became part of Rowntree, which became part of Nestlé. The first two companies were seen as irreproachably ethical, Quaker firms with a social conscience. When Nestlé took over Rowntree, he saw continuity rather than discontinuity in what we would now call the corporate social responsibility. Even if campaigners carry on campaigning against Nestlé and former executives continue to believe that they were employed in an ethical company, such an encounter is itself an invaluable learning opportunity for everyone involved, including students and staff.

A university should be such a meeting place for the clash of ideas and world views. There are limits and exceptions, especially as universities have duties of care to students and a commitment to the pursuit of truth. There are, therefore, sometimes grounds for banning illegal or highly disruptive groups from activities on a campus, and it can be necessary to prevent a malevolent few from spreading untruths or showing a reckless disregard for the truth. In general, however, a university can make a difference in advance of any particular ethical dilemma by the culture it has developed of approaching controversies with open minds, courteous argument and respect for diversity. If this is a minimum expectation, then the next step might be developing such awareness of international volunteering opportunities that no student or member of staff can be unaware of ways in which our least privileged fellow human beings can be better supported. If our highest-profile example is Leeds Met Africa, there are many others. The work of Leeds Met students and play work expert Dr Fraser Brown with orphaned children in Romania, for instance, touches the lives of the wider university in diverse ways. In a research conference in 2006 on ethics and children, Fraser Brown raised a dilemma of uneasy global ethics. Should volunteers helping children in appalling conditions denounce the practice in another country's institutional orphanages of tying them to beds overnight, with the likely result of being excluded from encouraging the children to play during the day? We might then ask, is the urge to denounce, to distance oneself from a practice or perception, necessary for an ethical journey through life, or can it be too precious? In particular, if we are seeking change, do we not need to become fellow-travellers with those whose current practice might be anathema to us?

Case study: Leeds Metropolitan University

Ethical dilemmas discussion topic: child labour

Reading task

Prior to the seminar on ethical issues associated with child labour, please read the following reference material:

Dachi, H. and Garrett, R. (2002) *Child Labour and its Impact on Children's Access to and Participation in Primary Education*, London: Department for International Development.
DFID (1999) *Helping not Hurting Children*, London: DFID.
Kielland, A. (2006) *Children at Work: Child Labor Practices in Africa*, New York: Lynne Rienner.
Murphy, D. and Mathew, D., 'Nike and global labour practices: a case study prepared for the New Academy of Business Innovation Network for Socially Responsible Business', http://www.new-academy.ac.uk/publications/keypublications/documents/nikereport.pdf.

Refer to DFID (http://www.keysheets.org/red_5_child_labour.html), which stresses a complex debate on:

- whether the emphasis should be on all forms of child work or the worst forms, e.g. should the eradication of child work in any form be the ultimate goal?
- the impact of child employment on adult employment and wages;
- whether work and school are incompatible in the lives of children;
- what are the most effective interventions against harmful forms of child work, e.g. labour legislation, compulsory education, poverty reduction, social mobilisation?

- the pros and cons of trade sanctions against and consumer boy-cotts of the products of child labour;
- whether (and if so how) children should participate in decision-making processes;
- key alliances needed for effective policy implementation;
- links between poor health, mortality and child labour – particu-larly in relation to HIV/AIDS.

(http://www.keysheets.org/red_5_child_labour.html, p. 1)

Seminar task

On arrival at the seminar, working in groups of five, please read and consider the following:

Many would argue as a universal ethical rule that child labour is wrong. This has led to vociferous arguments in the case of the sports manu-facturing company Nike. In the 1980s it became known in the West that a significant part of the labour force for some of Nike's products was chil-dren or young adults working in Asian sweatshops. Nike have attempted, in response to activist groups, to address this, aware that condoning such practices could affect their Western sales, and the debate is still very much alive.

The argument against child labour is simply that it is a form of exploit-ation because:

- children should be in the education process, enabling them to develop personally and intellectually;
- children do not have any power and thus are unable to defend them-selves against exploitation;
- exploitation often involves using children in dangerous or difficult jobs. It estimated that 126 million out of 218 million child workers are in hazardous employment;
- children are not paid fair wages.

The opposing view suggests that:

- this is placing a Western perception on childhood which is not shared in different cultures. In a culture of poverty it may be that all members of the family have to earn money for the family to survive;
- it may be that such a culture sees it as a matter of honour and respect for the child to participate in making money for the family;

- in such a culture the idea of full-time education may not be critical or even available;
- it may be thought by the family that such labour is a better way of developing the child for the future, in terms of both responsibility and skills.

In your discussion with fellow students please consider:

- the relative autonomy of the children;
- how different options will affect the different stakeholders;
- how the issue of child labour links to wider problems such as health;
- how stakeholders might work together to take account of the different values.

Assessment task

Following your discussions, each student is expected to produce a short (700-word) individual article for publication in a specified newspaper of a specified country in which you argue the case for or against child labour.

Chapter 3

International Reflections and culture change

Elspeth Jones

Introduction

Since September 2003, an item has appeared daily on the Leeds Metropolitan University website, entitled International Reflections (http://www.leedsmet. ac.uk/internat/reflects/index.htm). These vignettes of exactly 200 words have helped to change the culture at Leeds Met and have both contributed to, and shown evidence of, a shift in mindset in the importance attributed to internationalisation in the institution. In recent years, the University's approach to internationalisation has changed from being one primarily of international student recruitment to a more values-driven approach which views internationalisation as fundamental to the work of the University and requires a radical reconsideration of how this affects all aspects of the University's life and work. Leeds Met adopted the definition of internationalisation as 'the process of integrating an international/intercultural dimension into the teaching, research and service of an institution' (Knight and de Wit, 1995). Given this thorough re-evaluation of approach, the Internationalisation Strategy (Leeds Met, 2003) was developed with six themes, only one of which relates to student recruitment:

- internationalising learning, teaching and research;
- enhancing the international student experience;
- enhancing the international experience of home students;
- developing and fostering international partnerships and alliances;
- developing staff capability for internationalisation;
- effectively recruiting international students.

International students are now seen to be at the heart of the University and a valuable source of cultural capital. They help to provide the means of delivering the strategy in that, amongst other things, they add to the diversity of the institution and offer focal points for themed activities, such as events celebrating particular cultures. However, it is recognised that an internationalised institution offers opportunities to enhance the global perspectives of all students and staff, not only those who are already in an international environment as a function of undertaking their education in another country.

This volume takes, as a premise, the notion that positive benefits can accrue from international and cross-cultural experiences, including those which take place 'at home', in one's own country of origin. Chapter 9 shows how cross-cultural capability skills can be developed, and enhanced employability skills can also result from such experiences (see Chapter 10). Webb (2005) offers fourteen strategies for 'normalising internationalisation of the curriculum' which extend beyond the narrow interpretation of curriculum into the student experience as a whole. He defines such 'normalisation' as 'turning the ad hoc and uneven efforts of a few enthusiasts into the normal expectations and requirements of the organisation' (pp. 115–17). He proposes that this should 'be seen as a dynamic process which ... affords staff and students the opportunity to own the processes of their own learning and knowledge production' (p. 115). The 'normalisation' challenge for Leeds Met was to move from an institutional mindset which placed the emphasis on international student recruitment, to one in which 'an international ethos pervades the University', thereby meeting the international Aim in the Corporate Plan 2004–2008 (Leeds Met, 2004, Aim 5). This chapter illustrates one means by which this culture change has begun to be both effected and reflected.

There is insufficient space here to consider the complex relationships between institutional cultures and change processes (see, for example, Kezar and Eckel, 2002) but, as should be apparent from my comments and those from readers and contributors to International Reflections which follow, I believe these daily postings have had an impact on the institutional culture, while at the same time reflecting change within that culture through their growing sophistication. As several of the comments on the process of reflection indicate, engaging in the reflective process and doing so in a public forum are fundamental to the broader culture of academia, and it may be for this reason that they have been so enthusiastically embraced, echoing one of Kezar and Eckel's conclusions that 'change strategies seem to be successful if they are culturally coherent or aligned with the culture' (p. 457).

The emergence and rise of International Reflections

Professor Simon Lee took up his post as Vice-Chancellor on 1 September 2003 and, soon after, announced that an International Faculty was to be created. The Faculty was to be responsible not only for delivering a range of existing subjects with a broadly international theme but also for fostering and leading internationalisation across the whole University. The development of new subject areas which would promote international understanding and global perspectives for home (i.e. British) students was to be a further focus of the Faculty's work. The emphasis on the international dimension was one aspect of the Vice-Chancellor's broader vision for the University. One means by which he chose to communicate this vision was through a daily reflection of exactly 200 words, VC Reflects, which began on the day of his arrival and has continued ever since.

Two weeks after VC Reflects began I, as International Dean, was invited to provide a one-week series of Reflections to mark the international student welcome week. Under the banner Leeds Met Equals, the theme of the week was intended to illustrate the importance of internationalisation as a defining characteristic of Leeds Met and was to be followed by other major themes. This marked an important turning point, as it was the first time the University had devoted a whole week to a dedicated welcome programme for its international students in advance of UK students arriving. Previously a series of activities had taken place in faculties with just a couple of days provided by the wider University. The result was differing student experiences in different faculties, some of which were more used to working with international students than others. It could also be difficult for students to meet those in other faculties and, where numbers from an individual country were low, did not always offer the opportunity of a contact point to their own culture, which can be so important during the settling-in phase.

Those first five pieces in Leeds Met Equals were aimed at supporting the physical welcome being offered and at signalling to the wider University community that here was a step change in our approach to internationalisation. The increased length of our welcome programme was symbolic of the increase in focus on the international dimension of the University. This was further emphasised by the new vision statement that Leeds Met was striving to become 'a world-class regional university with world-wide horizons using all our talents to the full'.

By the end of the week we had received excellent feedback and it was clear that continuing value could be obtained if we carried on producing pieces each day, so we decided to continue doing so for a little while longer, perhaps until Christmas. Now called International Reflections, the page was designed to explain, support and promote the broader, values-driven approach to internationalisation as this was rolled out across different aspects of University life.

At first some coercion was needed to ensure we had five pieces each week. This was supported by the introduction of a robust new travel authorisation process which both required those planning overseas visits on University business to say which of the six aspects of the Internationalisation Strategy they would be meeting and required travellers to submit a Reflection on their return. No international travel by staff at any level in the institution was sanctioned without this agreement. Some of these Reflections were simply reports of the visit without any real reflection, but the best began to show fascinating insights into the emerging internationalisation ethos. Students were encouraged to contribute by several enthusiastic staff members and we introduced an incentive with a £50 book token for the best student contribution.

Not only did we manage to stretch out the series beyond that first Christmas but, several years later, the page is continuing to thrive and the maturing nature of contributions has been fascinating to observe. Gradually the number of contributors grew until the competition for places was so fierce that many were destined to remain unpublished and only those which offered true reflection would be considered.

The items may offer tantalising glimpses of other cultures, or of different perspectives on life as an international student in the UK. Many talk of personal transformation or changed perspectives as a result of an international experience or encounter. Others help to raise awareness of global development issues or the need to understand better other communities and cultures, including the needs of our international students. Yet more mark a response to world events, including natural disasters which may have affected students' families. It is not only academic staff who write Reflections. Some of the best have been from support staff, including one who took part in a fundraising walk along the Great Wall of China.[1] Colleagues from international partner institutions and the British Council have made contributions, as have alumni and students on exchange overseas and incoming exchange students. There have been pieces from agents and representatives, and international visitors are encouraged to submit a Reflection. One parent of a staff member, who was at that time working within the Arctic Circle, wanted to describe this experience and so sent in a Reflection,[2] and there have been other contributions by family members of staff[3] and students.[4]

Taken as a whole the pages, which are all available through the online archive, offer real evidence that internationalisation at Leeds Met is about much more than recruiting international students. They have helped to support the kind of culture change which was needed in changing the mind-set of those who thought this was all that was meant by internationalisation. They have done this in part by providing evidence that students, staff and friends of the University are not only having international and intercultural experiences but are learning from these in ways which support and reflect the internationalisation process, and which may or may not be related to working with international students.

Some writers have been willing to offer thoughts and insights of such a personal nature that they have seemed more like personal letters from friends than public material read on several continents. Many colleagues have said how much they value International Reflections, one saying that the best of these 'transport' him to other countries or cultures. This, in turn, has led to an increase in the quality of the pieces submitted.

Mezirow (1991) suggests that reflection is significant when it 'serves a purpose, and purposes serve as organizing principles that give coherence and order to activities. Clearly, reflection is different depending on whether the learner's purpose is task-oriented problem solving, understanding what someone else means, or understanding the self' (p. 15). He distinguishes this from introspection which is, for him 'becoming aware of the fact that we are perceiving, thinking, feeling, or acting in a certain way' (p. 15). But it is the reflection of our assumptions that 'becomes crucial in learning to understand meaning' (p. 15). In the case of International Reflections, it is the challenging of existing assumptions that becomes crucial in learning to understand ourselves and others in the developing internationalisation process.

Developing practice through reflection

In many disciplines and professions, 'reflective practice' is widely embraced. The work of Donald Schon (e.g. Schon, 1991) has been influential in causing professionals to reflect on their practice, and in particular to commit their reflections to paper or screens not only so that the benefits of looking inward at one's practice are achieved, but also so that others can learn from the reflections. In the context of innovation in teaching in Higher Education, Cowan (2006) makes a strong case for the necessity of reflection on teaching practice, and on learning from the reflections of students in order to develop and improve the quality of their experience.

Race (2006) discusses ways of helping teachers in Higher Education to reflect on their practices in the context of assessment, learning and teaching, and starts with the following questions:

> 'But how can I reflect? What do you mean by reflection? How will I know when I've reflected well?' are questions which students and staff alike ask about the processes of reflection. Moreover their next questions are, 'how can I show that I've reflected successfully?', 'What will be deemed satisfactory evidence of my reflection?'

Race (2006) goes on to explore the value of clusters of 'starter-questions' as a way of prompting reflection, and adding focus and purpose to reflection. For example, in the context of reflecting upon teaching, his suggested question clusters include:

- What did I actually achieve with this element of teaching? Which were the most difficult parts, and why were they difficult for me? Which were the most straightforward parts, and why did I find these easy?
- What was the best thing I did? Why was this the best thing I did? How do I know that this was the best thing I did?
- What worked least well for me? Why did this not work well for me? What have I learned about the topic concerned from this not having worked well for me? What have I learned about the students through this not having worked well for me? What have I learned about myself from this

not having worked well for me? What do I plan to do differently in future as a result of my answers to the above questions?

- With hindsight, how would I go about this element of teaching differently if doing it again from scratch? To what extent will my experience of this element of teaching influence the way I tackle anything similar in future?
- What did I find the greatest challenge in doing this element of teaching? Why was this a challenge to me? To what extent do I feel I have met this challenge? What can I do to improve my performance when next meeting this particular sort of challenge?
- What are the three most important things that I think I need to do arising from this element of teaching at this moment in time? Which of these do I think is the most urgent for me to do? When will I aim to start doing this, and what is a sensible deadline for me to have completed it by?

(Race, 2006: 227–8)

Questions similar to those above could be designed for the context of International Reflections, allowing (for example) teachers to think more deeply into particular aspects of their practice in the context of working with international students or challenging our assumptions about other countries and cultures.

The processes involved in writing to an exact length and format are significant in developing the quality of reflection. Most often, a first attempt to write the required two paragraphs in exactly 200 words leads to a draft which is significantly over-length. The processes of reducing the reflection to exactly 200 words include:

- looking carefully at words and phrases, and deciding which are less important to the message of the reflection;
- making decisions about what ideas can be sacrificed – in other words, bringing quality control mechanisms to the content of the reflection;
- deciding what the reflection is *really* about, and focusing the content of the 200 words so that it is self-sufficient and coherent.

These processes are in their own right quality enhancers which deepen the very act of reflecting, in the course of working towards evidence of reflection in the adopted format of 200 words.

What do readers of the International Reflections think?

While, as Editor, I have my personal view on what makes a good Reflection, it was important to gain a better understanding of readers' views in order to provide feedback to those whose Reflection could not be used in its present form. This has allowed the development of a response to such submissions based on practice and evidence rather than simply the editor's personal view and often results in resubmission as it has allowed the writer to reflect on and reframe their piece, thus making it more publishable. This is essentially the third phase of the process, that is the event or stimulus for reflection and the writing and the rewriting – in this case, based on editorial comment. A consideration of the process from the writer's perspective forms the final section of this chapter, but first we will consider the views of readers.

A brief questionnaire was designed and, reached by a click from the main page, asked readers, 'What do you think of International Reflections?' The questions were:

1   How often do you read International Reflections?
2   What makes the best kind of reflection?
3   What should we do more?
4   What should we stop doing?
5   Do you have any other ideas for improvements?

A range of responses has been received to date. Some people choose to give their name; others prefer to remain anonymous. Some offer lengthy responses which have proved extremely helpful. This section considers a selection of the comments received for each of the questions in the survey.

1 How often do you read International Reflections?

It was gratifying, yet hardly surprising, to note that 85 per cent of those responding read the column either every day or most days. Of greater interest though are the qualitative comments which the open-ended questions have elicited, some of which are shown below.

2 What makes the best kind of reflection?

The vast majority of respondents find human or personal angles on the topic of greatest interest:

- 'Reflections that are reflective and written from a personal angle where you learn about perceptions of experiences and how they learned and developed from the experience.'
- 'I like the people stories though I think you have the blend just right (too many personal stories would spoil it).'
- 'When the author explains what they have learned and how this has enriched/changed their life/opinions/views.'
- 'Personal experiences; observations about culture and language; highlighting specific worldwide events and special days.'
- 'I enjoy all of them, especially the one on 19 December 2005 as it touched

me – it talked about displacement – which captured a feeling I have. Human stories (of families, feelings etc.) are what most draws me to the International Reflections. I particularly enjoy Reflections by students from this country and outside. Every day the Reflections open a different chapter, people experiencing the same things in the same country at different times – or new feelings and experiences. The Reflections are like a portal to different feelings etc. I do enjoy Reflections from people not immediately from the University but connected to the University for example staff from partner universities. Also, the article from Leeds Met South Asia after the Tsunami was especially poignant and brought that office and people – so many miles away – closer.'

Others enjoy Reflections which consider the relations or comparison between cultures:

• 'One which draws lessons out from cultural differences, making one think about (even challenge) one's own current thinking (or more often lack of thinking).'

The word 'insight' often appears in responses to this question. Examples include the following:

• 'Sharp insight, relevant connection and some element of surprise that makes me want to learn more about what was the core of the reflection.'
• 'Being given insight into someone's memorable events which they feel have benefited their understanding of different cultures.'
• 'Personal insights into the lives and customs of other countries or out-siders' views of British lives etc. The two that particularly stick in my mind were a student who was missing his young child and details of orthodox Christmas celebrations.'

Reflections from students are greatly appreciated by those responding to this question:

• '[I appreciate] [r]eflections from students either here or our own students studying or working abroad.'
• 'Student experiences of living and studying in Leeds, and the best ones are about different cultures and their celebrations i.e. what the Polish people celebrate at Easter and how and what Hindus do at Diwali and that kind of thing are great.'

Reporting on topical issues is also valued by readers:

• 'Pithy/witty or those which for one reason or another are topical, for example, an Irish student talking about St. Patrick's Day on 17 Mar. Also, poignant ones following a major event or crisis.'

- 'A reflection that goes beyond the simple reporting of a visit that considers challenges or topical questions.'

Reflection 1: Tuesday 28 February 2006

Studying in Finland was the most amazing and totally fantastic life-enhancing period of my life, and was definitely the best decision I have ever made! I had such a great experience, making friends with people from every country in Europe. One of the most special things was how cross-cultural I have become, accepting many different views and opinions about so many different issues. It was an interesting and challenging experience studying in a foreign university, as the working methods are different. There was more group work and assessments were more regular, in the form of group reports and presentations. It was interesting and fun though! I also feel that it will be useful when I apply for jobs, as I can say I have lived and studied overseas, experiencing different things.

I could not have made more from my experience than I did, taking every opportunity. I did lots of travelling, visiting countries that I have lots of interesting stories to tell of – Russia, Sweden, Lapland, Estonia and Latvia. I would recommend study abroad. It is something you wouldn't regret, but just leave with lifelong memories, many new friends, and as a changed person in a very positive way.

Nicola Riches studied in Helsinki, Finland, as part of the Erasmus programme 2004/5.

Other comments on this question are indicative of the variety of the Reflections and of a similar variety of response to these:

- 'Reflections which indicate some local or obscure information which would not be readily available to the ordinary traveller!'
- 'Something that brings new information to light and can be used in research or for the students.'
- 'For me one of the most positive aspects of International Reflections is the opportunity they provide to enlighten staff and students about other cultures and other perspectives than their view of the world. Staff should be encouraged to write with this in mind and staff should encourage students to read the Reflections and on the most appropriate occasions

use a reflection to engage students in discussion, e.g. poverty, standard of living, transport, education, medical care. The International Reflections are one way to take a global perspective.'

- 'Those that help us to recognise how we are the same as well as learn from and celebrate how we are different.'
- 'Articles that cause me to consider the lives of others and reflect upon my own position.'
- 'A good Reflection is one which is truly reflective. But does anyone agree on what being "truly reflective" actually entails? For me, it involves all of the following: critical self-examination (i.e. what happened to my self-concept?); critical examination of what was learned (what was new? How did this change my understanding?); impact on future practice (what will I now do differently and how will it be an improvement on what I did before?). But I never write a Reflection for the web with all that in mind. For a start, it would be incredibly po-faced and alienating for most readers, even assuming you could do all that in 200 words. So, I like a Reflection most if it makes me smile (or even laugh), if it tells me something that I find genuinely stimulating (i.e. enlarges my understanding), if it contains no platitudes, and if the writing is energetic and inventive. If it can also achieve at least one of the three characteristics of "reflection" listed above, I am delighted.'

3 What should we do more?

Responses to this question are often linked to those for question 2. However, there are also a number of other suggestions, some of which are now being introduced:

- '[Add information on] [w]here to find out more e.g. links to other web based info pictures/documents/video etc. . . . . so if it's of particular interest we can find out more easily.'
- [More student contributions:] 'Students' Reflections are often very perceptive and moving.'
- 'Encourage Reflections that deal with current topics and events globally – perhaps ethically or philosophically. These would provide an additional opportunity for intellectual debate.'
- 'I would like to see more "light-hearted" Reflections that can give a greater sense of the place being visited. There is an occasional dryness to some of the Reflections (which isn't a problem, but it is good to see these balanced out).'
- 'Reflections from children??'
- 'I like the idea of themed Reflections – e.g. ethical, development, environmental and some spiritual stuff – just periodically – how about a one-off on poems by students and staff on their Leeds Met Experience?'

4 What should we stop doing?

The majority of responses to this question seem to encourage severe pruning of those which are not reflective. These examples are fairly typical:

- 'Accounts of people's business trips – they are a little boring unless they have experienced something cultural.'
- 'Perfunctory reporting of tedious conferences because the reflection was part of the deal but the writer's heart wasn't in it.'

Reflection 2: Friday 15 September 2006

Today we mark three years of International Reflections

International Reflections take me to new cultures and give me insight, not into how we view others, but how others view us. An example was from **Kobon Moses Togo**[5] reflecting on the support he received from inspirational individuals at Leeds Met. My favourites are those that send a message or make you sit back and think, such as the empty chair at the table for a missing loved one, in my all time favourite reflection from **Teresa Pioro**.[6] What Reflections have done for me is best summed up by **Karen Griffith**,[7] where she talks of her son and a couple of students in hospital beds next to each other, 'They have shown consideration and compassion and have recognised each others' diversity . . . [this] is another example of how essential integration and understanding can be'.

I believe that International Reflections have made the world a smaller place for me, made me understand diversity and given me the impetus and courage to go beyond boundaries by visiting Mexico last year and later this year Brazil. I could pick ten books on various countries in the world but I am more likely to remember ten 200 word Reflections. Thanks to everyone who has contributed.

Brian Bolton
Campus Services Manager and Staff Governor

---

5 Do you have any other ideas for improvements?

This elicited further ideas, again some of which have already been implemented:

- 'Think that there is a variety of Reflections, including some from students, staff etc. – and the variety is important. People will reflect what they perceive to be the most interesting thing. Keep up the good work.'

- 'How about a map of the world with the location of all the Reflections added to it?'
- 'A themed archive – or at least some themes in addition to the chrono-logical archive. A weekly Reflections Board in [the International Faculty] – either printouts on a notice board – or screen prints as part of the electronic display. Best of the month might similarly appear on other public display screens around the institution.'

What is the impact on the writer?

Boud, Keogh and Walker (1985) begin their volume on reflective learning by asking, 'How do you introduce a diverse collection of articles on "Reflec-tion: Turning Experience into Learning" when many of the contributors have not until now used the term "reflection" or "reflection in learning" to describe their own activities?' (p. 7). Soon after this they continue, 'we drafted an introduction . . . [and] . . . as we reread it we became increasingly dissatisfied with what we had written' (p. 7). This offers an example of one way in which reflection deepens the writer's sense of discovery, that moment of discomfort when reviewing what has been placed tentatively on record and questioning whether the record indeed reflects his or her intention. While International Reflections was not specifically initiated with this in mind, several of the authors have suggested that the process of reflection and the writing of their item have indeed contributed to their own learning process.

A survey of frequent contributors to International Reflections was con-ducted, with questions as follows:

1   How do you choose a topic for an International Reflection?
2   How does the 200-word limit affect the way you approach the writing of a reflection?
3   Can you describe your thought processes as you are composing the piece?
4   Are you influenced by feedback you have received on previous Reflections?
5   To what extent does your personal reaction to other International Reflections (either positive or negative) influence the piece you write?
6   Do you have any other comments which might be useful?

I How do you choose a topic for an International Reflection?

Responses to this question indicate a broad range of stimuli and often men-tion the fact that conscious awareness that a Reflection was expected of them caused the author to view the place they were visiting in a different light or to notice things which otherwise they might not.

- 'Writing the reflection actually does encourage me to take the time to reflect on what I am finding strange, interesting, irritating or exciting about where I am.'
- 'I take whatever strikes me as being the most notable about a country or culture, maybe the traffic congestion, or the food, or the aroma, or the atmosphere, or the way that people interact with each other.'
- 'I choose a mental souvenir; this is what I shall remember about this place.'
- 'There was one that was stimulated by an Australian student's reflection that I didn't like, so I wanted to be a bit provocative and present an alternative view.'
- 'I tend to choose topics from the pile up of ideas that appear, uninvited in my mind, as a way of clearing my mind to do other things.'
- 'When I stop and think, when I reflect, I give myself the space to deliberate upon that of which I want to make sense. If, say, it is the impact on me of the way another, from another culture, has behaved, my reflection may be based upon the fact that I felt that behaviour as "impact" and question why it has this "force". In other words I observed the behaviour, the behaviour was in some way different to my expectations and this "forced" me to stop, and think about it.'

2 How does the 200-word limit affect the way you approach the writing of a reflection?

The constraint of writing exactly 200 words in two paragraphs has been mentioned by some as too difficult a challenge, although those who work with students who are not native speakers of English say this is a useful learning task which helps students to gain greater understanding of English grammar in use. Those who responded to the survey generally found it an interesting personal challenge:

- 'Shorter is not easier. The limit means only the essence can be included and every word must count . . . Much time is spent crafting those last four or five words in or out. The key discipline is to make a couple of points powerfully.'
- 'The 200-word limit provides a good discipline for writing, however this can on occasion create difficulty in retaining meaning where the issues addressed are complex.'
- 'It's a welcome challenge and a discipline.'
- 'Sometimes the editing to get down to 200 words takes almost as long as writing the piece itself.'

3 Can you describe your thought processes as you are composing the piece?

Responses here show a number of motivations and ways of approaching the task. Some focus on the message and others on the reader:

- 'I am conscious that I want to tie things together ... I sometimes write the last line first, though I then will often end up changing that line.'
- 'Ideally there should be something new and interesting ... something that deserves reflection, which readers will actually want to read. The creative process involves finding that essence. It's an act of story telling.'
- 'Generally the process revolves around the need to communicate an international issue in a clear and meaningful way, but also that encourages others to think or do something themselves.'
- 'It is a creative process, it is a rare opportunity for creative writing as contrasted to the dull academic reports which we so often write. I have even written in verse.'
- 'I tend to think that the first paragraph has the stimulus and the second has the message . . . Other things I would add relate to intrusive thoughts about whether it is any good and how will it be received. I also try to think about any ways I can promote the University (or a section) internally and/or externally without sounding like a PR student.'
- 'Reflection on the experience of the trip as a whole to begin with and then focus on certain aspects of the trip. I also think about the audience reading the reflection and try to make it as interesting and readable as possible.'
- 'I want to get some main points across but don't want to sound patronising.'
- 'Not really a process. Always go through it in my head, usually when I am travelling abroad then write it.'
- 'I begin by writing freely about my topic, aiming at around 200 words. Then I leave what I have done to simmer for a while. After that I carefully read what I have written, often "out loud", partly because I find that doing so helps me to spot places where I have been longwinded ... I re-type the text, incorporating corrections and additions, thus beginning a round of reading, editing and rewriting, of which there may be twenty, before I feel satisfied and have reached 200 words.'

4 Are you influenced by feedback you have received on previous Reflections?

Colleagues are encouraged to respond to Reflections they find interesting, and clearly this provides encouragement for some authors:

- 'Yes, sometimes by the positive nature of the response but also occasionally challenged.'
- 'If I get feedback, I've got it wrong. The best pieces have their own rhythm and feel natural. I love the fact we get a chance to publish our images – I would like to be encouraged to share short video clips.'
- 'Not really. Praise is welcome, but writing is really a selfish pursuit, one writes for personal pleasure.'
- 'Having people encourage me to start writing in this way and congratulating me when something gets accepted has been very good for my personal development as a young academic. It has been a good place to start thinking about writing concisely, getting a point across and considering the audience.'

5 To what extent does your personal reaction to other International Reflections (either positive or negative) influence the piece you write?

While authors clearly find International Reflections interesting, few responded that their own writing is influenced by other contributions to that page. They are more likely to be influenced by the example of the Vice-Chancellor, who continues to write 200 words each day in VC Reflects.

- 'We have a research community here which strives to share via the reflective process. Many of the Reflections are really excellent, make you think or laugh. If I find it tough then I am humbled by [the Vice-Chancellor's] output. He writes one every day and there is a real risk that they could become perfunctory but they never are, so that is the marker. I also like the fact that some of the best Reflections have been by support staff who relish putting their experiences and thoughts into print. That knowledge that the process is shared by all is an encouragement to do better since people do look at them to make a bit more sense of what else other people are doing here . . .'
- 'The International Reflections serve as a constant reminder of the global context in which we both live and work, they remind me of the diversity of our students and of the breadth of the activity of the University.'
- 'Probably the biggest thing influencing my Reflections is the way [the Vice-Chancellor] writes his.'
- 'Each new reflection makes me feel confident that I am managing to interest people and I guess that makes me feel confident about continuing to write in my own rather unacademic style.'

6 Do you have any other comments which might be useful?

This question elicited a number of interesting additional comments, some with suggestions and others commenting on the value of International Reflections as a resource:

- 'I wonder if the editor's choice of all the year's Reflections could be printed and inexpensively bound.'
- 'One of my senior colleagues really impressed upon [us] the need to be productive and to make sure people knew we were and he pushed us strongly to make sure we were contributing Reflections for our own internal marketing . . . If you want to know why people write Reflections, it can be a motivating factor . . . I find the Reflections to be an interesting part of our uni – they serve many purposes to many audiences and contributors.'
- 'International Reflections are useful as they provide us with insights into what the University is doing abroad as well as personal reactions, cross cultural knowledge and experiences which can help in the understanding of our own international students and possible country contacts for our next visits.'
- 'They are a useful university-wide communication tool . . . They are also a way of showing to outsiders, e.g. potential students, that we are a dynamic University. Some other universities' websites seem so static somehow.'

Conclusion

The process of daily reflection in a public form, as has been demonstrated by responses from both readers and authors of International Reflections, appears to be serving its purpose in driving, supporting and reflecting internationalisation at Leeds Metropolitan University. Research Reflections, Assessment, Learning and Teaching Reflections and Ethical Reflections have all been introduced and are serving similar purposes in respect of those issues. All the Reflections have become a significant feature on the University's website, and ensure that there will be daily changes to the site to keep readers coming back. In addition, there has been a growing sense of pride as, increasingly, staff submit paper copies of their contributions in job interviews and students alert family and friends around the world when their piece appears.

This chapter has considered learning points from this particular aspect of culture change in one university and has given examples of actions that can be implemented in other contexts. In undertaking this reflection on Reflections, it is timely to consider how the concept can be taken to a higher level. The feedback given by both readers and writers, illustrated by the examples here, represents further opportunity for development as well as heartening evidence that internationalisation is becoming firmly embedded in the lifeblood of the institution.

Acknowledgements

I am indebted to all those who have contributed to International Reflections and to the readers and writers who have responded to the questionnaires. Particular thanks go to Jo Appleton, Brian Bolton, Steve Cockerill, Gavin Fairbairn, Max Farrar, Chris Garbett, Eddie Halpin, David Killick, Dawn Leggott, Adrian Schonfeld, Rai Shacklock, Richard Smith, Phyllis Stewart, Steve Wright.

Notes

1 http:sh/www.leedsmet.ac.uk/internat/reflects/jan06/jan17.htm
2 http://www.leedsmet.ac.uk/internat/reflects/dec04/dec17.htm
3 http://www.leedsmet.ac.uk/internat/reflects/apr04/apr20.htm
4 http://www.leedsmet.ac.uk/internat/reflects/apr05/apr20.htm
5 http://www.leedsmet.ac.uk/internat/reflects/may06/may18.htm
6 http://www.leedsmet.ac.uk/internat/reflects/dec04/dec24.htm
7 http://www.leedsmet.ac.uk/internat/reflects/mar04/mar05.htm

Chapter 4

Globalisation and sustainability

Global perspectives and education for sustainable development in Higher Education

Dorron Otter

In the UK, global perspectives and education for sustainable development can be seen to be a development of political education, civic education and their most recent forms as embodied in the term 'education for citizenship'. It is the increased awareness of globalisation that has led to this development using the terms 'global perspectives' and 'education for sustainable development'. The history of political education and citizenship is one marked by mutual suspicion across the competing ideological viewpoints between 'radicals', who take a 'broad' view of education in enabling individual students to challenge and ultimately act to transform the nature of the society in which they will live and work, and 'conservatives', who see education in the 'narrow' functional sense of creating efficient worker citizens.

Global perspectives and education for sustainable development have at their heart this radical agenda. Education not only has a role to play in the development of the functional knowledge and skills within and beyond the immediate educational subject area being followed by students, but must also enable them to develop a set of values that transform them, both now and in the future, so that they can challenge and change the deep-seated problems that they will confront in the society and worlds of work in which they will operate.

In *Values in Higher Education* (Robinson, 2005), Fryer reminds us that the Dearing Report of 1997 saw the purpose of the university to:

- inspire and enable individuals to develop their capabilities to the highest potential throughout life, so that they grow intellectually, are well equipped for work, can contribute effectively to society and achieve personal fulfilment;
- increase knowledge and understanding for their own sake and to foster their application to the benefit of the economy and society;
- serve the needs of an adaptable, sustainable, knowledge-based economy at local, regional and national levels;
- play a major role in shaping a democratic, civilised, inclusive society.

For Fryer it is this last aim that has been largely forgotten, which is surprising given that it is this last aim that so clearly focuses on 'their responsibilities towards the rest of society' and given that Dearing argued that 'higher education can legitimately, it is suggested, become a vehicle for social justice' (Fryer, 2005: 74).

For Fryer:

> According to this view, universities should play a pivotal role in the education and development of citizens and enlarging social inclusion, especially in the lives of those who might be expected to provide leadership of all kinds in civil society, if this doesn't sound altogether too grand.
>
> (Fryer, 2005: 76)

Dearing explicitly recognised that there was a need to move beyond the notion of there being a fixed common culture and set of values to a world which recognises the plurality of cultures and the possibility of competing value systems. Universities have a vital role to play in developing the knowledge, skills and values to enable students to participate as global citizens in such a world. It is argued that it is through embedding global perspectives and education for sustainable development that students in Higher Education can genuinely attain a global citizenship education for the twenty-first century.

Policy drivers

In the Foreword to the UK government strategy document *Putting the World into World-Class Education*, the then Education Secretary, Charles Clarke, argues:

> *Developing and maintaining a world-class system begins with understanding the world in which we live:* the values and cultures of different societies; the ways in which we are increasingly dependent upon one another; and the ways in which we all, as global citizens, can influence and shape the changes in the global economy, environment and society of which we are a part. One cannot truly educate young people in this country without the international dimension being a very significant and real part of their learning experience.
>
> (DfES, 2004)

Focusing on the issue of sustainable development in particular, the Higher Education Funding Council for England's (HEFCE) consultation for the policy development of sustainable development argues that:

> Higher education has a pivotal role to play in helping society to develop sustainably. This is because sustainable development is fundamentally a

process through which we can learn to build our capacity to live more sustainably. It is a process which everyone needs to participate in, but the involvement of higher education is particularly important because graduates will go on to occupy the vast majority of managerial and leadership positions in this country. Thus the role of higher education far outweighs the size of the sector in terms of its resources.

(HEFCE, 2005)

It is clear that the perceived threat of potential environmental catastrophe has led to the development of calls for education for sustainable development. It was the Brundtland Report, *Our Common Future*, that first sought to define the term 'sustainable development' (WCED, 1987). This report was then followed by the so-called Earth Summit which took place in Rio de Janeiro in 1992. The Rio Declaration formulated 27 principles for sustainable development and an action plan known as 'Agenda 21'.

Agenda 21, whilst mainly concentrating on the practical environmental management measures, did consider the possible role of education in both the formal and the informal sector. In 1993, the International Association of Universities issued the Kyoto Declaration on Sustainable Development, and in Europe in the same year the Copernicus University Charter for Sustainable Development was issued. The role of universities in terms of sustainable development was further emphasised in 1998 with the UNESCO World Declaration on Higher Education. In 2002 at the Summit for Sustainable Development in Johannesburg the role of education was seen as being critical if practical change was to occur, and this commitment ushered in the start in 2005 of the Decade for Education for Sustainable Development.

In the UK, the Toyne Report (Department of the Environment, Department for Education and Employment, and Welsh Office, 1993) immediately followed the first Earth Summit. However, despite this recognition of intent, it has been argued that, in the UK, the actual education and skills agenda has been keen to stress the 'narrow' or functional role of education as a means of improving individual performance and enhancing national competitiveness.

Since 2003 there has been a change in the policy response of the UK government. The *Sustainable Development Action Plan* published by the DfES in 2003, as well as the White Paper *21st Century Skills: Realising our Potential* of the same year, began to link the improvement in the functional skills base of the population with the recognition that this needs to be linked with wider social goals. In 2005 the role of all education sectors in promoting sustainable development was set out in the UK government's sustainable development strategy, *Securing the Future*.

Within the Higher Education (HE) sector this challenge has been picked up. The Higher Education Partnership for Sustainability (HEPS), established in 2000, resulted in a number of guidance papers for HE institutions (see www.heps.org.uk). One example of this in 2005 was a consultation paper prepared by HEFCE (HEFCE, 2005), which has been subsequently followed up with the publication of a report by the Higher Education Academy assessing the progress that is being made in embedding sustainable development in the sector (Dawe *et al.*, 2005).

In terms of global citizenship a range of development NGOs has been active in trying to foster approaches to development education and, within the education profession, practitioners have been actively involved in introducing global issues into the school curriculum and in teacher training programmes. David Hicks has surveyed the development of what he now prefers to call 'global education' both in the UK and internationally (Hicks, 2003). From the 1960s onwards there emerged a loose network of practitioners in the UK who began to adopt the name 'world studies' to characterise their approaches to introducing a global dimension into the curriculum. From 1973 to 1980 the World Studies Project brought together a community of interest of NGOs and educational practitioners within a conceptual framework that world studies would enable a transformative process to occur both for students and in their future actions in society. The role of values was a fundamental part of this process, as was the belief that the global dimension covered the four areas of poverty, environment, oppression and conflict.

In 1980 the World Studies 8–13 Project was established, primarily targeted at middle school students, and its pedagogical approaches were disseminated in the book *World Studies 8–13: A Teacher's Handbook* (Fisher and Hicks, 1985). In 1988 the World Studies Trust was established to take this work forward, and this resulted in the Global Teacher Project based at Leeds Metropolitan University, which ran from 1999 to 2005 (see www.globalteacher.org). Allied to this work was the work of the Centre for Global Education at the University of York led by David Selby and Martin Pike. Initially aimed at student teachers in secondary education, their work was then rolled out across a large section of the secondary schools sector.

Development NGOs have been keen to promote an awareness of development issues. Organisations like Oxfam and the Development Education Association (www.dea.org.uk) and their close links with DFID have had their efforts rewarded by substantial recognition in terms of UK educational policy. This was explicitly recognised in 1999 with the publication of the strategy paper *Building Support for Development*, which argued that development education must go beyond 'compassion and charity' by:

> establishing a real understanding of our interdependence and the relevance of development issues to people's everyday lives. We need to strengthen public confidence in and support for the fight against global poverty, acceptance that it matters for our future, that great progress is possible and that the behaviour of each of us can make a difference.
>
> (DFID, 1999a)

Operationalising global perspectives and education for sustainable development in Higher Education in the UK

What then is the current state of play as to the approaches being taken regarding global perspectives and education for sustainable development in the HE sector in the UK?

Definitions of global perspectives

Oxfam sees the Global Citizen as someone who:

- Is aware of the wider world and has a sense of their own role as a world citizen;
- Respects and values diversity;
- Has an understanding of how the world works economically, politically, socially, culturally, technologically and environmentally;
- Is outraged by social injustice;
- Participates in and contributes to the community at a range of levels form the local to the global;
- Is willing to act to make the world a more equitable and sustainable place;
- Takes responsibility for their actions.

(Oxfam, 2000)

For the Development Education Association, development education:

- enables people to understand the links between their own lives and those of people throughout the world;
- increases understanding of the economic, social, political and environmental forces which shape our lives;
- develops the skills, attitudes and values which enable people to work together to bring about change and take control of their lives;
- works towards achieving a more just and sustainable world in which power and resources are more equitably shared.

(McKenzie *et al.*, 2003)

Incorporating global perspectives into the curriculum is seen to involve the development of active and participative approaches to learning but also changes at the different spatial levels within any institution. For the DEA, global perspectives involves defining not only a range of learning outcomes but also a range of performance indicators by which institutions can be measured in terms of their commitment to global perspectives. This can be seen in relation to the institutional ethos, the social and environmental accountability systems and the purchasing and investment decisions of the institution.

Definitions of education for sustainable development

There are many different interpretations of what is meant by sustainable development and so it is not surprising that there will be different conceptions as to what might be required of education for sustainable development. For the UK government sustainable development is:

- Social progress which recognizes the needs of everyone;
- Effective protection of the environment;
- Prudent use of natural resources;
- Maintenance of high and stable levels of economic growth and employment.
  (http://www.sustainable-development.gov.uk/what is sd/what is sd.htm)

For many critics of this definition it is simply not tenable to include the last aim, as that fundamentally undermines our ability to meet the others. It is the nature of this challenge that also forges a clear link between the practice of global perspectives and education for sustainable development.

Rao (2000) reminds us that people are selective in their use of Brundtland's definition of sustainable development by only referring to the first sentence below:

Sustainable development is development that meets the needs of the present without compromising the ability of future generations to meet their own needs. It contains within it two key concepts: the concept of 'needs', in particular the essential needs of the world's poor, to which overriding priority should be given; and the idea of limitations imposed by the state of technology and social organisation on the environment's ability to meet present and future needs.

(WCED, 1987: 43)

It is the inter-generational aspect of the impact on future equity that is often the focus of debates about sustainability as reflected in this first sentence. However, this begs the question as to the implications of development for present generations. If the needs of future generations are to be compromised by the development agendas of today, what then about the plight of the present poor? As Solow argued in the UN Development Report of 1996, 'those who are so urgent about not inflicting poverty on the future have to explain why they do not attach even higher priority to reducing poverty today' (Solow, in Rao, 2000: 86). Principle 25 of Agenda 21 makes this point even more explicit: 'Peace, development and environmental protection are interdependent and indivisible.'

In the consultation plan commissioned by HEFCE to look into the support strategy for sustainable development in HE, it adapted a model developed by Meadows (1999) (see Figure 4.1).

This model is based on a systems view of the human condition. It emphasises the transformative process by which natural capital, through the application of science and technology, is turned into built and/or human capital. The processes and institutions of the political economy in turn change this capital into output in the form of private and public goods and services, and corresponding income and wealth, and then finally through our ethical and religious systems we achieve our ultimate ends of identity, community, fulfilment and progress (HEFCE, 2005). Quite clearly at the heart of both global perspectives and education for sustainable development is a recognition that it is not enough simply to look at the underlying knowledge and skills needed to come to terms with the global environment but what is needed is the development of a set of values that will encourage people to take the active role needed to transform this environment and their own behaviour.

As will be seen, it is argued that if education is to encompass values and be seen as enabling the individual learner to undertake a (life-long) transformative process then this has fundamental implications not only for the content of curricula but also for the processes of all aspects of the educational process. One key aspect of this is to develop the critical thinking and reflective practice skills of students, and this approach to pedagogy underpins both the learning and the teaching approaches of both global perspectives and education for sustainable development. Scott and Gough (2003) explore this relationship at length and emphasise the need for learning to encompass the experience of learners within, without and beyond the immediately defined formal education context. The implication for curriculum planners within this context is to draw on these wider experiences and equip the learners for the skills of life-long learning when they leave this context.

Stephen Sterling has argued that hitherto learning has been experienced by students in discrete subjects but that education for sustainable development

Ultimate ENDS	Well-being
through theology and ethics	
Intermediate ENDS	Human/social capital
through political economy	
Intermediate MEANS	Built/human capital
through science and technology	
Ultimate MEANS	Natural capital

Figure 4.1 Systems view of the human condition.

requires the adoption of a systems-based learning approach which seeks to reintegrate all elements of decision making. This fundamentally requires the embedding of education for sustainable development not as a grafting on to existing curricula but as a recognition that responses to systemic change in turn require systemic changes in our approaches to learning and teaching and the institutional context (Sterling, 2001). Sterling has gone on to develop these views further. For Sterling the emphasis is on *sustain-ability*. One aspect of this ability is the response-*ability* that education can encourage. In Sterling's view education should indeed be transformative. In relation to education for sustainable development such responses could range from no response, to accommodation with unsustainability (putting on a 'green gloss'), to reformation (contemplation of serious reform) or ultimately to transformation, when there would be a deep recognition of the need for world system redesign (Sterling, 2004).

Such an approach implies that it is not enough to go down the road of either confining sustainable development to a subject in and of itself or else of regarding it as having a natural home in a narrow range of disciplines but as of necessity being integrated into all courses. Ron Barnett has written about the need for education to deal with 'supercomplexity' and that in order to do so we must highlight the transformative role that education can play (Barnett, 2000). What global perspectives and education for sustainable development both have in common is that they are in a sense seeking to bring the 'outside in' to the curriculum and lifeblood of institutions of Higher Education.

Just as the DEA emphasises the link between the objectives for global perspectives as being curriculum change through specified learning outcomes and institutional performance indicators, so a joint report by the Higher Education Partnership for Sustainability and the Forum for the Future prepared by Parkin *et al.* argues that as well as sustainable literacy needing to be embedded into the content and delivery of all courses and all disciplines so too institutions need to set the context so that there is a clear strategic approach to sustainable development in the way that resources are used and in their wider community involvement. They must practise what they preach. It uses the Five Capitals Model to help to understand sustainable development. In this model resources are categorised into five types: natural, human, social, manufactured and financial. As sustainable society seeks to maintain and invest in the stocks of these so as to ensure the flow of benefits from each without diminishing the size of the original stocks/capital so Higher Education institutions might use the Five Capitals model to assess their contribution to sustainable development (Parkin *et al.*, 2004).

In terms of learning and teaching there is now a large and growing body of research in the area of education for sustainable development. The HEPS report (Parkin *et al.*, 2004) argues that, on the basis of this research and its own work, there are five principles that could be considered when thinking about how to embed education for sustainable development into the curriculum:

- The 'at the same time rule' should be applied.
- A learner-centred approach works best.
- Ethics and values matter.
- Sustainability literacy should be integrated into the content and delivery of all courses.
- Good learning practice is essential.

The 'at the same time rule' confronts head on the problem faced by those wanting to promote sustainable literacy in terms of being on the outside trying to get into the curriculum. This principle would involve education for sustainable development not being seen as an 'add-on' in terms of courses and curricula but, no matter what the individual subject discipline, the student should be able to recognise the resource/capital dimensions of that aspect of the discipline.

As a result of the consultation undertaken by HEFCE there have been a number of developments: HEFCE has funded two centres for excellence in teaching and learning (CETL) to help develop sustainable communities. One focuses on professional development for the built environment professions, and the other looks precisely at how the whole university can be transformed through education for sustainable development. Furthermore the Higher Education Academy commissioned research to investigate the current position of universities in relation to education for sustainable development and how they could best be supported in embedding education for sustainable development. This research culminated in a report, *Sustainable Development in Higher Education* (Dawe *et al.*, 2005), and a shorter briefing paper (Higher Education Academy, 2006).

In earlier research Martin and Jucker discovered the gap between rhetoric and reality in relation to the sustainable literacy within the university sector (Martin and Jucker, 2005), and this most recent research confirms this but is much more optimistic in terms of possible future progress. The research was conducted across the twenty-four subject centres of the Higher Education Academy and found:

> substantial work in progress, a range of good practice, but overall a patchy picture with sustainable development being marginal or non-existent in some influential disciplines but increasingly higher profile in others. There is universal acknowledgement that a wide range of skills and knowledge are required to create an action-orientated sustainability literate graduate body.

The research contains many 'vignettes' of good practice across many disciplines including Engineering, Initial Teacher Training, MBA programmes, Religious Studies and, as one might expect, Environmental Science. The report in surveying the literature and including the case studies highlighted the following three aspects of education for sustainable development and then sought to assess the degree to which the case studies show the practical implementation of these:

- The teacher as a role model and with the interest to act as a catalyst to introduce sustainable literacy. Here the case studies, whilst broadly supportive of this approach, did throw up concerns of teacher bias and the danger of teachers as preachers and the dangers of sustainability being seen as an ideology.
- As has been explored above, a strong aspect of education for sustainable development is the need to adopt an experiential approach to deal with the 'messy reality' that is thrown up by the complexity of the world. Generally the case study examples supported the need for such approaches and indeed argued that it was important for students to engage critically with the institutional and wider local community engagement.
- The need for systemic or holistic thinking. Again there was broad support for this but a recognition of the difficulty of introducing critical thinking to students who hitherto have experienced the curriculum through the reductionist approach adopted in schools.

The research points to subject areas such as Engineering and Materials, English, Geography and Earth, and Environmental Sciences (which one might reasonably expect) as having substantially embedded education for sustainable development into the curriculum. Other subject areas such as Bio-Sciences, Economics, Philosophy and Religion, and Tourism, Hospitality and Leisure have only made limited progress. In areas such as Information and Computer Sciences, Mathematics and Operational Resource there is little evidence of sustainable literacy skills being developed despite a professed interest.

It is useful here to look at the reason why this limited progress might be the case and, by identifying the barriers, explore ways in which the education for sustainable development agenda can be taken forward. On the basis of the research the following four barriers were highlighted:

- an overcrowded curriculum;
- perceived irrelevance by academic staff;
- limited staff awareness and expertise;
- limited institutional drive and commitment.

It is interesting to compare this research with that of the ongoing work of the Development Education Association (www.dea.org.uk) and the research of the Royal Geographical Society commissioned by the Department for International Development (www.dfid.gov.uk) to look into global perspectives in Higher Education. This report has been published and is available at www.rgs.org/globalperspectives. This study looked at the current status of global perspectives by looking at the discipline and department levels as well as the institutional responses. In terms of the disciplines and department levels the research was able to highlight evidence that in many areas there is an increasing profile for the global dimension as measured by conference themes and research projects and the increase in the global networks of interested academics. In its review of undergraduate programmes there is evidence that knowledge of the global dimension is being included but less evidence of the development of skills and values. At the institutional level there is a minority of institutions which have sought to embed global perspectives in their ethos, practices and provision. Many universities have sought to gain Fairtrade status from the Fairtrade Foundation and to ensure that their purchasing and estates policies are both ethical and sustainable. These examples of good practice, which are profiled in a series of case studies, certainly provide much encouragement and help for those operating across disciplines and departments and institutions that want to see an increase in the global dimension to see how best practice can help.

However, it is clear that, at the moment where this is happening, it is, for the most part, down to the efforts and commitment of individual teachers or groups within institutions. Even where there is this commitment there is the gap between rhetoric and reality referred to above and the problem of adding to what is seen to be an overly crowded curriculum. In many programmes the modules which incorporate global perspectives are relegated to the option space after the core curriculum has been dealt with. In many areas global perspectives is perceived to be a vague or woolly subject or indeed positively resisted as being overtly values-driven. At the institutional level internationalisation is still seen as being primarily about creating the environment in which to recruit international students successfully.

It is clear that education for sustainable development and global perspectives share the same agendas in terms of the challenges they face in being embedded in Higher Education and therefore the same agendas for future change. There are now strong external drivers at government policy level to encourage universities to introduce these approaches into the curriculum and there are internal drivers seeking to do so. Networks of interested practitioners are being formed and in some cases aided by both formal networks, such as the Higher Education Academy and its work through the subject centres, the centres for excellence in teaching and learning referred to above, the Development Education Association and the Forum for the Future, and the informal academic networks, such as the Global Perspectives Network in HE coordinated by Leeds Metropolitan University (www.leedsmet.ac.uk/gpn).

This could be helped with the review of subject benchmark statements to incorporate the addition, to highlighting areas in which each subject can help to promote education for sustainable development and global perspectives. There is an increasing academic literature on the role that education can play and, as has been argued, in so doing universities can rediscover the role that they can play in the fostering of global citizenship. There are now numerous examples of good practice that can be disseminated, and some institutions are seeking to incorporate education for sustainable development and global perspectives through their ethos and practice and their ALT strategies. The future for both education for sustainable development and global perspectives looks hopeful, the external environment has never been more promising, and the need has never been so urgent to effect change. It is up to the internal actors in the Higher Education sector to take up this challenge.

Conclusion

Whilst global perspectives and education for sustainable development have a different focus they are linked conceptually in relation to the full definition of sustainable development as outlined in the Brundtland Report and then further elaborated in Agenda 21. The focus on the possible inter-generational conflicts between present and future generations also brings into immediate focus the inter-spatial conflicts between the present rich and poor parts of the globe. It has been shown that both global perspectives and education for sustainable development aim to develop students as global citizens. The pedagogical implication of this is that due attention must be paid not only to the knowledge and skills required in a global environment but also to the values that will enable students to transform the nature of the societies in which they live and work so that they can fulfil their responsibilities as global citizens.

These developments are in line with the radical tradition in education and are subject to the same problems in terms of their ability to permeate the ethos and curricula of Higher Education institutions. They are both attempting to bring the 'outside in' to the academic world as experienced by students, but this can mean that they face the problem of being on the outside and looking in whilst the immediate demands of the subject being studied and the short-term goals of the institutional frameworks within which they operate serve to squeeze out cross-curricular themes.

This chapter has explored the developments of global perspectives and education for sustainable development and has shown that, despite the possible obstacles, changes in both the internal and the external environment in the UK Higher Education sector are providing the opportunities for practitioners to embed these themes within the ethos and curricula of their institutions.

Acknowledgement

With thanks to Stephen Martin for his advice and support on this chapter.

Part II

Perspectives on assessment, learning, teaching and student support

Chapter 5

Assessment and international students

Helping clarify puzzling processes

Sally Brown and Gordon Joughin

The importance of assessment

There is no doubt about the high importance of assessment for all students, and the particularly vital role it plays for international students and their teachers. Assessment is an important basis of esteem and the key measure of success; it determines progression and ultimately graduation, while providing students and tutors alike with vital information about students' developing understanding and skills. For international students who have made significant financial, emotional and family commitments to studying overseas, the assessment stakes can be particularly high.

Equally importantly, assessment is at the heart of student learning. Boud (1995), Brown *et al.* (1997) and one of the authors (Brown and Knight, 1994) *inter alia* have argued that it is potentially of even greater importance in terms of its impact on the student learning experience than just about any other aspect of their pedagogic experiences:

> Assessment defines what students regard as important, how they spend their time and how they come to see themselves as students and then as graduates. Students take their cues from what is assessed rather than from what lecturers assert is important.
>
> (Brown *et al.*, 1997: 7)

While the importance of assessment is undeniable, equally indubitable is the often problematic nature of assessment of students studying away from their home learning environments in another country, whether they are US students horrified by what they perceive as the low grades they receive in the UK, where marking conventions are different, students from some Pacific Rim countries who find that their approaches to presenting written arguments do not find favour in Australia, or UK students studying in Scandinavia or Northern Europe where they discover that they are expected to defend their work frequently in viva voce (oral) exams.

Usually, this is seen by those assessing as a problem that students have to solve, since they are the ones who are perceived as 'different' or 'wrong' in their approaches. Certainly students do need to adjust to their new environment, but we would like to argue here that the root of many of their problems with assessment is largely cultural – there is a mismatch between the assessor's expectations about accepted behaviour or ground rules for assessment, on the one hand, and students' experience, skills, and perceptions of assessment formats and tasks on the other. Such problems may arise when students are confronted with unfamiliar formats and unfamiliar or uncomfortable tasks, e.g. when they are required to be critical before they have established basic knowledge and understanding. Some students may simply lack the intellectual skills required by certain tasks because they have never had the occasion to develop them. A good starting point is for assessors to recognize that international students are bearers of culture, not bearers of problems (Ryan and Carroll, 2005), and that approaches to knowledge, learning and assessment can be highly culture-specific.

Assessment and culture

In her very useful *Guide to Teaching International Students* Ryan proposes that variations in approaches based on cultural factors might centre around:

- the extent to which historical texts and previously accumulated knowledge are respected;
- how far authority figures, including teachers, are respected (or not);
- how far it is acceptable to be overtly critical of authoritative texts or figures;
- whether a 'correct' answer is sought and the extent to which alternative responses are acceptable;
- issues about avoidance of making mistakes or losing 'face';
- how far students are expected to speak up or to listen quietly;
- how far personal opinions are valued (or whether this implies arrogance); and
- the importance of harmony and cooperation within the group over the interests of the individual within it.

(adapted from Ryan, 2000: 11)

Each of these factors has immediate implications for how students approach assessment and can help explain the actions of particular students. Ryan (2000) exemplifies this with reference to one broad group of international students:

Students from Asian cultures are generally portrayed as having a more 'conserving' attitude to knowledge than an 'extending' one. Western universities generally expect students to demonstrate creative, challenging and questioning learning behaviours, whereas in Eastern societies, harmony and compromise are highly valued for survival and social well-being. Asian students may therefore tend to rely more on the work of recognised 'sages' in constructing their arguments in essays, rather than seek to quote from newer, less well-known authors who may seem to be espousing radical or unfamiliar ideas.

(p. 17)

Such different approaches to learning and assessment are often deeply embedded within a culture. Ryan quotes Hofstede (1991) in arguing that there are four distinct areas in which cultures vary and which might impact on differing conceptions of assessment:

1   *power distance* – the extent to which less powerful members of the society accept inequality of power distribution;
2   *individualist/collectivist* – individual: where people look after themselves and their immediate family; collectivist: where people belong to 'strong cohesive in-groups' which protect them and to which they are loyal;
3   *masculinity/femininity* – 'male': social gender roles are clearly defined; 'female': roles overlap;
4   *uncertainty avoidance* – the extent to which the members of a culture feel threatened by uncertain or unknown situations.

Our assessment practices are likely to reflect our own home teaching and learning culture and our views on the four issues above. When our students are used to learning and being assessed in one culture, they may find working to a different set of grounds rules from those in use at home problematic when they find themselves in a new and unfamiliar context of study. A key task for assessors, then, is to make explicit the tacit rules under which assessment is sometimes seen to run, and to anticipate (and if possible eradicate) unpleasant surprises for students and staff.

Assessment 'surprises' and cultural factors

Cultural factors in assessment often emerge in the form of 'surprises' – behaviours from international students that we would not anticipate and that would not be expected from local students (Ryan and Carroll, 2005). Carroll asks us to notice and use 'surprises' in relation to student behaviour:

When British lecturers are asked, 'What do international students do that you don't expect from home students? Are there any unexpected behaviours?' lecturers mention behaviours such as:

• giving presents;

- answers all my questions with 'yes';
- handing in 4,000 words for an essay with a 2,500 word limit;
- writing very personal coursework with the main point on page 3 and lots of unnecessary background;
- repeating verbatim my lecture notes in the coursework;
- coming into my office after I have given the marks to argue loudly that I should give them higher marks – several times;
- coming up after the lecture for a 1:1 discussion and seeming to expect me to stay for as long as it takes even though I said 'Any questions?' in the lecture;
- deferring to my opinion, even when a preference would be appropriate (e.g. Me: 'which essay will you do as coursework?' Student: 'Please, you say').

(Carroll, 2005: selected from list on p. 29)

These surprises demonstrate lack of shared expectations between students and staff about what is required in assessment. They express particular cultural understandings of teacher–student relationships, the valuing of effort versus achievement, and respect for the authoritative nature of the teacher's views.

What follows, derived from comments made or reported to us in our work on assessment in more than twenty-five countries, is the kinds of remarks that staff make about surprises they have had in assessing their students:

- 'I couldn't believe that the pass mark for the exam was so low in your country. How can you have doctors qualifying with a pass mark of 50 per cent (or even less). Does that mean your doctors can practise knowing less than half the curriculum material?'

    The issue here is about different expectations of what constitutes successful student achievement. For example, medical schools in Scandinavia have pass marks of 70 per cent or even 80 per cent, which some of their UK counterparts would find surprising. This becomes problematic when marks from one country are aggregated with those from another without mutual understanding of what standard of achievement is being reflected in each.

- 'This work is absolutely full of errors: the verb tenses are all over the place and the definite and indefinite article seem to be used more or less at random (when they are not omitted altogether!).'

    The issue here is whether the work was full of errors, or a couple of errors repeated many times. Some languages, for example Chinese, do not have articles (definite or indefinite) at all and there is no single/plural distinction for nouns. Consequently, students may have great trouble with single/plural issues in languages that do. Similarly, verb conjugations work in lots of different ways and so errors with verbs can be frequent.

- 'Several of them share a flat together, and when their work came in it was all very much of a muchness. I took the matter up with them and they were very defensive, saying that was how they worked, all helping each other, especially with getting the language right. It was really hard to mark them fairly and I worried a lot about whether I had let them get away with plagiarism.'

Here the issue is about lack of clarity concerning the boundaries between collaboration, collusion, cooperation and cheating. It is really difficult to make judgements on whether joint production of assignments is intentionally trying to break the rules, or whether it is a sensible coping strategy demonstrating the kinds of behaviours we would often privilege in work-based contexts.

- 'After the Christmas vacation, one of my overseas students brought me back an expensive gift from home. And she alluded to the possibility, in an email, that I might like to visit her family back home for "social and professional reasons". It was just before the Semester One exams. What was I supposed to make of that?'

What is at stake here is around mismatched cultural expectations. It is probable that the student would be horrified to think that the tutor might misconstrue the gift and invitations as bribes offered to engender high marks. However, students might need alerting to that fact that gift giving is unacceptable in some cultures while welcome in others.

'Surprises' from the student perspective

The following comments, all again drawn from our own experiences or those reported by colleagues, give a flavour of the kinds of things that students encountering assessment regimes very different from those back home find surprising.

On dealing with unfamiliar assessment formats

- 'I couldn't believe it when they told me there was no written exam. At first I thought it was wonderful but now I'm really worried because I don't know what I am supposed to be doing.'
- 'I've never given an oral presentation before. Back home all our exams were written ones, so it was very nerve-racking for me to have to stand up in front of everyone, with them all looking at me. It made it really hard for me to concentrate on what I was saying, even though I had done lots of preparation.'
- 'In my country, you only really get to do a viva for a postgraduate qualification so it was a shock to me to find that I was expected to do them for my course on my year abroad.'
- 'Back home exams only last a couple of hours, or three at the most. Here they are six-hour marathons, sometimes more. It's really exhausting.'

- 'I haven't got my own computer and I've only just learned how to use PowerPoint. It was very scary doing the presentation as I had never used a data projector until I came to this country and I had to ask for help to get my presentation running. It made me feel stupid even before I started speaking.'

On language

- 'I've never been asked to write an essay as long as this before. Back home I was getting on really well with my written English, but what they asked for was usually only around 1,000 words long. This just takes so much time to get it right.'
- 'I went to my tutor and asked him to proofread my dissertation but he refused to help me. I am paying so much money as an overseas student here and I expected them to be more helpful to me.'

On religious issues

- 'We had two exams in one day, both lasting three hours. I had difficulty concentrating in the second one as I had been fasting since dawn. I didn't really feel I did my best.'

On ways of relating to others

- 'Home students are at such a great advantage over us. They seem to laugh and chat with the teachers in a very familiar way. We feel like outsiders and I think we are disadvantaged when it comes to the tests.'
- 'The tutor went through the criteria for the presentation with us, emphasising things like body language and eye contact but he didn't understand that that would be a problem for me to look straight at all the male students.'

On the authoritative role of the tutor

- 'It was a shock for me to find that I wasn't going to be marked by the tutor but by other students. How can they possibly be able to do that? The tutors should be doing this because they have the knowledge that we don't have.'
- 'In our OSCEs [Objective Structured Clinical Examinations], we had to examine a patient whose comments on my proficiency formed part of the assessment. How can that be right? They know nothing of clinical matters.'
- 'They tell us to read around the topic and give us long book lists to help us prepare for writing essays, but how do you know where to start? I

wanted to know which was the best book for me to concentrate on but no one would help me find it. In my country the books we need to study properly are indicated and everyone knows what they are.'

- 'In the lecture she gave us information about three different approaches to the subject, but she never told us which one was the right one. When I asked her about it, she said it was up to me to decide. How am I supposed to do that? She is the expert! So now I just don't know what to write in my essay.'

On expectations of a supportive relationship

- 'He told us we could come to his office if there was something we didn't understand, so I went, but after only half an hour he said he had to go off to a meeting, so I didn't feel he had really helped me much.'

Surprises about the assessment context

- 'I can't imagine anyone back home bringing their families along to watch them presenting university coursework, but here they all come along, aunties and cousins and grannies. I felt rather lonely doing mine all on my own.'
- 'The fees were cheap but we got no support since we paid only for lectures and examinations. In the lectures there were several thousand students and no chances to ask questions. I had to pay a tutor privately to help me prepare for the exams. And the question papers seemed to have nothing to do with the lecture topics.'
- 'He gave me a B-minus for my essay. Back home I never got less than an A or maybe an A-minus so I went to see what the problem was, and he more or less brushed me off, saying it was fine. But it's not fine! It'll play hell with my Grade Point Average when I go back home.'

These surprises draw our attention to a number of issues, including the following:

- Different marking and assessment cultures from nation to nation.
- Different pedagogic paradigms and contrasting philosophies of what learning at HE level comprises. Students may be surprised by the idea of multiple meanings and lack of a single authoritative voice. The teacher may be expected to give clear and definitive direction.
- Differences in 'distance' between staff and the students they teach.
- Shocks for students encountering novel (for them) means by which they are to be assessed, often with little preparation about what constitutes high-quality outcomes.
- Mismatched expectations about what level of support for learning

students can expect. More initial direction may be expected by students who may have had little experience to date of setting their own learning parameters.
- Lack of sensitivity about cultural mores: for example, setting demanding or multiple exams in a day during major religious festivals can be problematic.

Feedback

In the UK, results from the first National Student Survey on the learning experiences of British students showed a widespread dissatisfaction with the amount and type of feedback they receive. Much of this unhappiness stems from mismatched expectations, with lecturers perhaps feeling that they give plenty of feedback but that students don't make the effort to read and use the comments given, and students feeling that what they get back is tardy, sometimes peremptory and insufficiently personalised. Just as there are national cultures around assessment practices, so too are there variations in expectations internationally of feedback. Students who expect their tutor to spend time with them talking through how to improve their work may be shocked if they find their tutor unavailable or not keen to work with them individually for more than a few minutes. Similarly students working in a second or even third language may find handwritten comments, often in the form of personal shorthand or of single words in the margin which might have multiple meanings, to be just about valueless. They are likely to really value typed or emailed text in unambiguous language – but then again so might local students (particularly if they are dyslexic or have visual impairments)!

Carroll argues for an explicit, sensitive approach that acknowledges students' efforts and guides them to a more acceptable performance:

> Feedback that concentrates on what students have not done ('confusing argument', 'no links') or that implies rather than states what is required ('Is this your own words?', 'What about the Hastings reports?') is not helpful. It assumes the student knows the preferred behaviour, can decode the question, and could do what you suggest if they wished . . . Explicit feedback describes positive behaviour ('Put the main idea first then provide examples of how the idea would work in practice' or 'Tell the reader when you move from describing the method to discussing whether it is a good method or not' or 'If you are using someone else's words, you must enclose their words in quotation marks to show they are not your own words' or 'You should have referred to the Hastings report because it . . .').
> (Carroll, 2005: 33)

Once again, good practice for international students is clearly good practice for all.

Mini-case study: Assessment and 'the Chinese learner'

The perception of Chinese students as rote learners, lacking in initiative and tending to simply reproduce what they have read or heard in class rather than offering their own critical analysis and perspective, is perhaps one of the most widely held stereotypes of international students in Western countries. Much has been written about 'the Chinese learner' in Asian cultures, particularly in mainland China and Hong Kong. Here are some of the points worth noting from this literature (for example Biggs and Watkins, 2001; Gao and Watkins, 2002; Lee, 1996; Pratt et al., 1999) and from the experience of one of the authors in teaching and assessing Hong Kong Chinese students:

- Chinese school assessment is based on a highly competitive external examination system. Consequently students entering university have experienced a limited range of traditional assessment formats. *Students need to be introduced to new assessment formats.*
- Students are adept at working out what is really required by assessment and studying accordingly. Moreover, students tend to be highly motivated to achieve, and attribute academic success to their effort (rather than innate ability). *If students can come to grips with what is required by their assessment, they are likely to work hard at it.*
- What appears to Westerners to be rote learning usually isn't (Biggs, 1998; Marton et al., 2005). Chinese learning involves an intricate interplay between memorising and understanding. (This explains why Chinese high school students consistently outperform Western students in comparative tests of understanding in maths and science.) *Chinese students will tend to adopt deep approaches to learning when assessment requires it, and will often seek understanding at the same time as memorising material.*
- Chinese students and teachers value the mastery of basic knowledge. If there is a typical pattern of Chinese learning, it may be (i) acquiring basic knowledge and understanding; (ii) learning to apply this; and, only then, (iii) analysing, critiquing and developing personal perspectives. *Assessment that seeks critical analysis before mastery of basic content has been established may be problematic. Students may be reluctant to participate in tutorial discussion if they have not mastered the material in advance.*
- 'Teaching from the text' is a common practice in high schools, while the 'teacher as text' indicates the respect accorded to teachers as

authoritative experts. *Students may treat texts as authoritative statements of accepted knowledge. They may need to develop a critical approach to their reading, and learn to question their teachers. Some may need to develop appropriate citation practices.*

- Chinese conceptions of teaching include a closer relationship, outside class, between teacher and student. *Students may expect their teachers to take an interest in both their learning and their personal well-being.*

- While university assessment in Hong Kong is dominated by examinations and essays, a wide range of alternative assessment methods has also been used successfully. *With support, students are able to adapt to alternative assessment methods; there is no reason to believe that Chinese students are less capable than Western students of mastering new or unfamiliar assessment formats.*

Gordon Joughin, University of Wollongong

Biggs (1996) argues powerfully that we need to make a distinction between rote learning, that is, repetition without understanding what is being learned, as one might when repeating sentences in a language one doesn't understand, and learning by repetition, with understanding. He cites the example of the calligrapher who repeatedly makes the same strokes of brush on paper to form letters, intensifying meaning by contemplation. A further example might be the répétiteur working with an opera singer, helping the artist to add colour to the aria by variations in phrasing or intonation. Practice makes perfect. And even rote learning can have its place (those born in the 1950s know their multiplication tables in sing-song voices in their heads, but rarely make mistakes when purchasing multiple items or calculating their winnings at the bookmakers!).

Briefings on an assignment need to be clear and unambiguous from the outset. Asking questions of the tutor about criteria or expected outcomes is completely acceptable in some nations but would be embarrassing in others. In Chinese contexts, this could also be considered a matter of respect. To ask questions is to imply that the tutor has not explained clearly and is therefore inadequate (hence the tutor might lose face) or an admission of stupidity by the student for not understanding (hence the student might lose face). Students might be more likely to ask for clarification after they have gone away and studied the material, which can cause annoyance if the tutor can't understand why they didn't sort things out during the briefing session.

Plagiarism

Plagiarism is a hugely contentious area, with allegations often made that international students are the worst culprits. Such claims are often made with little realisation that different attitudes to originality exist around the world, and that what is acceptable in one context is frowned on in another (and vice versa):

> International students may have been previously rewarded for academic performance which drew heavily on the work of others. In some cultures this is regarded as a compliment to those whose work they copy (and is sometimes referred to as 'following the master'). In their new environment international students may find themselves being criticised and penalised for not being independent, or worse, being accused of plagiarism or cheating.
>
> (Ryan, 2000: 55)

We also don't know with certainty why those who plagiarise do so:

> Some studies identify the problem of plagiarism being greater among international students, but it is worth noting that the evidence is equivocal on this point. Where there is evidence of higher rates of plagiarism among international students, they are also more likely to be affected by a range of mitigating circumstances such as poverty, isolation and financial pressures requiring long paid working hours and/or embarrassment at not knowing how to do the task.
>
> (Dunn et al., 2004: 63)

It is often difficult to distinguish academic malpractice (deliberately setting out to use others' work fraudulently) from poor study techniques that home students get involved with as well (patchworking bits and pieces from various texts through a combination of lack of confidence in one's own voice and failure to fully understand the material). Assessors need to take into account the possibility that students might be writing in their second or even third language, when the paraphrasing and summarising they could readily do in their first language become very difficult.

We should aim to make a distinction between deliberate cheating and not understanding the conventions in the place of study. Students can become angry or confused if the behaviours they have been encouraged to develop are regarded as inappropriate or suspect in a new nation of study. Greek students, for example, who have been encouraged to focus single-mindedly on an authoritative text with the expectation that they use it extensively word for word in a subsequent exam may be astonished to find that this is frowned upon by markers who are expecting to find 'originality' or 'flair' (however ill defined) in students' work. Such students may ask 'Why reword something that is already expressed clearly and authoritatively?' Others, used to a deferential approach to authority figures, may ask 'Who am I to try to improve upon the words of a distinguished and celebrated teacher?'

I give students simple descriptions of plagiarism and collusion:

- Copying – reproducing or imitating;
- Collaboration – working with others;
- Collusion – agreement to deceive; using the words or ideas of colleagues or other students and passing them off as your own;
- Plagiarism – stealing someone's words or ideas and passing them off as your own.

I then give the students real examples of each of these.

(Lecturer, University of Strathclyde, quoted in Ryan, 2000)

Solutions and mitigations

- Make the rules of the assessment game explicit and don't expect everyone to get the hang of them all at once. It is a matter of having very clear expectations, showing examples, and discussing what is required with students. Of course, this will benefit all students, not just those from different countries.
- For students, being clear about what they need to do may not suffice. 'Seeing what to do is only part of the story; you also have to know how to do it' (Tang and Biggs, 1996). This involves providing opportunities for practice before the real thing.
- Be explicit about the extent to which the accuracy of written language is a criterion for assessment, and don't mark down work on the grounds of poor language if this is not explicitly part of the mark scheme. The aim should be to establish where a student stands in relation to the concepts and abilities being assessed. If language issues prevent a student from demonstrating where they stand, the validity of the assessment is in question.
- Assessors should inform themselves by finding out more about assessment practices elsewhere. One way to do this is to talk to students about the kinds of assessment they are used to. Another thing to do is to reflect on our own assessment practices and why different students may respond to them in different ways. Ultimately, it is important to recognise our own practices as culturally determined.
- Assessors in subjects other than languages or journalism, say, should consider the extent to which they mark the English language of students.

We advise that they only mark down the language if it's in the assessment criteria and students are aware of this. It's worth noting that many home students are also poor at expressing themselves, so the criteria should be applied to both home and international students equally. We suggest that occasional grammar lapses do not always result in communication being ineffective, since arguments are often easy to follow even though something is clearly not written by a native speaker.

- Provide multiple and diverse opportunities for assessment so it isn't a matter of 'sudden death' at the end of a module when the student encounters a novel assessment practice for the first time.
- 'For an assessor it may be difficult to work out whether a student does not know the material or simply cannot express it as expected. When the cohort is particularly diverse, this may be quite a problem. One solution is to provide a range of assessment items – perhaps involving portfolios or presentations, so the student understanding can be gauged in a variety of ways' (Dunn et al., 2004: 50). However, we need to be aware that this could also exacerbate the problem by introducing even more unfamiliar and threatening formats. One could argue that the range of formats should be limited so that students can become familiar with them.
- Encourage, or require, students to submit early drafts of assignments for feedback, particularly in the early stages when students are 'learning the ropes'.
- Provide opportunities for peer assessment (for feedback rather than marking), since this can help all students to develop their sense of what is required.
- Where appropriate, use cultural diversity positively by encouraging students to write about their own contexts in assignments, thus valuing what might otherwise be ignored.
- Consider how you allocate students to groups when you are using group assignments, to ensure diversity. Left to their own devices students choosing groups may stick with their friends and co-nationals, which can have some benefits in terms of mutual support, but will have disadvantages too if students feel excluded or disadvantaged. If clumsy group allocations are made (perhaps making each group of predominantly home students include one international student), this can be equally inappropriate. Perhaps the best approach is to ask students to identify at least one person with whom they would like to work and then combine pairs into larger groups which combine diversity with mutual supportiveness.

Conclusions

We argue that good practice for international students is good practice for all. Janette Ryan and Jude Carroll talk about international students being useful indicators of the health of the learning organisation:

> Harkening back to the time when coalminers took canaries into mines to monitor air quality, if the canaries died, they knew that the atmosphere threatened the miners' well-being, too. We are also at a 'coalface'. The international student 'canaries' thankfully show us their difficulties in less dramatic ways but nevertheless point out aspects of our teaching that all students will probably experience as challenges. By paying attention, we can change conditions to make sure that everyone can thrive in the Higher Education environment. If we improve conditions for international students, we improve them for all learners.
>
> (Ryan and Carroll, 2005: 9–10)

If we manage to make our assessment approaches fit for purpose with international students in mind, home students will also benefit since they too often have trouble coming to grips with assessment requirements and may interpret requirements in unintended and unhelpful ways. Within these approaches, making things explicit is imperative, including, critically, providing examples that illustrate good work and discussing these with students, as well as providing opportunities for students to practise the format in realistic contexts but in a climate where they don't feel foolish or exposed if they get things wrong first time. Students need to learn about assessment, just as they need to learn about subject content.

At the same time, this good practice requires an awareness of the culturally determined nature of some crucial aspects of assessment. When students from particular cultural contexts consistently experience problems with assessment, we need to consider the role that culturally based factors may be playing and respond to these appropriately. This calls for an awareness of and respect for other assessment cultures and a realisation that our local culture is not the only one, nor necessarily the best.

It is important to note that the recognition of cultural factors in assessment does not imply a lowering of expectations. While cultural and language issues may partly explain some of the problematic behaviours described above, they should not be seen as an excuse for students' inappropriate academic practices. We should have confidence in our professional practice of assessment, convey high expectations to all of our students, and expect, and require, international students to adapt to the practices of the teaching and learning culture in which they are studying. This is a vital aspect of their learning and development.

We began this chapter by noting that assessment is at the heart of learning. Tom Angelo has exhorted us to do assessment 'as if learning matters most' and given us some guidelines for acting on this principle (Angelo, 1999). If we apply these guidelines to our international students, we will see assessment as a vehicle for actively engaging our international students in their academic work, and for developing regular, fruitful interactions between us and these students and between them and our local students. It will become a focal point for feedback that actually helps learning. Perhaps most importantly, it will become a means for students and tutors alike to recognise their own beliefs, values, and ways of learning based on prior experience, while opening the way to 'unlearn' habits and practices that are not appropriate in new cultural contexts. And, in doing this, we will surely be improving the quality of assessment practices for all.

Chapter 6

Support and guidance for learning from an international perspective

Jude Carroll and Jo Appleton

Introduction

The literature on cultural migration is extensive. It usually concentrates on the consequences of moving to unfamiliar contexts and, often, the negative aspects of cross-cultural travel, using labels such as 'culture shock' and detailing the impact of encountering so much that is new. The positive side of placing oneself in a new culture is mentioned less often, yet, for many cross-cultural travellers, observing and experiencing others' ways is, on balance, more interesting than it is painful; it can prompt better understanding of one's own assumptions and beliefs in the same way that the first astronauts to the moon looked back and saw the Earth as a blue sphere.

The experience of moving from familiar *academic* contexts to unfamiliar ones is less commonly discussed and less often anticipated by students moving to a new academic setting. This may be one reason why students have fewer strategies to deal with new ways of learning and teaching than they do with new food or new banking systems. Cortazzi and Jin (1997) describe how pedagogic practices and expectations seem normal and remain invisible to those who stay within familiar academic systems. If students who were 'blind' to their own academic assumptions then arrive in a new system, they may continue to use strategies and expectations that served them well in the past, assuming they will be equally useful in the new context. The result may be academic 'culture shock' and it can happen when students progress from secondary school or decide to leave professional practice and return to academic study or move to a new country. Students from any of these groups may encounter new expectations and behaviours and ask themselves questions such as: 'What are students meant to be doing here when they study?' 'What are the teachers testing when they set essays?' 'What do teachers mean when they tell us to "be original", "use a wide range of sources", "take a critical view" . . .?' 'How do teachers expect me to use my time between lectures?' and so on. Tutors, whether of international students or of those admitted with non-standard entry qualifications, may wonder: 'What might I realistically expect from a student with this level of language competence?'

'Should I be using more "basic" English?' 'What can I do to get everyone talking in the seminars and not just the UK students?' amongst many other questions.

This kind of reaction and confusion has grown more common and more widespread from the mid-1990s in Western universities as the international-isation of universities in Western Europe, Australia, New Zealand and, to some extent, Canada and the US gathered momentum. Many who describe these changes (the authors included) see the changes as enriching and an opportunity to improve all students' learning, whether they are called 'inter-national/overseas' or 'home' students. However, benefits are not automatic, nor do they flow from simply having international students on campus. Students' cultural capital needs to be exploited appropriately, and support is necessary for both teachers and students if the potential benefits are to be realised.

In this chapter, we review students' needs for support and guidance, espe-cially those who arrive in Western universities from other academic cultures. We acknowledge that all students who are new to Higher Education must learn new study skills and adapt to different assumptions, but only inter-national students must do so in a totally new culture, perhaps in a new language and, in some cases, requiring them to take on skills or activities that directly contradict ones that had previously been encouraged and valued. So, for example, Greek students may have learned to study one text in great depth, reading it again and again until they were completely familiar with its context and ideas and then use the familiarity to ensure success in an exam. Put the same students in an Australian university and, to be a 'good student', they must access a wide range of sources, select ideas and short statements from the sources they decide are appropriate and then weave the extracts and comments together into an argument which they write independently over a few weeks. It is not immediately clear how someone who is skilled at the former learns to do the latter.

Similar examples abound. Indian students in their home country have probably invested years in memorising answers for examinations, secure in the knowledge that an accurate reproduction of an answer which derives from a reliable tutor will be assessed for top marks. Put the same students in a Canadian or British university and they must solve problems independently using a range of resources, one of which could be a tutor who serves more as a 'guide on the side' than a 'sage on the stage'. To some extent, these shifts can be predicted, but often students find the change confusing or unexpected. Americans may assume the differences between a US and UK pedagogic culture are minor, yet American students who have spent years mastering the art of multiple choice questions and pithy short answers are often just as unsure how to proceed as the Greeks when they are expected to decode an essay title which is in itself a puzzle and which is designed to trigger 3,000 'original' words.

These and other examples illustrate differences in academic cultures. In this chapter, we suggest alternatives to assuming students in new academic cultures will decode and make sense of others' surprising behaviour (though some can do so). Instead, we suggest they are offered guidance and support, and cite instances where different levels of support have been tried at different stages in students' tertiary study. Whilst concentrating on students' needs, we recognise that teachers often have needs too, and might find support and guidance equally useful. Advice on teaching culturally diverse students is widely available. Teachers can seek out suggestions on inclusive teaching methods designed to make all students more able to learn (for example, Carroll and Ryan, 2005) and/or focus on meeting the needs of specific groups such as Chinese students (Edwards and Ran, 2006). They can focus on teaching specific skills, such as Indian students learning Western writing requirements (Handa and Power, 2005), or use a book such as this one to guide internationalisation activities. Students, on the other hand, cannot always seek help widely and are perhaps less well served by the literature.

For both students and teachers, it is unlikely that any one solution will suit all cases or that conditions for guidance and support will be optimal. Both students and teachers are probably making the best of what is on offer, and we describe some of those situations below. We do so in the hope that those forced to rely on such approaches can anticipate common problems and, hopefully, be more expeditious in devising strategies for dealing with them.

Offering no specific help or guidance

Many students have only a day or two of general induction to help them adapt to university study. It is common for their teachers to expect them to learn the ropes quickly, perhaps even within a week or two of arrival. Some teachers regard offering guidance on pedagogy as outside their responsibilities ('I teach Geology and it's up to them to learn it'), and many, if they do offer advice, would see no need for it to include academic cultural differences. Some may have little or no knowledge of their students' varied pre-university experiences, perhaps because they were 'home students' themselves and have only taught within their own national system. Some assume their subject is 'culture-free' ('I teach computing. A computer works the same in China as it does in Cleveland') and overlook the fact that, as soon as two people talk about computing or make judgements about the other's mathematical abilities or communicate about a lab instrument, then culture inevitably enters into the interaction.

Zero support does not mean zero student success. Students can and do arrive, survive and sometimes even thrive in an unfamiliar HE context, especially where international incomers are relatively few in number, thus keeping open the option of individual attention and additional personal effort by students and teachers. This kind of unplanned, opportunistic approach to support is often used in American universities where classes have only one or two international students. It can work in small, specialist institutions where students can become known and integrated members of the community such as happens in small, isolated institutions. It was common in the past when students were admitted after vetting and coaching in their home countries, as was commonplace in the UK until the mid-1990s. 'Sink or swim' approaches might continue to produce good swimmers in elite institutions that select between a number of highly qualified applicants. However, where overall numbers are above 20 per cent on any one programme (as is the case in the UK, Australia, New Zealand and many countries in Western Europe) and where the diversity within cohorts is growing, it is no longer viable.

Offering no support to students who arrive with minimal qualifications, from very diverse backgrounds, in significant numbers such that the cohort includes percentages in double figures and can be well over 20 per cent will cause problems for teachers and students. It is likely to trigger demands from tutors for different admission policies and identify the students as the problem. Students must expend considerable energy to be successful and often experience high levels of stress and even mental and physical illness (Sakurako, 2000). Perhaps most worrying, providing no support to incomers can mean that home students see international students as threats to their grades and as frustrating to work alongside rather than the stimulus for global understanding that some campaigners for internationalisation argue will happen when students from around the world study 'together'.

So, if you or your institution decides to opt for this level of (non-) guidance, then as a minimum there needs to be staff and student awareness-raising of the difficulties of operating in another language and culture and actions designed to encourage empathy for those who travel to learn and for those teaching them.

Pre-arrival support and guidance

Another kind of support and guidance is provided by pre-arrival or pre-course interventions, usually aimed at foundation-level and pre-masters students. Pre-sessional programmes can be a compulsory admission requirement for students who are just beneath the subject knowledge and/or English language entry requirements. Some pre-sessional courses offer a qualification and guaranteed entry on to undergraduate programmes upon successful completion, thereby shaping students' study plans and direction. However, the majority of pre-sessional offerings are optional, with the goal of improvement rather than remediation.

Pre-sessional programmes for students who have met minimal requirements and who know what substantive programme they intend to follow are typically a few weeks in duration (or somewhat longer if located in the student's home country, as costs are lower). Programmes aimed at students with minimal qualifications can be marketed at reduced or even no cost in recognition of their value as a recruitment inducement and as a way of enhancing students' learning. For example, the University of Central Lancashire in the UK has a four-week-long programme that combines generic teaching, aimed at orienting the student to Britain, with academic skills development in the student's cognate area. Discipline-specific study skill help on this programme is especially welcomed by students who must cope with the specific vocabulary and writing requirements in their chosen field of study. When marketing the programme, it is important to stress their benefit rather than implying any compensation for skill deficits. One example is a two-week pre-sessional for students planning to study Tourism, Hospitality and Events Management at Leeds Metropolitan University, where marketing literature stresses that only those with minimal requirements may attend and where the purpose is clearly stated that attendees will receive guidance in Academic English and study skills to alert them to university requirements.

Somewhat longer pre-sessional programmes are provided for students whose language skills fall just below the minimum. These programmes are typically about a semester in length in the new country of study and somewhat longer in the student's home country, offering students time and specialist help either to focus on their language development or to improve their subject knowledge alongside Academic English and study skills.

Successful completion of pre-sessional programmes probably leads to a greater chance of success and lower rates of attrition for students entering their substantive programme of study. This is certainly the claim made by those providing such services. Tutors of students who have had pre-arrival or pre-sessional support notice the difference that exposure to concepts such as plagiarism, independent learning and critical thinking has on students new to Western university education. Teachers claim that these students spend the early weeks of substantive study attending to the demands of the course rather than decoding English and/or trying to make sense of unfamiliar teaching methods. However, pre-sessional programmes, even those lasting many weeks or months, are unlikely to 'graduate' students who are fully ready for their substantive tertiary study.

Students leaving pre-sessional support continue to benefit from organised 'buddy systems', linking them with more experienced peers who are drawn from students of the same nationality or, sometimes, from a generic 'international' pool, as happens at Oxford Brookes University where students designated as Guiders offer new students information and support in the early weeks. At the University of Central Lancashire, mentors in the form of experienced students answer new students' questions and generally welcome and support them during the first few weeks of semester. And the University of Melbourne offers a wholesome 'Transition Programme' which provides advice and support not only for new students themselves but for schools, parents and university staff.

Another way to help students make the transition to 'real' study is by developing close links between pre-course tutors and those in the students' substantive areas. At the University of Northumbria, great efforts go into building links between those teaching their ELAN programme, offering English and Study Skills foundation courses, and tutors on the students' undergraduate programmes. Students are tracked over the six months after they leave the ELAN programme, and their subsequent successes and struggles inform programme development for all.

Whilst it can be challenging to provide pre-sessional programmes, it is even more so to persuade students to attend them. Barriers such as time, cost, marketing decisions and perceived competition between providers will mean the majority of students opt out or persuade themselves the support is not needed. It can seem very sensible to a student to assume that hard work and the confidence that comes from knowing the university admitted them will suffice. Indeed, it is complex enough to convince international students that they make the grade for entry but then again somehow do not and need additional support. For this reason, it will always be a minority who attend. Even where pre-sessional support is offered, students' skills will remain tentative. It may take years and almost always many months before students working in a new academic culture (and often a new language) will feel confident of doing themselves justice.

Support after admission on a substantive programme

Extra teaching, additional study skills modules and intensive English language classes are sometimes offered to all students and/or targeted at international students after enrolment. Support after admission can be relatively unproblematic compared to the problems of persuading students to pay more money and take more time before they start to study. However, here too organisers have difficulties with organising provision, sourcing extra help and convincing the students who most need it to attend. Hard-pressed students who have not yet had any assessment feedback may not see the need and those who are already struggling with the demands of the course may judge their time better spent elsewhere. It is often helpful to organise support after an early diagnostic activity within the student's cognate area, perhaps asking for 1,000 words within the first four weeks and providing feedback on how it was produced, rather than focusing on the content or what was said. This ensures students are alerted to their study needs rather than waiting until the first assessment point, by which time several months have passed, unacceptable habits such as copying texts may have been reinforced, and the student risks a failure from which it might be difficult to recover. When commenting on early diagnostic tasks, it is important that assessors remain focused on entry-level skills rather than comparing the newcomers' performance to what will be expected upon completion of the programme. This kind of activity may need to be repeated at other times in the student's university career and, again, appropriate skills identified for development.

If students are persuaded or compelled to access additional support, this will be more successful if it is designed to mesh with the demands of students' substantive study and if students who attend are not marked out as remedial. Students often find it difficult to fit in additional, non-assessed classes, so designing them over time, perhaps as two-hour 'mini-courses' focusing on different areas (e.g. 'Writing references and bibliographies', 'Effective reading', 'Presentation and seminar skills') and offering them weekly over four weeks, would allow students to select those of greatest use and to have several opportunities to fit one into their schedule. To promote attendance, reflection on the benefits gained could be assessed through the students' main course of study (e.g. through progress files) and certificates or letters of attendance could be awarded to those with 100 per cent attendance.

Support and guidance that are carefully organised and specific to the discipline are widely welcomed by students and, increasingly, expected by many. Indeed, many wonder where their fees go if they see that all students, regardless of their contribution, are treated the same. Tutors, too, are grateful for the extra help and can develop very collaborative relationships with whoever is offering the extra support and guidance. For example, the University of Kent offers 'Value Added Learning in University Education', which is a partnership initiative between students, participating academic departments and the Unit for the Enhancement of Learning and Teaching. The aims of the programme are to develop students' academic knowledge and understanding, key skills and learning strategies.

These arrangements work when English language specialists, study skills advisers and discipline-specific tutors work together and when early diagnostic activities are used to identify where students need to set aside skills and beliefs that have served them well and adopt new ones appropriate to the new setting. They ensure the students who need the help get it and that the help is tailored to the specific context of the programme.

Even when effective, there are risks in putting all the emphasis on the first few months and all the emphasis on the students adjusting and adapting to the new academic culture. Front-ending support seems to imply changes can happen quickly if the student works hard and puts in the effort to adapt. The reality is that a student cannot develop English competence or perfect new skills quickly no matter how hard he or she works at it (Volet and Renshaw, 1996). Those unfamiliar with language learning may think it is only a matter of building vocabulary and studying grammar, but Hedge (2000) lists many conceptual changes and challenges that confront a 'good language learner'. Hedge lists attributes such as willingness to take risks, and being creative/experimental that could be seen as inherent to the student's personality though other characteristics can be learned over time such as noting that good language learners organise opportunities for practice and make sure they learn from errors. They develop ways to live with uncertainty 'without wanting to understand every word' (Hedge, 2000: 77) and draw upon the context to aid guessing. Effective language learners use knowledge in their first language to illuminate aspects in the new one and develop their use of chunks of language and formalised routines – this helps them perform 'beyond their competence' and appear more 'native-like' or 'natural'. Hedge goes on to cite their ability to use different styles of writing and speech to adapt to formal and informal situations and also to find ways of communicating without language. Finally, she suggests that good language learners must 'enjoy grammar'. If this somewhat daunting list is placed alongside the demands of the substantive course, it becomes clear that time and effort are required rather than any 'quick fix' solution in a few weeks.

Front-ending also risks ignoring needs that develop later as academic demands change. For example, students who move from year one courses to year two may encounter more complex texts and more difficult cognitive demands. Students tackling a thesis or dissertation will need more support as will those about to go on placement or to undertake their first field trip. These new situations and demands will require new things of students, and they may or may not recognise this or have the skills to do what is required.

An alternative to front-ended, specialist guidance and support?

It is possible (though relatively rare) to regard supporting international students as everyone's responsibility and as achievable within current workloads. They will need clear messages about what to expect, appropriate feedback about whether they have met those expectations and honest interventions when they do not. Librarians, departmental secretaries and front-line staff may be able to meet this requirement, as well as tutors and students' supervisors. However, the tutor a student encounters day in and day out is probably the one with the most influence on the student's ability to learn and use English appropriate to academic study and the language of the discipline. Students will need practice, feedback, encounters with acceptable examples and many chances to try out the new ways of demonstrating understanding and creating high-grade work, e.g. through a student's academic/personal tutor, which needs to be profiled into that tutor's workload, as otherwise the student can feel that the tutor is always too 'busy' to help.

This sounds like a demanding requirement and, to some extent, it is. However, the challenge is not doing *more*; rather the challenge is to do things *differently*. Where tutors are willing to develop a greater awareness of their own expectations for students and where they adopt a relatively small number of different practices, it is possible to move from a 'just fit in' or 'just go away and be fixed' way of seeing the interaction between tutor and student to something more appropriate to the changed Higher Education environment of the last decade or so. The rest of this chapter suggests ways in which tutors can develop their meta-awareness of their own beliefs with a view to making them more explicit to students. It also draws on case study evidence that shows which changes in practice seem most effective in helping international students and, indeed, all students learn what is expected and develop the skills to meet those requirements.

Learning the 'rules of the new game'

As students move about the world in ever larger numbers to institutions that are prepared not just to admit them or even to help them thrive but that begin to see Higher Education as a community of practice where all adapt, change and draw upon the ideas and experiences of everyone, it may be that in future no special approaches will be needed. Such institutions, should they ever exist, would be very different places from those in which students and tutors now operate. Using explicit, skills-focused, culturally aware guidance and support is likely to best ensure students and tutors operate effectively in the universities we now have. Here are some suggestions about how you as a teacher might help your international students learn the 'rules of the Western Higher Education game'.

Early-stage rules

- Provide honest pre-arrival information about what the student can expect to happen and what specific methods are designed to do. Provide 'induction' as more of a process rather than as one-off days. For an example of good generic international student pre-arrival guidance see Northumbria's 'Coming to study' guide.
- Become more explicit about the make-or-break issues of being a success-ful student. Induction programmes or initial classes could include discus-sion sessions about the expectations of students in Higher Education in general, moving on to what makes a successful student and/or language learner.
- Provide early opportunities for students to discover how they measure up. This could be in the form of an academic skills test with general questions: How would you reference this quote? What are some of the main features of academic writing? What is independent learning?
- Attend in the early days and weeks to the English you use and seek to lighten the students' cognitive load. Make use of plain English, hand-outs, running glossaries, student mentoring/befriending/budding/guiding opportunities, social events, etc.

Mid-game rules

- Use multiple channels for information and advice. A mixture of written guidance, discussion-based exploration of meaning, online tools and resources, and reading from texts chosen for their uncomplicated language all help – especially at the start. Leeds Metropolitan University offers online training for students through its 'Skills for learning' package.
- Take every opportunity to get to know students as individuals and seek to understand their perspectives and expectations. This can be achieved through personal tutorials and social events (encourage students to help organise local events) and by asking students to evaluate the support and guidance on offer.
- Ensure support and guidance are rooted in the discipline and specific to the real task students will experience. The specific materials and texts chosen are crucial to engaging the learner and creating a meaningful and enjoyable learning experience. Teaching content through process and by building confidence in the learners by starting with what they already know and using meaningful tasks and outcomes is likely to enhance the learning experience as a whole (Tomlinson, 1998).
- Provide not just the expectation but also the rationale and the values that underpin the requirement. (We want students to speak in seminars because we assume it helps them explore and clarify their ideas. We think speaking, even if you are wrong, helps to lead to more understanding.) Staff resources could help tutors find clear links between theory and practice to help explain the purpose behind different tasks. See, for example, the University of Northumbria's staff resources.

Rules of assessment

- Ensure that the first few assessments are safe and recoverable. For example, International Foundation Studies at Leeds Met offers students minimally weighted assessments on a continuous basis as well as final assessment. This offers useful feedback to both student and tutor during the early stages of the course. To maintain this kind of assessment workload, peer assessment can be used.
- Provide specific behavioural feedback telling students what they should do rather than listing what they did wrong. ('You need to put the key idea in the first few paragraphs and then explain . . .' instead of 'Badly organised'.) Students also appreciate seeing models of what a 'good one' would look like.
- Find ways of meeting students halfway, e.g. by using more innovative assessment methods or with tutors learning to speak 'international English' to aid student comprehension rather than expecting students to

understand all the idioms, idiosyncrasies and strong accents of the British Isles.

General rules

- Provide staff development workshops on intercultural awareness and competency.
- Offer language learning opportunities for staff and home students or language and culture courses in a particular language.
- Encourage staff to take part in international/EU teaching mobility schemes.

A final word

Daring to change our own and our institutions' ways of thinking is not always an easy option, but can produce rewarding results. Managing international student expectations and also managing staff expectations of international students often involve a mindset change. Several chapters in this book refer to ways of promoting an ethos of internationalisation within the university.

Daring to help our international students adapt to cope with the demands of Higher Education in the UK may seem a tall order indeed, but the emphasis must be on tackling issues in a different way, rather than feeling them an 'extra burden'. The examples given here provide some encouraging ways in which institutions are moving towards an agenda to enhance the teaching and learning experience for all our international students.

Case study: Michael Lanigan and Mick Reid, Waterford Institute of Technology, Ireland

Waterford Institute of Technology (WIT) devised its Bridging Course for International Students as a Higher Education transitional programme for overseas/non-EU students. The students were mainly Chinese but included some from the Indian sub-continent. This piece concentrates mainly on the Chinese group, as this cohort constituted the entire first semester and the majority of the second. English levels needed to be IELTS 5.5 to enter our undergraduate programmes; this course requires that it be IELTS 4.5; however, some had a much lower *active* English competence.

Passive learning styles, relying on rote learning, and a marked learner/lecturer distinction – the typically didactic approach – were identified within the cohort. This contrasted with our widely egalitarian, participatory Irish/EU approach seeking to achieve understanding and ultimately independence. Students were reticent when confronted by enthusiastic native speakers. Their rationale for remaining silent was confidence – 'I wasn't sure if I had the correct answer so I didn't answer.' This suggested their English was worse than it really was.

Lecturers complained about students' written English – poorly structured with 'idiosyncratic' grammar, and no tenses or articles: weaknesses needing attention. Students commented, 'I don't know what to write, how to begin or how to conclude!' As for referencing, this meant lifting text unacknowledged – plagiarism.

The course, split into two semesters, aimed to improve their IELTS score, help them to adapt to learning in the Irish/EU education system, develop their confidence, improve grades in their target courses and offer an internationally recognised computing qualification, namely the European Computer Driving Licence (ECDL).

Semester I subjects included Communications, Study Skills and an introduction to Business (Mathematics and Accounting). The second added EU Society (locating their language in our culture), Critical Thinking and IELTS preparation. Each semester included a course in Supplementary English for weaker students. Remarkably, we found that the stronger students utilised this facility more often than the weaker ones, a phenomenon not too dissimilar to behaviour noted from Irish/EU students at the Institute. Perhaps the students are blending in better than we realise?

From a learning and teaching perspective, staff were briefed on what they might encounter, and a gentle transition from Chinese to Irish/EU self-directedness was encouraged. One-hour sessions included fifteen minutes for student/lecturer consultations. This proved difficult to promote: the students' 'reserve' inhibited them from asking for help conspicuously, and lecturers' 'old' habits, on occasions, impelled them to conclude classes without a consultation period.

Furthermore, the original learning environment proved problematic – more students enrolled than our first room accommodated comfortably. This forced students into tight rows (as in Chinese classrooms). Those on the back row welcomed this, protected from staff visitations to check on their work. Eventually, this was solved and the group relocated to a more suitable room with loose furniture and increased space.

Our apparent inability to establish the importance of speaking English in class disappointed us. We were reluctant to prohibit Chinese but our liberal generosity encouraged them to use it. Repeated exhortations were ignored. Further desperate warnings to practise English were rejected. One plus was that they were contributing: but mostly not in English.

A final objective unrealised concerned out-of-class learning. We offered support that was not taken up. Extra assignments were issued but rarely worked upon. Weak students were encouraged with strategies we thought might help. Mostly our initiatives were rejected – they simply seemed to 'bounce off' them. As a result staff became somewhat demoralised and exasperated.

In the final analysis, are we to abandon the Bridge? Far from it: that great ancient Chinese philosopher Tsung Xi stated 'Know your enemy.' We have learned:

- Group work is still a reluctant chore that occasionally bemuses.
- Examinations are the ultimate motivators but subject to examiners' 'random whims'. An IELTS examiner was asked, 'Exactly what should we learn to pass your examination?' They wanted finite content rather than the infinite possibilities of English.
- We should reconsider our approach to self-directed learning. Free rein is too free; prescriptive scheduling is unpalatable. A compromise may work.

In conclusion, the gap is not yet bridged. But we anticipate that, the more we learn and the more responsive we become in our methodologies of teaching and learning, the fewer the differences between our students' and our own aspirations will be. Our teaching will become more effective. We will reflect, adapt and be better prepared. Tsung Xi would be proud of us.

Links to web pages referred to in this chapter

The following web pages were all accessed in October 2006.

University of Central Lancashire

- http://uclaninternational.org/main/collect/system/11/
- Experienced students answer new students' questions and generally welcome and support them during the first few weeks of semester: http://www.uclaninternational.org/studentsupport/60/

University of Kent

- 'Value added learning in university education', http://www.kent.ac.uk/uelt/learning/value/index.html

Leeds Metropolitan University

- Language and Culture Fiesta, www.leedsmet.ac.uk/lsif/sol/SOL_Fiesta.htm
- Staff and student resources, http://www.leedsmet.ac.uk/lskills/
- ECIS (English and Cultural Studies for International Students), http://www.leedsmet.ac.uk/lsif/sol/ecis.htm
- 'Skills for learning', http://www.leedsmet.ac.uk/lskills/
- International Foundation Studies, http://www.leedsmet.ac.uk/lsif/sol/foundation.htm
- Pre-masters programme, http://www.leedsmet.ac.uk/lsif/sol/prema.htm

University of Melbourne

- Transition programme provides advice and support for new students and for schools, parents and university staff: http://www.services.unimelb.edu.au/transition/index.html

University of Northumbria

- 'Coming to study' guide; pre-arrival information: http://northumbria.ac.uk/brochure/international/ready/
- ELAN programme, http://northumbria.ac.uk/brochure/international/gl/eng_lang/
- Staff resources, http://northumbria.ac.uk/sd/central/library/marcet/

Chapter 7

International teachers and international learning

Betty Leask

The basis for this chapter is qualitative research conducted in two small projects in Australia, Hong Kong and Singapore in 2003/4 and 2004/5. These projects provided insights into the expectations students had of their teachers as well as those skills and abilities most highly valued by the teachers themselves. They also provided insights into how these characteristics might be developed in academic staff. In both projects extensive literature reviews were conducted spanning internationalisation and Higher Education internationalisation of the curriculum, professional development in Higher Education and transnational teaching and learning. In the first study, which investigated constructions of internationalisation of the curriculum at an Australian university, a small number of sixteen staff and students involved in a business programme taught in Adelaide and Hong Kong were interviewed. The interviews were part of a case study seeking understanding of the relationship between teacher and student understandings of internationalisation of the curriculum through the analysis of a variety of information from a range of sources. In the second study, conducted in 2004/5, questionnaires were sent to over 100 students and staff involved in transnational programmes in Hong Kong and Singapore, and follow-up interviews were conducted with sixty-one students and staff. In this study fifteen essential and desirable characteristics of teachers in this setting were identified (Leask *et al.*, 2005). These research projects provided some insight into the characteristics of 'the international teacher'.

The settings

International education occurs in a range of settings, and international classrooms are as varied as those who teach and learn in them. International classrooms include those in which students from a variety of cultural and linguistic backgrounds come together in a predominantly English-speaking environment and are taught in English (e.g. in the UK, Australia, Europe, Canada and the US) and classes in which students from a common linguistic and cultural background come together in their 'home country' to be taught by a teacher from a different cultural and linguistic background, often in English (sometimes called 'transnational' classes and common in Hong Kong and Singapore). Students, teachers and programmes today are increasingly mobile for both short and long periods of time. This has resulted in an increase in the number and range of 'international classrooms', learning environments in which culture, language and curriculum are the key variables. These three variables are central to teaching and learning in any international classroom, and the way in which they interact requires specific knowledge, attitudes and teaching skills in those who teach in the international classroom.

Interaction between students and students and students and teachers in these settings is the key to internationalisation. However, interaction in such settings is intense and requires significant effort on the part of those involved. It also has several risk factors associated with it, including risk of embarrassment and risk of failure. Individuals involved in any interaction need to have the motivation to expend the effort required to interact and the skills to enable the interaction to succeed. Teachers in this environment need to be both effective intercultural learners and effective managers of an intercultural learning environment.

Teachers as intercultural learners

The international classroom requires teachers to be skilled managers of a complex teaching and learning environment. They must not only possess the abilities associated with 'good teaching' but be efficient intercultural learners who use cultural diversity in the classroom as a learning resource. They must be able to adapt their teaching to an international, culturally diverse teaching and learning environment rather than expecting learners to adapt to a 'monocultural', inflexible environment. This requires that they engage with and learn from other cultures and that they themselves become interculturally competent so that they can take on the role of being an intercultural educator.

International teachers must therefore be highly self-reflective and willing to critically examine the interactions and communications they have with students from different cultural backgrounds. In this way they will be able to develop their understandings of how the languages and cultures of their students influence their thoughts, values, actions and feelings as well as their understanding of the ways in which their own language and culture influence their actions, reactions, values and beliefs. The international classroom is in many ways a 'third place' (Lo Bianco et al., 1999: 13), a meeting place between different cultures where there are not necessarily any shared values or beliefs about learning and teaching, roles and responsibilities and where it is therefore vitally important that there is recognition of what cultural difference means for the way those involved think, feel and act.

International teachers need to be able to engage students with the course content. This means that teachers have to be able to locate and incorporate a range of culturally appropriate materials into their teaching. It also helps greatly if students can see themselves in the curriculum. In an international classroom this means, for example, including a diverse range of examples and case studies to which students can relate and ensuring that where this is not possible students are provided with assistance to understand the cultural framework within which the case operates. This involves the teacher having an understanding of the way in which what they are teaching is culturally constructed and framed, for example how the roles of accountants, social workers, nurses or teachers are constructed in different cultures, why this is so and what this means for teaching and learning as well as for professional practice.

Thus international teachers must be able to:

- identify and incorporate a range of international content and perspectives in the programme through examples and case studies;
- seek, evaluate and respond to feedback of different kinds (written, verbal and non-verbal) from students about the effectiveness of their teaching;
- change their teaching approaches to achieve different course objectives in different ways, depending on the needs of students;
- reflect on and learn from teaching experiences.

International teachers must also understand:

- that their own culture affects the way they think, feel, act and interact with others;
- the social, cultural and educational backgrounds of students;
- the cultural framework of the discipline;
- how professional practice in the discipline is influenced by cultural and national contexts.

Ideas on how to put this into practice could include the following:

- Seek out scholarly papers written by international colleagues from different cultural and linguistic backgrounds from your own.
- When travelling, read local newspapers and start an article file that you can use later in the development of regional and international case studies related to your discipline.
- Make connections with staff of international partner institutions working in the same area or with similar research interests. Wherever possible team-teach and -research with them.

Teachers as managers of intercultural learning environments

Teachers in the international classroom must manage not only their own intercultural learning but also that of their students. This requires an understanding of diversity in the learning styles of individual students. While generalisations about culturally based learning styles are common, individual students will learn in many different ways, and assumptions about the learning preferences of individual students based on their cultural background may be of limited use in the international classroom. International teachers need to be able to recognise when there is a cultural block to learning and act to overcome this. The international teacher must understand the way that their own cultural context has shaped all that they feel, do and believe, including the way they approach teaching, their expectations of students and the judgements that they make about them.

Cultural diversity can be a valuable resource in the international classroom, but international teachers need to be skilled in using this resource effectively, for it will be of little use unless the international teacher requires that students engage in intercultural interactions with other students. The ability to manage multicultural group work, to stimulate and encourage students from diverse cultural backgrounds to work together productively and learn from each other, is a skill that is highly valued by students in the international classroom. Designing tasks that can be more efficiently and effectively completed in mixed-culture groups, such as analysing intercultural issues related to the course content and objectives, is an important part of the work of the international teacher. However, groups may not always work effectively, and so the international teacher also needs to prepare students for this and provide them with guidance on how to get the best out of the diversity in their group. Cultural diversity within the student body is a valuable resource for internationalisation of the curriculum, but careful planning and management are needed in order for the benefit to be realised.

The ability to provide effective feedback on student learning was the most highly ranked characteristic of the international teacher. International teachers must be able to provide all of their students with useful feedback on their learning, recognising that in different educational systems the roles of teachers and learners may be quite different and that there is little that can be taken for granted.

Management of an intercultural learning environment requires flexibility, a willingness to learn from and with students and recognition of the critical role played by language and culture in learning.

International teachers must be able to:

- communicate effectively with students from diverse cultural and linguistic backgrounds;

- adapt learning activities to suit the needs of students who learn in many different ways;
- write assessment activities that enable students from a variety of cultural and educational backgrounds to demonstrate what they have learned;
- provide feedback on student performance which tells each student exactly what they need to do to improve their learning;
- use a range of different tools and strategies to assist student learning;
- engage students from different cultural backgrounds in discussion and group work.

> To put these ideas into practice you might like to try conducting a small survey of your class concerning their linguistic, cultural and national background and use this information in planning teaching and learning activities related to international objectives.

International learning

Changes in the external context in which universities operate, including the rapid increase in the movement of people, money, services, goods, images and ideas around the world associated with globalisation and the global nature of work, have resulted in universities focusing increasingly on preparing graduates for life in a rapidly changing and increasingly interconnected world. An internationalised culture and globalised economy require interaction with people of different cultures within and across national boundaries and inter-cultural competence. Universities are thus increasingly focused on developing international perspectives in all students.

International perspectives are knowledge, skills and attitudes which assist students to understand and work with the diversity of cultures that exist within countries, communities and institutions across the world. It is common for universities, as demonstrated in the first part of this book, to strive to develop some or all of the following in their students:

- knowledge of other cultures and appreciation of cultural diversity;
- international perspectives on the field of study;
- ability to work effectively in settings of social and cultural diversity;
- ability to think globally and consider issues from a variety of perspectives;
- ability to communicate across cultures;
- ability to engage positively with cultural others in both their professional and their private lives;
- responsiveness to international communities;

- awareness of their own culture and its perspectives and how and why those are similar to and different from other cultures and their perspectives.

Across institutions there is variation both in the balance and scope of these 'international perspectives' and in the levels of importance attached to them by different institutions. Some highlight international and global perspectives as key areas of responsibility; others describe them as subsidiary skills, contributing to the development of higher-order skills such as the development of ethical and social understanding. However, there is no doubt that the development of international perspectives is seen as important in today's world and that their development is connected with cultural understanding, self-knowledge and a range of skills, attitudes and knowledge. This makes the role of the international teacher in facilitating and assessing international learning a very important one.

A review of course objectives is a good place to start thinking about international learning. The following are common, generic outcomes of Higher Education courses:

- Communicate effectively in a variety of situations.
- Critically evaluate knowledge and ideas presented by others.

If these outcomes are 'internationalised', the focus of learning and teaching is significantly changed. For example, 'Communicate effectively in a variety of situations' could become 'Communicate effectively with people from a range of cultural backgrounds in a variety of situations.' 'Critically evaluate knowledge and ideas presented by others' becomes 'Critically evaluate knowledge and ideas presented by others from more than one cultural perspective.'

To put these ideas into practice, you might like to explore how the following outcomes could be internationalised:

- Collaborate with others in professional practice.
- Demonstrate a commitment to being a responsible and ethical practitioner.
- Demonstrate knowledge of professional standards.
- Contribute to the knowledge base of the professional community.
- Effectively gather and evaluate information from a variety of sources.

By internationalising the objectives, the focus of learning is significantly altered. A different range of learning activities will be necessary to provide students with the practice they need to be able to achieve the objectives.

> To put this into practice you could design a learning task that would assist students to develop one of the 'internationalised' objectives listed above.

Assessing the level of development of international perspectives was identified by students and staff participating in the research projects as a significant challenge. The realisation of international objectives requires a planned and systematic approach which includes active engagement with other cultures and assessment of both progress and achievement. Bowden *et al.* (2000a: 13–19) describe four qualitatively different approaches to the development of any generic capability:

1   *scoping level:* defining the scope of the capability;
2   *enabling level:* developing certain skills related to the capability;
3   *training level:* elaborating or establishing the meaning of the capability within a particular discipline or field;
4   *relating level:* developing understanding of the relation between the meaning and the context.

These levels provide a useful focus for the development of teaching and learning and assessment tasks and activities at different levels of a programme. An interpretation of the levels in relation to the achievement of international perspectives is included in Table 7.1.

This hierarchy has several implications for the work of the international teacher. As with any programme of learning, students will not necessarily move in neat progression from one level to another. Teachers will need to recognise that there is likely to be movement backwards and forwards between levels as students' knowledge and skills develop. They will need to be prepared to provide many opportunities for students to receive feedback on their learning from both the teacher and their peers. In the international classroom everyone needs to be able to use a variety of resources for intercultural learning and to provide feedback to others on their achievement of learning goals. International teachers have a specific responsibility, though, to provide a range of learning tasks designed to challenge students and assist them to develop and demonstrate their level of achievement of international perspectives in a planned and coordinated way across an entire programme. They will need to ensure that the complexity of the assessment tasks reflects the complexity of the learning tasks introduced at different times in a programme. This will ensure that students are provided with valid feedback on

Table 7.1 Levels of development of international perspectives

Level	Focus of tasks
Scoping	Ability of students to identify the range and significance of cultural and national perspectives, e.g.: – different cultural and national perspectives on past and current issues; – the relationship between cultural and national perspectives and attitudes, values and actions; – ways in which their own cultural and national perspectives influence their attitudes, values and actions.
Enabling	Extent to which students have the skills necessary for effective communication across national and cultural boundaries, e.g. their ability to: – identify ways in which others' cultural and national perspectives influence their attitudes, values and actions; – understand other cultures and communicate across cultural boundaries.
Training	Extent to which students: – understand the relationship between cultural and national contexts and different approaches within their discipline area; – understand international standards within their discipline area.
Relating	Extent to which students are able to adapt their behaviour to deal with different contexts, e.g. by: – using cross-cultural communication skills to negotiate outcomes within the discipline area; – reflecting on the relationship between international standards in discipline areas and their local and international contexts.

their progress towards achievement of the desired learning outcomes of the course and programme in relation to their international learning. Learning experiences and assessment tasks will therefore need to be planned and coordinated at programme level as well as course level. This in turn involves the international teacher in communicating effectively and efficiently with what is likely to be an increasingly culturally diverse teaching team.

To put this into practice you could design an assessment task that requires students to work in a cross-cultural group and tests one of the objectives you internationalised in the task at scoping level.

Conclusion

International and intercultural learning are important today and likely to be even more so in the future. University classrooms are, in many ways, a reflection of the world in which we all live – increasingly diverse and complex.

In order to manage student learning in this environment, international teachers need to understand themselves as intercultural learners, see learning and teaching as an intercultural conversation and be able to manage their own and their students' intercultural learning. This requires that they be critically reflective of their own practice and aware that many of the interactions they have in the international classroom will be intercultural encounters.

Chapter 8

Using a quality enhancement audit approach to review provision for international students

A case study

Vicky Harris, Julie Brett, Stuart Hirst, Zoe McClelland, Elizabeth Phizackerley-Sugden and Sally Brown

Introduction

Holmes and Brown established a themed approach to quality enhancement audit at the University of Northumbria in 1998/9 (Holmes and Brown, 2000) in order to review university activities across a number of themes. Essentially the methodology involves asking a small team of university staff volunteers to scrutinise closely what an institution says about itself in its published documentation and on its website, and then to interview staff at all levels, students and other stakeholders to see how far actuality matches aspiration. This approach was subsequently used with modification in a number of contexts, including Higher Education institutions (HEIs) in New Zealand and Ireland, and has more recently been adopted as a means of identifying good practice and areas for action at Leeds Metropolitan University. This chapter outlines some of the outcomes of such an internal quality enhancement audit on the experiences of international students undertaken during the academic year 2005/6.

The quality enhancement audit of international students' experiences at Leeds Metropolitan University

The audit was commissioned as a result of the introduction of the University's Assessment, Learning and Teaching Strategy (Leeds Met, 2005), which requires the University to: 'Set up short-life working groups to undertake proactive thematic Quality Enhancement reviews twice each year.' The specific aim of the audit under consideration here was to investigate University, course and programme documentation to evaluate what claims are made in relation to the experience of international students and to assess how far the stated ambitions are achieved. The project ran between February 2006 and July 2006.

The University context

Leeds Metropolitan University, one of the largest universities in the UK, has a commitment to internationalisation which is espoused in its vision to be 'a world-class regional University with world-wide horizons, using all our talents to the full'. The University is one of the first in the UK to develop an Internationalisation Strategy (Leeds Met, 2003) which goes beyond just international student recruitment. The definition of internationalisation is taken as: 'the process of integrating an international/intercultural dimension into the teaching, research and service of an institution' (Knight and de Wit, 1995). This has been further refined into an explicit strategic aim, within the University's Corporate Plan (Leeds Met, 2004), 'to develop students' international opportunities and global perspectives, ensuring that an international, multi-cultural ethos pervades the University'.

The process of internationalisation right across the University is a relatively new concept. Previously there have been pockets of international activity where particular international champions have worked hard in the delivery of consultancy projects, off-shore delivery of courses, and recruitment of international students to study in Leeds. At this early stage, the strategy was primarily one of income generation by increasing the number of students coming to Leeds to study. This resulted in sustained recruitment activity, and a significant growth in student numbers was achieved (see Table 8.1).

However, the achievement of such significant growth in a relatively short period gave rise to a re-evaluation of the benefits of internationalisation to the student body as a whole and to the broader ethos of university life. The Internationalisation Strategy both reflects and drives this broader interpretation, taking a values-driven approach which encompasses six interrelated areas:

- internationalising learning, teaching and research;
- enhancing the international student experience;
- enhancing the international experience of home students;
- developing and fostering international partnerships and alliances;
- developing staff capability for internationalisation;
- effectively recruiting international students.

Table 8.1 Growth in international student numbers

Year	Numbers
2001/2	2,580
2003/4	3,405
2004/5	3,515
2005/6	4,160

Source: Higher Education Statistics Agency.

As international students have become a significant feature of University life and an increasing emphasis is now placed on making the University an international experience for all, it was judged timely to analyse the perceptions of international students and to consider their views about their experience at the University. This was the first time that a quality audit of this type had taken place within the University. It was also the first time that any review of the total experience of international students, separate from their UK counterparts, had been carried out.

Claims made in the University's published materials, including the prospectus and marketing materials, as well as the University's website and the faculty pages, include:

- 'Leeds Met is a University with world-wide horizons.'
- 'At Leeds Met you will be studying in an international environment.'
- 'Leeds Met has a truly international atmosphere.'
- 'We make every effort to ensure that your time with us is memorable.'
- 'There's a warm and friendly welcome for everyone.'
- 'Our caring, experienced staff will do their best to make your time here rewarding and enjoyable.'
- 'Our courses are of a very high standard.'
- 'Before you arrive at Leeds Met we will send you welcome information containing everything you need to know about study and life in the UK.'
- 'When you arrive in Leeds we will meet you.'

(Undergraduate Prospectus 2007)

The primary objective of the audit was to source student views on whether international students felt these claims were being achieved. However, it was thought appropriate by the project team, in addition to questioning the students about the above statements, to find out more about students' experiences of Leeds Met in relation to the other aspirations of the Internationalisation Strategy.

The audit methodology

As this was the first time that any audit of international students had been undertaken, one of the first challenges was to design a set of research instruments which, given the timescales for the research, were realistic and flexible and could be conducted in a relaxed and non-confrontational manner.

Initially it was planned to run a series of international student focus groups from schools across the University. However, the first challenge for the project team was that not all students actually used their Leeds Met email accounts. Initially international students were invited, through these email accounts, to an event to give feedback on their time at Leeds Met. As this meeting was held towards the end of the academic year, the project team named this event the 'outduction'. Of the 715 invitations that were sent to student email accounts, thirty responses were received and thirteen confirmations of intention to attend. The actual number attending was nine on the day. This was very disappointing.

Originally the focus group was planned to begin with all attendees filling in the printed survey, with the project team on hand to help if required. Refreshments would then be available to enable students and the project team to chat in a relaxed manner. Around the room a series of flip charts would be available, each with a different topic. Students would then be divided into small groups and asked to spend a short time brainstorming their thoughts on each topic before moving on to the next. Owing to the small number of students who attended, the process was changed on the day. Students completed the written questionnaire and then the whole group came together to discuss issues, guided by members of the project team. A record was made of the themes raised and individual comments. Those who attended the event ensured a lively and constructive debate. Students were very concerned to highlight good practice, as well as drawing attention to areas where the University could improve its performance and make a positive impact on the experience of international students at Leeds Met.

Although the focus group worked well and some very useful information was derived from the event, it was felt that the number participating made it difficult to draw reliable conclusions. As a consequence, it was decided to extend the sample by the use of a quantitative survey based on Survey Monkey online survey software. The strategy was to undertake a survey which would take no more than ten minutes to complete and that results would already be in electronic form for easier analysis.

Through the International Student Social Programme database held by the Leslie Silver International Faculty, 420 students were contacted by email. All students were 'blind-copy' recipients to ensure confidentiality of personal data. This email was sent to each student:

Dear International Student

This survey has been commissioned by the Pro-Vice-Chancellor responsible for Assessment, Learning and Teaching at Leeds Metropolitan University. Your responses, to this survey, are extremely important to us and will remain anonymous. The results will be aggregated in order to provide a broader understanding of international student experiences at Leeds Metropolitan University. Please spend 15 minutes of your time filling in the (10 questions) survey at this web address: http://survey_address_given.

Thank you in anticipation of your contribution.

Leeds Metropolitan University

There were twenty invalid addresses. The survey was made available on the internet for three weeks, resulting in sixty responses (most of these in the first week); of these, forty provided data of an appropriate quality.

Concurrent with the student surveys, a quantitative survey of the heads of school was undertaken, this time using the WebCT virtual learning environment. This survey aimed to establish the views of middle managers on the level of international activity within the schools and also established progress on the implementation of the University's Internationalisation Strategy. The response rate was disappointing, with only 48 per cent responding.

Results of the research

As this was the first time that an audit of this type had been carried out, one of the key problems was communication with students. This meant that the methodology had to be adapted in order to achieve a reasonable sample on which to base conclusions. Nevertheless, some key themes and areas of importance were suggested by students, and these are supported by a range of qualitative comments.

The findings have been separated into those from the online questionnaires and those from the 'outduction event'.

The online questionnaire

Student feedback from the online questionnaire could be categorised into four major themes: examining student expectations; evaluating whether student expectations had been met; identifying students' experience of the assessment, learning and teaching experience; and seeking student opinions on their experience of Leeds Met teaching staff. The analysis of the data identifies key features and then presents examples of the feelings, thoughts and reflections of the students in their own words.

The major expectations of the students were indicated as a desire to gain a high standard of education in line with the University's reputation. They respected the qualification that would be achieved and believed this would improve their employability:

- 'Good quality education which goes along with international standards. Good career opportunities. Experiencing of a great culture.'
- 'Excellent learning facilities and very good faculties, excellent career prospects.'

What also proved important to the students was the gaining of particular subject/course knowledge and wanting an international perspective to their studies:

- 'That I would enjoy a new experience that would open my eyes to the world. I wanted to also gain knowledge in my field of study that I might not be able to achieve while at my home university.'
- 'Getting to know information about media studies. See English methods in learning and teaching.'

Finally, students expected to improve their English language skills and receive an international or specifically UK experience with the opportunity to meet a wide range of people from the UK and other countries in a safe, welcoming and supportive environment:

- 'I wanted to improve my language, meet new people and of course study business in international dimension.'
- 'My major expectation was to get in contact with British and international students and their cultures, to improve my language, to get more flexible in thinking, benefit from business competencies.'
- 'Friendly people, including tutors plus other students. Good surroundings and atmosphere and easy to settle down as I never been away from home. Also, safe environment to live.'

Results to the question 'Have your expectations been met?' were ambivalent, with a small majority saying that they had. Only 20 out of 74 respondents provided any qualitative data, and responses were varied. However, some indication of the type and range of feedback is noted below:

- 'Quite difficult to meet local people because they seemed conservative and feel like they are not interested in meeting people from other countries.'
- 'Efforts for international social life is excellent. Welcome Week and Social Trips were well organised and a good opportunity to find friends at the beginning and during the semester.'
- 'Not very sure about the career prospects. Uni should hold programs to explain students that after completion of course, where does the opportunities arise.' [*sic*]

Results on questions relating to assessment, learning and teaching were more encouraging but leave no room for complacency (see Table 8.2).

In the free response section, the general areas of importance were indicated as feedback, staff support and value for money in relation to fees paid. Some students believed they should get more benefits, ranging from free books to free sports passes. Selected examples are recorded below:

- 'The service level at Leeds Met is excellent. All the tutors and

lecturers were available for questions and mostly their answers were very helpful.'
- 'The staff was very flexible and very kind. I had a really good feedback about my work. We could ask all the questions we wanted.'
- 'Majority of the international students are still not aware about the grading and assessment methods. University must take steps to rectify this problem.'
- 'Actually in our country we have enough time with staff to discuss but here staff are not getting enough time we cant explain our problem still lot stuff to discuss.' [*sic*]

A number of these comments can be read in the light of the mismatched expectations students have about the kinds of support they can expect, as discussed in Chapter 6.

Comments about teaching staff were generally heartening (see Table 8.3).

In the free responses, the key area of importance to the students was the level of staff support for international students. It was evident that the experience was variable, and again the kinds of negative surprises detailed in Chapter 5 are evident in some comments:

- 'Staff are certainly very helpful but it is difficult to say that they understand fully the international students.'

Table 8.2 Results on questions relating to assessment, learning and teaching

	No	Yes
Were you made aware of the learning styles in UK study?	36%	64%
Have you found it difficult to learn at Leeds Met?	74%	26%
Do you understand the Leeds Met assessment grading system?	32%	68%
Do you get useful feedback, from staff, on how you might improve your grades?	55%	45%

Table 8.3 Comments about teaching staff

	No	Yes
Do you think that Leeds Met staff understand the needs of international students?	28%	72%
Have the staff been helpful in assisting you to understand what is required for your assessments?	23%	77%
Do the staff use international examples in their teaching?	32%	68%
Are you able to contribute your experiences of your own country into class discussions?	23%	77%

- 'Majority of the tutors are well aware of the needs of the students and go out of their way to assist. They are obviously highly knowledgeable and dedicated.'
- 'I feel that the staff could be a bit more understanding to international students, as for us it is a bigger step than for English students and I feel some of them are unaware of this.'

A mixed picture in relation to the use of international examples and opportunities to share experience was presented, as the sample comments show:

- 'All of them gave plenty of international examples which I liked.'
- 'Some tutors, they tended to focus on European cases more than in Asia, and as a result of that, if people from Asia, sometimes we found the European case studies difficult to understand.'
- 'Too much discussion of the UK on an international course!'

Focus groups

The feedback from the focus group could largely be categorised into three sections. A primary area of importance and concern for the students was accommodation. A number of students felt that not enough thought was given to the mix of students in residences. Several felt that accommodation should be organised so final year and postgraduates are together in a more studious atmosphere. Suggestions were made that there should be more flexibility in tenancy agreements so that people could move to more suitable accommodation if their original allocation wasn't appropriate. Other comments focused on features of student life common to both home and international students, including security and travel information. Students also commented that there was a need for a communal area in addition to the bar for socialisation, and better IT facilities.

The second significant category of comments concerned the timeliness of information received on living and studying in Leeds. In some cases, students left home early, so the welcome packs sent out by post arrived after students had left their country. While all this information is readily available and easily accessible through the website, there is a need to draw attention to this more effectively.

Some students had used the 'meet and greet' service, and one commented: 'They couldn't be better! Staff were very kind and friendly and gave me lots of info about Leeds.' Others felt that even more could be done to welcome students arriving from outside the UK. A range of information is given in the welcome week packs and through the International Freshers' Fair. However, some students had ideas for additional information which could be provided for those unused to the UK environment, such as the location of affordable shops and restaurants, different banks and better information on public transport routes from accommodation to campus.

There were further ideas for better information on academic matters, particularly in relation to assessment criteria and feedback. This information hunger is common to home and international students alike, but as Chapter 5 indicates there is a particularly strong information need for those unused to unfamiliar assessment regimes.

The third category of comments concerned integration with UK students. Some students expressed disappointment that they had not been able to make friends or feel integrated with UK students. They also acknowledged that, even within the very diverse international student population, groups tended to form by nationality and therefore tended not to mix. A number of students would have welcomed having a mentor who knew the University and the locality who could have guided them through the early weeks of their arrival and their settling in period both at the University and in Leeds.

It should be noted that there were only nine participants in the focus group; therefore the key themes and indeed individual comments noted here cannot be used to reflect the experience of the whole international student population. Even in this small sample, the students had encountered a mixture of experiences. Nevertheless these areas were indicated as important to the students and provoked lengthy but constructive debate and are worthy of consideration in reviewing services to students.

A number of questions were asked which tested the extent to which the University is meeting the claims made in its published material, which received mixed responses in a small sample. One particular area, however, which received a positive response concerned whether they considered the University to be a warm, friendly and welcoming place (see Figure 8.1).

Heads of school survey

The results of this survey indicate a diverse profile of individual and school-based activity in relation to internationalisation. The responses showed that there is a rich mix of activity within schools which, over time, will contribute to the achievement of the Internationalisation Strategy. However, inevitably, schools are at different stages of development. Key points which could be derived from the research are:

- Sixty-seven per cent of those responding indicated that they were involved in international initiatives in some way.
- Only 25 per cent of those responding would consider themselves to be 'experienced internationalists', suggesting that there may be a need for a more sustained development programme for senior managers within the University.

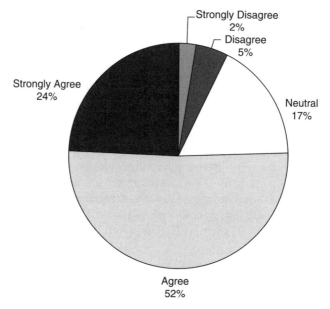

Figure 8.1 The extent to which the University is seen as a warm and friendly place.

- Seventy-five per cent of schools were able to give examples of staff development initiatives for international activity. These ranged across courses on teaching international students, shadowing opportunities, deployment to conduct international research, staff exchange, sessions on internationalisation and cross-cultural capability.
- All schools make use of the induction programme provided by the International Faculty, and a small number at the time of the survey provided separate welcome events for international students within the faculty or within individual schools. In 2006 this number increased significantly.
- Two schools indicated that they provide specialist support for international students through international student liaison officers. One school has a principal lecturer with specific responsibilities for international students, while another deploys a senior lecturer to provide learning support for students. It is worth noting that from 2006 all faculties have a dedicated International Teacher Fellow to promote understanding of the assessment, learning and teaching needs of international students and broader internationalisation initiatives across the University.
- Several schools provide social events for students, particularly around Christmas and Chinese New Year, while others relied mainly on those provided by the International Faculty.

- One school is launching an international student database to 'support the integration, interchange and professional development' of its students.

Following the audit

The principal purpose of a quality enhancement audit is to enable an institution to celebrate its good practice and to look for opportunities to enhance provision in the targeted area. This quality enhancement audit gave us no room for complacency but enabled us to feel confident that we have good practice to build upon. The following recommendations were made by the Audit Group and are now under active consideration:

- Develop, in collaboration with international students, additional survival information that students need in their first few hours and days in Leeds.
- Promote the availability of welcome pack information on the Leeds Met website.
- Develop a buddying scheme for international students.
- Encourage the development of the Global Friends initiative (a pilot scheme to promote links with families in the local community, begun in September 2006).
- Promote the out-of-hours contact numbers offering assistance in the early weeks of each international student start date.
- Provide additional social events both across the University and within faculties to promote contact with home students.
- Enhance the staff development programme for internationalisation offered for staff at all levels within the University.
- Create a network across the University of those, such as the international student liaison officers, who are working closely with international students in order to align the University's efforts more closely with the expectations of students.
- Analyse the views of international students on an annual basis for the purpose of continual improvement in services and information provided.
- Review the accommodation allocation strategy.
- Develop a series of cross-institutional initiatives for staff to encourage involvement with and commitment to international students.
- Provide enhanced information on assignment procedures, assessment and grading.
- Introduce additional learning materials for international students and specialist workshops in assessment, learning and teaching practices.

Conclusions

Whilst the project reports the views of a relatively small sample, general themes and areas of concern for international students were highlighted. These included accommodation allocation, assessment guidelines, criteria and feedback, support in the early days and the availability of additional supporting literature. Those who participated had a generally positive attitude to the University and were constructive in their discussions and responses. Therefore the results offer the opportunity to consider the areas indicated and to enhance further the international experience for students at Leeds Met as it strives to be a world-class regional university, with world-wide horizons, using all its talents to the full.

Part III

Perspectives on curriculum enhancement

Chapter 9

Internationalisation of the curriculum

Elspeth Jones and David Killick

Introduction

This chapter considers ground which has been highly contested (for example, see Chapter 12 for a divergent view), covering, as it does, the concepts of both curriculum and internationalisation. We will make clear our interpretation of curriculum and present a brief review of both rationale and features of internationalised curricula with reference to recent literature and university position statements (see Knight, 1994, 2004 for broad reviews of internationalisation). This will provide the context for a case study outlining the rationale, strategy and process for the implementation of a curriculum internationalisation process in one institution. The major tool for the case study process is a Guidelines Document for academic staff engaging in the review process; this is presented in full as an appendix to this book, as it outlines much of the context and the ethos behind that institution's articulation of internationalisation.

Definition of curriculum

In contrast with most other descriptions of curriculum internationalisation, our interpretation of curriculum is very wide. We do not see this being restricted to the content of a student's formal programme of study. Course content, teaching methodologies, learning strategies and assessment mechanisms are important, but so too are the extended curriculum activities enabled and encouraged (or disabled and discouraged) through a course. Obvious examples of this are student exchanges, volunteering, interactions with students beyond culture or comfort groups and engagement with clubs and societies. Equally important are those symbols and messages which convey the institutional ethos in which students study and which demonstrate a commitment to global perspectives and diversity, of which internationalisation is one element. These include visible celebrations of diversity, ethical purchasing policies, sustainable environment practices, appropriate food services, and respect of multi-faith perspectives and practices. In short, we take a broader definition of curriculum than is usual in reviews of this kind and see it as encompassing all the experiences which inform a student's development (cognitive, attitudinal and affective) while undergoing their Higher Education studies. It will be clear from this broad definition that we view internationalisation of the curriculum as relevant to all students, not only those studying outside their home country.

Section I: Review

Rationale for curriculum internationalisation

Interest in an internationalised curriculum seems to come relatively late in the development of the notion of an international university, generally being articulated following a focus on international student recruitment, student exchanges, study abroad, off-shore delivery and, perhaps, related staff development. Webb (2005) suggests that, 'without significantly changing the curriculum, the first modern phase of internationalisation included attempts to ensure the survival of international students'. He quotes van der Wende's (1996) classification of international curricula[1] and proposes four phases in internationalisation of the curriculum:

1 international students studying alongside home students;
2 systematic curriculum development for internationalisation;
3 transnational operations and internationalisation of the curriculum;
4 normalising internationalisation of the curriculum: 'turning the ad hoc and uneven efforts of a few enthusiasts into the normal expectations and requirements of the organisation'.

In some universities, the focus initially may be on designing a curriculum which better meets the needs of the international student body (e.g. Callan, 2000), but more attention may then be given to developing a curriculum which meets the needs of all students. There may even be a recognition that most home students are much less well prepared for the complexities of a culturally diverse world than are those international students who do, after all, function across cultures throughout their study period overseas and often in a foreign language. In some cases, consideration of both home and international student bodies in relation to curriculum development has resulted in a view that responding effectively to the diversity of international students and responding effectively to the diversity of home students are in fact not two agendas but one. As Knight (2004) notes, 'internationalization is also about relating to the diversity of cultures that exist with countries, communities, and institutions' (Knight, 2004: 11). As institutions gain a more sophisticated model of internationalisation, internationalisation of the curriculum can be seen as the pivotal work, without which other actions are destined to remain peripheral and transformation unrealised ('curriculum is the back-bone of the internationalization process' (Knight, 1994: 6); 'curriculum is . . . the major area for developing international and intercultural knowledge, skills, and worldviews' (Paige, 2003: 56)). Summarising several national body reports in the USA, a Michigan State University task force notes: 'A primary goal referenced by these reports is to mainstream global, international, comparative experience and content throughout the curriculum' (Michigan State University, n.d.).

Rationales for curriculum internationalisation will typically be either pragmatically based or values-based, or will be a hybridisation of the two (see Knight and de Wit, 1997; Leask, 2003, 2005a; Bremer and van der Wende, 1995 for examples of variations on the typology of rationales). Pragmatically based rationales refer to students needing *skills* and *understandings* in order to *work* (and sometimes to *live*) in a globalising world. The focus is on gradu-ates who can *perform*. Such rationales sit comfortably with the notion that the function of a university is to produce a successful workforce which will enable a country to maintain or grow its international competitiveness and influence (see, for example, HEFCE, 2003). In the USA in particular, this underpinning national interest is extended into bolstering national security, as students are given *insights* which will allow them (and thereby enable the state) to better understand other (potentially threatening) cultures, while at the same time spreading good will towards the mother nation through a kind of junior ambassador role while on study abroad or volunteering experiences, a view only occasionally overtly challenged, as in Haigh (2002): 'the challenge for course developers is to design a curriculum that serves global rather than national priorities'.

By contrast, values-based rationales will typically align themselves to notions of global citizenship, responsibility, ethics and justice, and are likely to include references to global issues such as poverty reduction, human rights and sustainable futures. In practice, the *content* and the *skills* which each rationale will aspire towards may be little different, but the values-based approach will seek to develop an underpinning set of *attitudes* to inform the application of both knowledge and abilities: 'a range of values that include openness, tolerance, cosmopolitanism' (Rizvi, 2000); 'promotes . . . multi-culturalism' and 'giving globalisation an informed and moral core' (McTag-gart, 2003); 'graduates . . . with cultural and environmental sensitivity' (Aulakh *et al.*, 1997), 'social inclusion, cultural pluralism and world citizen-ship' (Haigh, 2002); 'broadmindedness; understanding and respect for other people and their cultures, values and ways of living; understanding of the nature of racism' (Nilsson, 2000); 'Respect (valuing other cultures), Openness (withholding judgement), Curiosity and discovery (tolerating ambiguity)' (Deardorff and Hunter, 2006).

Haigh (2002), arguing for an *inclusive* curriculum rather than one which is specifically internationalised, summarises other work by Gibson, Dobbert

and Morey in a table of five deficit models of curriculum internationalisation, ranging from 'Bringing the foreigners up to speed' through 'Benevo-
lent multicultural segregation – separate development' to 'Multicultural
education'.

Features of an internationalised curriculum

The features of internationalised curricula reflect the varied rationales behind
them; early and less developed models will focus exclusively on content, but
more complex models encompass references to knowledge and skills, sometimes to behaviours and, where the rationale is values-based, to attitudes.
Most models will look specifically at outcomes, and to date relatively few
'involve an examination of the appropriateness of conventional western
pedagogical approaches to contemporary, more globalised and culturally
independent contexts for both domestic and international students' (Ryan
and Louie, 2005, online version p. 2).

Outcomes may include things such as: 'an understanding of the global
nature of economic, political and cultural exchange', 'demand culturally
inclusive behaviour', 'see change as positive' and 'engage critically with the
global plurality of knowledge' (Rizvi, 2000); 'how knowledge is constructed
differently in diverse cultures', 'an awareness of their own cultures and perspectives' and an ability to 'identify ethical issues that may arise in their
personal and professional lives in international and/or intercultural contexts'
(McTaggart, 2003); 'recognition and appreciation of different cultural perspectives on the same issue; valuing of cultural and linguistic diversity and
difference' (Leask, 2005b); 'can apply critical thinking skills to problems
with an international or intercultural dimension', 'can demonstrate specific
knowledge of similarities as well as differences in the professional practices in
their field among different cultures', 'content includes topics on ethical issues
in globalization' and 'through encouraging students to reflect critically on
their own cultural identity and its social construction, provides emancipatory
learning experiences' (Whalley et al., 1997); 'enhance the international understanding of our students, and to give them opportunities to reflect on their
society through the eyes, insights and critiques offered by others' and 'contribute to the search for solutions to major global problems (e.g. global
environmental change)' (University of Saskatchewan, 2003).

Pedagogies

The aims and objectives, curriculum content and learning outcomes associated with internationalisation require a consideration of the assessment,
learning and teaching strategies through which they are to be realised. Taylor
(2004: 157) emphasises the importance of this, summarising the approach to
internationalisation at the University of Western Australia as requiring 'a

fundamental re-examination of teaching provision'. In part, this may be a matter of developing practice which meets the needs of a diverse student body, but more fundamentally it will involve developing practices which can meet the objectives of an internationalised curriculum.

The more complex models of curriculum internationalisation would suggest that students need to *experience*, to *reflect* and to *make strange* (the basis of ethnographic techniques) if they are to develop the personal awareness associated with intercultural and global perspectives. Whalley's taxonomy of curriculum areas includes best practice lists for teaching and learning strategies and for assessment strategies which range from the minimalist 'avoid reinforcing cultural stereotypes' to a focus on methodologies such as 'problem-solving exercises in international or intercultural contexts', 'self-reflective writing' and 'discovery-based "contact" assignments with people from different cultural backgrounds' (Whalley *et al.*, 1997: 18). These later strategies can be allied to a more general recognition in teaching and learning theory that learners need to be challenged both cognitively and affectively if learning is to be transformative.

Leask (2001: 108) and others comment that the teaching and learning strategies associated with internationalisation, while often arising from a consideration of the needs of international students, bring about improvements in teaching and learning 'for all students from all educational and cultural backgrounds'. The process of reviewing teaching and learning strategies for appropriateness with regard to internationalisation, if approached holistically, can go further and lead to the development of practice which is 'inclusive of the diversity of all students' practices, values and beliefs' (Abu-Arab, 2005: 23). As already indicated, we would extend this to suggest that the whole process of curriculum internationalisation, but in particular the opportunities for critical self-reflection, is likely to be of most significant benefit to our stay-at-home domestic students.

Within the range of tools, techniques and resources available to help pursue effective learning and teaching within an internationalised curriculum, the most obvious, and perhaps least utilised, is the diversity of the student body itself. Effective cross-cultural integration is something which is rarely effectively achieved (take a glance around the student groupings on your campus). Improving on this is both an outcome of the process of curriculum internationalisation and a mechanism for helping to achieve it. Indeed, it may be seen as fundamental; 'engaging Canadian students with their international peers in the mutual construction of international knowledge deserves recognition as a central pillar of an internationalized methodology' (Whalley *et al.*, 1997: 6). In this context, once again, we can and should be looking more broadly than the cultural diversity in the international student community to that of the home student population, too. Internationalisation, actually, relates to multiculturalism and is, as indicated above, able to play a significant role in the broader objectives of an inclusive education.

In referring to normalising the internationalisation of the curriculum, Webb (2005) makes the important point that while 'the development of organisation-wide systems is necessary for this to happen . . . such "culture change" cannot be effected by university edict alone, but only through the creative utilisation of the imagination and agency of those who comprise the university'. The case study which follows illustrates how Leeds Metropolitan University has sought to engage both institutional and individual perspectives in internationalising the curriculum.

Section 2: Case study

The approach to internationalisation presented in the case study sets out to be inclusive, has a values-based underpinning, and has the potential to be transformative for the institution, its staff and the whole body of students it serves. The institution is a member of the Development Education Association, and parallels between its vision of *world-wide horizons* and the DEA's view on the role of education are clear within the rationale outlined in the Guidelines Document:

> As educators we have a unique opportunity and a clear responsibility to help prepare our students to be responsible citizens of the future. The fate of our planet and all its life forms lie in their hands. The question, therefore, is how do we prepare the global citizen?
>
> (McKenzie *et al.*, 2003: 3)

The process of curriculum review is intended to challenge the academic community to engage with their curricula and their pedagogy to become 'interculturally responsive' (MacKinnon and Manathunga, 2003). The term 'cross-cultural capability' has been coined to describe the attributes demanded of graduates and educators if we are to be able to respond appropriately, both personally and professionally, to the cultural diversity which globalisation increasingly throws together; in the case study, it is allied to the underpinning values brought through *global perspectives.*

Leeds Metropolitan University originally began to develop the notion of cross-cultural capability in response to the need to revitalise modern languages education, in part as a result of growing evidence that modern language students were often ill equipped to benefit fully from their year abroad but, more significantly, because neither a utilitarian approach to language teaching nor an area studies approach was providing students with the ability to perform effectively as linguists in the modern world.

From a series of conferences around this initial focus, the International Association of Languages and Intercultural Communication[2] was born. Echoing in microcosm the broader trends within internationalisation referred to earlier, the second iteration of the notion of cross-cultural capability focused on international cultures, seeing cross-cultural capability as particularly relevant to international students, students on courses with a strong international focus, and staff dealing with either or both of these. It was then not a great leap to see that all courses should be preparing all students for a more globalised world.

As we continued the internal debate on cross-cultural capability, however, colleagues working on other priorities, in particular on the demands of the widening participation and diversity agendas, helped us to the realisation that the requirements to deal effectively with cross-cultural contact are central to the broader agenda of inclusivity. Our Guidelines Document is, therefore, headed with a list of key concepts to emphasise this broader conceptualisation.

Cross-cultural capability demands a growth in self-awareness, in our understanding of culture and its influences upon our identities, our values, our attitudes and our behaviours, and an appreciation of the far-reaching impacts which can arise when dissimilar cultural rules of engagement collide. Some of this can be learned theoretically, but much of it must be experienced to be meaningful. Our Guidelines Document, therefore, includes more examples of 'experience' which may help develop cross-cultural capability than it does of 'knowledge'.

We believe cultures to be equally deserving of respect; we believe better cross-cultural engagement will enable our graduating students and ourselves to live more successfully with those around us; we believe the major issues to face our students in the future will be largely incapable of solution at a regional, national or even supra-national level and will therefore require collaborations based on respect and understanding of the 'other'. Because of these values and principles, we believe education which does not seek to prepare students to meet the global challenges ahead cannot be considered adequate. Cross-cultural capability is our formulation of the personal attributes of somebody who is prepared to begin that journey.

Putting cross-cultural capability into practice across the University presents a formidable challenge, requires a strategic approach with support at the highest levels, and must be articulated consistently through relevant key policies. In the case of Leeds Met, these include our

Internationalisation Strategy and our Assessment, Learning and Teaching Strategy, both of which support the University's Corporate Plan. As such, they have the approval of the Board of Governors, and their implementation is open to external scrutiny, for example by external examiners, professional bodies, the Higher Education Funding Council for England and the Quality Assurance Agency. Such high-level corporate support is a key to successful institutional reform and, we think, unusual in respect of internationalisation in UK Higher Education to date. Aim 5 of the Corporate Plan is: 'To develop students' international opportunities and global perspectives, ensuring that an international, multi-cultural ethos pervades the university.' The associated Outcome 5.2.1[3] requires all programmes in the University to have been reviewed against the Guidelines Document by 2008.

Using the process of programme review as a mechanism for driving internationalisation provides several advantages:

- Educational programmes are our core business. Taking them through review ensures internationalisation is directed at core practices.
- Academic staff feel a strong sense of programme ownership; if successful, programme review will provide academic staff with ownership of the internationalised curriculum.
- Through undertaking the process of programme review, academic staff need to understand cross-cultural capability and global perspectives not only in the abstract but also in the context of their own discipline and their own assessment, learning and teaching mechanisms.
- Every student is involved in a programme of some kind.
- Programme evaluation – both internal and external, peer and top-down – is a regular part of our activity, thus ensuring that our development and implementation are open to scrutiny.

The review process began in 2004/5, following consultations with each head of school in which they agreed initial programmes for review along with a schedule for all courses to meet the Corporate Plan deadline. Reviews were completed against a template, based around key questions, though the document was clear that review teams should not see this as a tick-list exercise and should modify or add to the questions as appropriate. Reviews were continually collated and, along with other feedback and further consultation with colleagues from faculties, Chaplaincy,

Community Partnerships and Volunteering, Employability, and Ethics, a revised version was produced for the substantive reviews to follow. Reviews continue to be collated, and are available on the intranet to inform ongoing work. With the process under way, each faculty now has an International Teacher Fellow appointed to ensure that pedagogy, partnerships, content, and student mobility opportunities are developed to embed and support the work.

Not surprisingly, perhaps, the degree to which the review process is embedding cross-cultural capability and global perspectives is differential across subjects and between individual course teams. However, development is taking place across the institution, with requests for staff development to support the process being a good indicator of engagement. Table 9.1 shows a sample of responses to selected key questions to indicate something of the range of interpretations and innovations, and something of the breadth of our understanding of what internationalisation encompasses. While these may reflect existing practice, they will form the baseline for the next stage of development.

Table 9.1 Questions evaluation

How does the course seek to incorporate the knowledge and understanding brought to it by students from diverse backgrounds?	From the induction course onwards, all students are asked to share their experience and point of view on the world and why they want to write what they do. They tell their backstories in the first week, and international students' experiences are compared to those of UK students. We also select films from a range of countries to study on the course, and the cultural context is one of those explored. Finally, we run a series called Movie Magic every year, which this year will be open to everyone in the University, in which only international films may feature and a student-led seminar is held in which the country as much as the film is investigated in discussion. This year we shall be bringing in international students from outside the course to participate in the delivery of these sessions.

Continued

Table 9.1 continued

In what ways are students helped to examine their own values, compare them with the values of others, and engage in respectful debate where differences occur?	Exploring and understanding alternative ethics and value systems are closely related to pursuing an informed response to a design project. This promotes healthy debate in various parts of the course curriculum and in turn helps students develop a rounded personal design philosophy, responsive to contemporary society.
How does the course enable other knowledge/perspectives to be recognised and valued?	One of the key areas identified as a Personal Development Planning attribute within the Social Science programme is that of Social and Ethical Awareness. Specifically the aim of the programme and all courses therein is to: – accept the culture and values of others; – respect different views and perspectives on shared issues; – be capable of rational and courteous challenge to views and values; – be capable of rational and courteous argument to support their own views and values.
How does a student on this course benefit from/contribute to the broader social context?	Most routes within the scheme bring in external perspectives by the use of guest speakers. Students are required to demonstrate an understanding of how aspects of the subject impact upon a group/context other than their own. The scheme actively seeks to recruit students from diverse cultural and socio-economic backgrounds.

Conclusion

Having defined our concept of curriculum, in this chapter we have considered rationales for an internationalised curriculum, features of such curricula, and a range of related pedagogies. We have offered a case study of curriculum internationalisation at Leeds Metropolitan University, and the Cross-cultural Capability Guidelines Document, which forms the basis of curriculum review for internationalisation in that institution, is reproduced in full in the Appendix.

Notes

1 Van der Wende (1996) (cited in Webb, 2005): (1) curricula with international content; (2) curricula that add a comparative dimension to traditional content; (3) career-oriented curricula; (4) curricula addressing cross-cultural skills; (5) inter-disciplinary area study programmes; (6) curricula leading to internationally recognised professions; (7) curricula leading to joint or double degrees; (8) curricula whose parts are offered at off-shore institutions by a local faculty; (9) special curricula designed exclusively for foreign students.
2 http://www.ialic.arts.gla.ac.uk/
3 Outcome 5.2.1: 'An agreed percentage of courses in each faculty will be reviewed against "Guidelines on Cross-cultural Capability" in 2004–05 through the Annual Review process . . . with all programmes having been reviewed by 2008.'

Chapter 10

Internationalisation and employability

Dawn Leggott and Jane Stapleford

Context

Increasing numbers of students world-wide are opting to complete part of their studies in another country, either as fee-paying individuals or through schemes such as the Erasmus programme. Whilst there are several reasons why students choose to study abroad, many of them do so primarily in order to enhance their employability. Those students who are unable to participate in international study in this way also need to develop the skills associated with study abroad, so that their employment prospects can be improved as well. This chapter looks, in part, at how this can be achieved through the development of a suitable internationalisation strategy and the embedding of employability skills into the curriculum.

After outlining what is meant by 'employability' and identifying skills and attributes that graduate employers require, this chapter will explore the nature of students' perceptions of their employability skills development by drawing on data obtained during a five-year research study. It will then offer ways of embedding employability and internationalising the curriculum in order to enhance the employability and career prospects of all students. There is substantial variation in students' understanding of, and orientation towards, their employability skills development, often depending upon their home context.

There is a plethora of definitions of 'employability', but we favour the one offered by the National Co-ordination Team for Student Employability (Higher Education Academy/ESECT, n.d.), now subsumed within the Higher Education Academy. This definition is comprehensive and appropriate to Higher Education. Employability is a 'set of achievements, understandings and personal attributes that make individuals more likely to gain employment and be successful in their chosen occupations'.

It is widely recognised that enhancing students' employability is vital to a knowledge-driven economy (Hawkridge, 2005) and that academic knowledge alone is no longer sufficient to satisfy today's employers. The nature of graduate employment is changing, with the result that new types of companies, different types of work, the globalisation of markets and a climate of rapid change have made the graduate labour market more unpredictable and difficult to navigate. It is now more critical than ever that all students are aware of, and work towards, enhancing their own employability and that they understand the nature and importance of continuing professional development. There is therefore a need for HE institutions to take a more employability-oriented, internationalised approach to the curriculum, fully considering the different global contexts in which students are likely to operate in the future. Efforts to address employability within a curriculum context need to respond to research and surveys of graduate recruiters which highlight the increasing need for graduates to develop a range of skills (Harvey and Green, 1994; Harvey et al., 1997; Yorke and Knight, 2004a).

The skills and attributes required by employers

Employers in the UK, Australia, New Zealand and other countries suggest that employability consists of a number of attributes or qualities and task-centred skills. These include: effective learning skills, self-awareness, networking and negotiation skills, transferable skills, self-confidence, interpersonal skills, team-working ability, decision-making skills and the capacity to cope with uncertainty (Yorke and Knight, 2004b). Such lists often include several 'skills', but employability is far more than just a collection of skills and it is often advisable to refer to employability attributes (Harvey and Knight, 2003).

There are numerous lists of employers' requirements or 'wish lists' arising from a range of research over the last twenty years, and some identify up to eighty attributes (Lester, 2003; Yorke and Knight, 2004a; Harvey and Knight, 2003; Association of Graduate Recruiters, 1995). These lists need to be treated with some caution, but certainly give an indication of employers' requirements and expectations and clearly demonstrate that far more attributes are needed than just subject-specific knowledge and skills. A survey carried out by the University of Dublin into employers' skills requirements in Ireland supported these findings. It found that the two most important attributes for employers when recruiting graduates were enthusiasm and personality. Work experience and a range of skills including oral and written communication, teamwork, customer service, time management and the ability to multi-task were also valued (Curry et al., 2003).

What is the situation in some non-English-speaking countries? The large-scale 'Higher education and graduate employment in Europe' (2000) study examined the relationship between Higher Education and employment across twelve countries by surveying 3,000 graduates from each country (CHEERS, n.d.). For example, in employment terms, Spain has been characterised by a history of high youth unemployment, a desire by graduates for job stability through a permanent work contract such as a civil service position and an emphasis on personal connections. Traditionally exam- and knowledge-based, the Spanish Higher Education system could be viewed as too far removed from the twenty-first-century labour market, and it has been argued that Spanish university students' development of generic skills within the Higher Education system is vital to facilitate their transition between education and employment (Mora *et al.*, 2000). Mora *et al.* (2000) have found that, in addition to specific subject-related skills and knowledge, employers in Spain principally require problem-solving abilities, independence, flexibility, adaptability and team-working skills. This echoes the requirements identified in the other studies referred to above.

Case study

The study officially entitled 'Higher education and graduate employment in Europe' and better known as the CHEERS project ('Careers after higher education: a European research survey') was developed between 1997 and 2000 by a consortium of nine universities and three European research institutes, as well as a Japanese university. It was coordinated by Professor Ulrich Teichler, Director of the International Centre for Higher Education Research of the University of Kassel (Germany), and funded by the European Union (through the Targeted Socio-economic Research Programme, TSER). Its main objectives were to investigate the current relationship between Higher Education and employment of graduates, as well as to find out and analyse graduates' perceptions of the deficiencies and virtues of the training they had received in the Higher Education institutions where they studied.

After designing a questionnaire which had to be translated and adapted to the individual educational and socio-cultural characteristics of the eleven participating European countries (Germany, France, Italy, Spain, Austria, the United Kingdom, Norway, Finland, Sweden, the Netherlands and the Czech Republic) and Japan, between the end of 1998 and the beginning of 1999 more than 36,000 graduates who had finished their university studies in the academic year 1994/5 (approximately 3,000 in each participating country) were surveyed.

The extensive questionnaire requested data about the graduates' socio-biographical background and academic history, as well as professional and job-searching activities, the relationship between Higher Education and the job they were currently engaged in, employability skills and their application, job satisfaction, continuous professional or educational development and finally a retrospective evaluation of the studies which they had finished in the academic year 1994/5.

What was particularly innovative about the study was the fact that it focused on the knowledge, skills and attitudes needed by graduates in order to meet employers' skills requirements. Therefore, issues such as 'To what extent do Higher Education institutions help students to develop employability skills or promote learning activities which will lead to the development of employability skills?' and 'To what extent do the graduates use these skills in the workplace?' were covered in the questionnaires, although precise definitions of the employability skills listed were not given.

As far as the main results were concerned, on a scale of 1 to 5, of the thirty-six employability skills listed as required in the workplace and acquired by the point of graduation, the most cited were working independently, problem-solving ability, oral communication skills and working under pressure (all with a score of 4.3), closely followed by self-responsibility, decision making and working in a team (4.2) and time management, assertiveness, decisiveness, persistence, accuracy, attention to detail, planning and organisation, initiative, adaptability, getting personally involved, loyalty and integrity (4.1). The graduates considered that their university studies had provided them with some foreign language proficiency, learning skills, discipline-specific theoretical knowledge and broad general knowledge, but cited a significant lack of negotiating skills, IT skills, economic reasoning, leadership and oral communication skills.

The data obtained have led to the publication of over 200 scientific documents (http://www.uni-kassel.de/wz1/TSEREGS/publi_e.htm) about very varying aspects of the study, including graduates' preferences when looking for work, sex discrimination, employees' opinions about Higher Education, the relationship between Higher Education and employers' skills requirements, regional differences and geographic mobility. In addition, many conferences, courses, seminars and discussions have taken place on different continents (http://www.uni-kassel.de/wz1/TSEREGS/conf_e.htm).

The relevance of the study for Higher Education institutions and university policy is considerable, because on the one hand it is the largest-scale comparative study to date into employability of university graduates and on the other hand the data collection methods used are conceptually and methodologically advanced and of relevance to future studies, particularly those conducted over large geographic areas. In conclusion, the wide distribution of the results of the CHEERS project has led many academic authorities to place a greater emphasis on the improvement of graduates' employability and meant that employability skills are now being taken more into account when new study programmes and methods are introduced into Higher Education institutions.

Dr José Sánchez Campillo
University of Granada, Spain

China is also facing a mismatch between its graduates' and postgraduates' knowledge and skills and employers' skills requirements. Many multinational organisations with branches in China are now aiming to employ more local talent rather than expatriates, but they are experiencing a severe shortage of suitably experienced and skilled managers (Spencer Stuart, 2004). Apart from the advanced level of English language and other language skills, other skill requirements include initiative, teamwork, negotiation, an aptitude for risk taking and creativity (*Economist*, 2005; *Financial Times*, 2005a, 2005b), again a familiar list of desirable attributes.

In general, therefore, employers' requirements seem to be broadly consistent internationally. This means that, on the whole, employability interventions in the curriculum which are devised for home students planning to work in one country are largely appropriate for both home and international students who are planning to work in another.

To what extent are students aware of their development of employability attributes and employers' skills requirements?

Student awareness and understanding of their employability attributes and employers' skills requirements formed part of a five-year longitudinal study carried out by one of the authors. The cohort under investigation consisted of thirty-five students, all of whom studied two languages and also a professional route such as Marketing, Tourism or Information Technology (IT) leading to the BA (Hons) Professional Language Studies after four years of full-time study. The students spent the third year of their degree programme working or studying in a target-language country. All of the students in the cohort completed a questionnaire annually (the return rate averaged over 90 per cent each year), and eight students were selected for a yearly interview. Those selected represented the diversity of students and ranged from 18-year-olds to mature students. The data from the interview tape-recordings were transcribed, labelled and categorised. This information then formed the basis for the design of the questionnaire. Both the qualitative and the quantitative results were presented and discussed each year in a report.

In their final year and again nine months after graduation, the students were asked which skills they felt they had developed in the course of the four years of their degree programme and which of these would be/had proven useful for the world of work. The skills included in Table 10.1 are not intended to represent an exhaustive list of employability skills, but merely

Table 10.1 Student perceptions of their own skills development and the usefulness of these skills for their future employability in their final year of study and nine months after graduation

Skill/Attribute	Percentage of students who perceived that they had developed each skill		Percentage of students who perceived that possession of the skills would increase their employability	
	In their final year*	Nine months after graduation*	In their final year*	Nine months after graduation*
Time management	65%	100%	69%	100%
Self-awareness	62%	100%	62%	86%
Language-learning strategies	57%	100%	50%	14%
Organisation and planning	42%	100%	54%	71%
Critical (evaluative) thinking and analysis	27%	86%	46%	57%
Self-confidence	39%	100%	39%	71%
Taking responsibility for own development	65%	100%	50%	71%
Decision making	39%	100%	46%	86%
Problem solving	34%	71%	42%	86%
Communication	No comments were made by students on this skill.	100%	No comments were made by students on this skill.	86%
IT	No comments were made by students on this skill.	100%	No comments were made by students on this skill.	100%
Team working	No comments were made by students on this skill.	100%	No comments were made by students on this skill.	100%

* All percentages are rounded up.

represent those mentioned by the students. The table summarises the students' perceptions.

As can be seen in Table 10.1, in the final year of their degree, less than half of the students felt that they had developed the skills of 'organisation and planning', 'critical thinking and analysis', 'self-confidence', 'decision making' and 'problem solving'. None of the skills were cited by more than two-thirds of the participants. Although many students seemed to fail to recognise their own skills development while they were full-time students, however, they were clearly better able to recognise it less than one year after they had completed their degree and started working.

Even by the final year of their degree, less than half of the respondents considered 'critical thinking and analysis', 'problem solving', 'decision making' and 'self-confidence' to be useful skills for the world of work. Even those skills most frequently selected for their usefulness for work ('time management', 'organisation and planning' and 'self-awareness') were not selected by at least a quarter of the students. Less than one year after graduation, however, the results indicated a marked increase in the participants' awareness of the usefulness of the skills listed, once they had finished university and entered the working environment. The only skill listed which did not show an improvement was 'language-learning strategies', probably owing to the fact that several of the former students were not using their language skills in their current employment situation. They seemed not to have realised that their general oral and written communication skills would automatically have been developed as a result of their language learning, even if they were not using their foreign language skills in their jobs, so it is important that students of languages are helped to make the link between language learning and their development of the generic employability skills of oral and written communication.

When students spend a period of time studying or working in another country, does it make a difference to perceptions of their development of skills and attributes and of employers' requirements?

All of the students interviewed during their year abroad agreed that their international experience would be of use to them in the future, and all of them mentioned at least one skill or personal attribute which they felt they had gained during the year.

> I have developed as a person and gained many valuable life skills during this year. I have gained in confidence as a person and hopefully future employers will take into consideration this completed year abroad.

Several students commented in a similar manner on the way in which their international experience offered them practical preparation for employment, thus increasing their attractiveness to employers.

It makes you truly independent and you have to be more organised with work and managing your time . . . I think it has helped me use my time more efficiently.

Others referred to metacognitive skills such as time management, planning, and organisational skills.

Not only has it [the year abroad] improved my Spanish beyond belief, hence aiding me in my final year, but more than that it has given me a lot of responsibility for my own life. I am more independent and grown-up, realising what is important in life, when and where you must take responsibility for yourself and that your parents can't and shouldn't do everything for you. The year abroad has given me confidence and practical work experience. I have learnt a lot about myself, which has to be advantageous.

The students clearly perceived their own development of such aspects as maturity, independence, sense of responsibility and self-confidence, and all of the students who had attended university straight from school mentioned at least one of these points. These personal attributes, though not strictly speaking definable as employability skills, contribute significantly to the students' employability.

The skills you learn while living abroad can be transferred to every walk of life, mainly responsibility, thinking for yourself, being reliant on yourself only, taking responsibility for your actions.

Increased cross-cultural awareness or intercultural competence was referred to by several students.

I have loved actually living in a different culture and feeling the effects of culture shock etc.

And of course, those who had tried to integrate into the target-language culture and improve their language skills specifically mentioned those.

The year abroad will be of use to me in the future because living in the country is the best way to absorb the language and really learn it.

The participants were clearly very well aware of some of the skills and personal attributes developed during their period abroad. Many realised that the benefits obtained from spending an extended period in a target-language country far exceeded those related to linguistic progress and were transferable from the study to the work context and more generally to their daily lives. The personal and professional outcomes stated above very closely reflect those of the taxonomy of the objectives of residence abroad (Coleman, 2004). Indeed it may be fair to surmise that many, if not most, of the students saw the year abroad as a life-changing experience – a process of discovery and self-discovery.

> The year abroad is different to previous years. I have learnt new skills that couldn't be achieved at home.

Although most of the students interviewed in this study were British students who were spending a year studying or working in another European country, the skills which they referred to as having developed can equally be developed by any student of any nationality who chooses to spend a period of time working or studying in any other country, for example international students studying in English-speaking environments such as the UK, Australia or the USA, or European students studying in any other European country as part of the Erasmus programme. What is crucial, however, is that any student embarking on a period abroad should be made fully aware of the resulting employability skills developed through this experience.

How can skills for employability be built effectively into the curriculum?

The various pieces of research cited above give an indication of the appropriate content for the HE curriculum for enhancing graduate employability applicable to a wide variety of countries, and HE institutions require a strategy for developing this content. To be effective, the commitment to both employability and internationalisation should be embedded in all aspects of the institution not just the curriculum. The AGCAS publication *Going Global* (2005: 16) stresses that employability should be 'at the centre of curriculum design and compatible with good learning in general'.

A major factor in successful curriculum development for employability and internationalisation is a commitment to embedding them both into the mainstream curriculum as opposed to providing sessions on a 'bolt-on' basis, whenever possible. Only this way does it become accepted and respected by both staff and students. 'Bolt-ons' tend to be seen as 'add-ons' and remain that way.

By means of an audit of the curriculum of a chosen course, gaps in provision and areas for improvement can be identified. Bespoke interventions of this kind are time-consuming but more effective, as they consider the unique characteristics of individual courses rather then providing a blanket solution. Internationalisation of the curriculum can involve, for example, the carrying out of a cross-cultural capability audit of all courses on offer in the university and encouraging the use of international examples and reading lists whatever the subject area. Employability aspects of the curriculum are frequently left until the students' final year of study, yet they should be embedded from their first year, as students need to be aware of the importance of gaining relevant work experience and reflecting and building upon it throughout their programme of study. Indeed Shah *et al.* (2004) found that the graduates they surveyed would have benefited from more careers advice. An audit often shows up a lack of student development of career management skills in the curriculum, through which the students are encouraged to engage with the employer recruitment process in an active and critical way and learn to sell their employability skills, including their intercultural competence, effectively to employers. These skills should be developed throughout the course, not just in the final year.

Some academic staff may be reluctant to incorporate what they see as 'mere skills' at the possible expense of their subject-specific content. An audit can help staff to recognise that their courses may already include the development of a range of employability skills, but that the existing curriculum needs to be enhanced and repackaged to enable the students to see clearer connections between their curriculum and the skills and attributes that employers are seeking. The staff involved should be supported in this process through staff development and the sharing of information about resources. The incorporation of personal development planning into the curriculum, which is now a major HE initiative in the UK (Quality Assurance Agency, n.d.), can help both home and international students to recognise the transferability of their skills and knowledge through reflection and synthesis of their learning. When both staff and students realise the learning is of value to employers and the academic skills are transferable to the workplace they tend to be less resistant to these aspects of the curriculum.

Key aspects of an internationalised curriculum are important for employability in the global labour market of the twenty-first century. Proficiency in at least one foreign language is viewed favourably by employers in the UK and as essential for employability in many other countries, not just because of the language skills themselves, but also because language learning automatically furthers the development of other skills such as communication skills and independence. Cross-cultural awareness and capability and an understanding of a range of global perspectives are highly desirable employability attributes which can be fostered through an internationalised curriculum addressing employability.

Work experience can be gained by all students through international exchange programmes or international volunteering through which students engage in a work-related project, perhaps as an alternative to a dissertation.

Without even going abroad, cross-cultural understanding can be gained through researching work-related topics and/or issues in another part of the world. Cross-cultural capability, employability and understanding of lifestyle and work practices in different cultures can be enhanced through intercultural volunteering, simulations based on experiences in other countries, or inviting visiting speakers from international companies.

Both language and cross-cultural capability can be enhanced by adopting a content language integrated learning (CLIL) approach. CLIL is an exciting learning and teaching strategy to enhance language acquisition by offering course content in the target language of the learner. This approach can be broadened from just language courses, where it is currently mainly used. It could also be offered more broadly as elective modules, thus enabling improvement for students who have some grasp of a language or encouraging students to take language electives. Employers look favourably on candidates with language skills, so this could enhance employability.

This approach can be particularly effective when linked with joint seminars or project work between home and international students.

International partnerships facilitating both staff and student exchanges will enhance the participants' understanding of similarities and differences in attitude, lifestyle and work practices in different cultures, thus contributing broadly to the institution's awareness and understanding.

A UK Higher Education Careers Services Unit (HECSU) research project explored how far careers services cater for developing employability attributes in international students studying in the UK but intending to work in their home country (HECSU, 2005). Overall this study concluded that there is a need for a more holistic and coordinated approach to the international student experience, including coordinated integration of services within institutions.

Employability and internationalisation of the curriculum are likely only to be taken seriously by staff and students if they are firmly embedded in the internal institutional quality assurance systems by means of specific programme learning outcomes for both aspects. Guidelines for internal course approvals and periodic review processes should explicitly refer to them. Such review processes can be used to encourage change, including internationalisation of the curriculum and the embedding of employability. Without these measures being firmly rooted in ongoing regulations for academic quality assurance, there is a danger that these aspects may disappear with the champion who introduced them.

Although personal development planning in the UK promotes reflection on both academic and work-related learning and aims to encourage habits leading to life-long learning, in other countries the focus on these areas may be much less pronounced, but recent interest from the USA, Denmark, Botswana and South Africa indicates that this is beginning to filter through. The concept of life-long learning is still very new in Spain, for example, but it is slowly gaining credence, and the possibilities of less formal learning, through work placements for instance, are increasing (Centro Europeo para el Desarrollo de la Formación Profesional, n.d.). Changes in the learning and teaching methods used in Spanish universities so that they include more work-based learning together with a greater emphasis on presentation skills, teamwork, field work and IT would help to create a better link between Higher Education and the world of work for Spanish graduates and therefore improve their employability (Jiménez Aguilera *et al.*, 2003). However, non-traditional programmes are not regulated by the state in Spain and are therefore not recognised at a national level (Mora, 2001).

In China one strategy increasingly being used is in-house tailored training of Chinese undergraduates, postgraduates or those who have completed additional education outside China (Spencer Stuart, 2004; *China Education News*, 2004; Chang, 2004). China is trying to remedy the mismatch between its Higher Education system and employers' requirements by increasing the funding for Higher Education in China and encouraging more Chinese students to study abroad (*Financial Times*, 2005b).

What can we do to enhance practice?

How can we help students to increase their awareness of their employability skills and maximise their development of them, so that they may be better prepared to work in the global marketplace in whichever location they choose? Suggestions are given under each of the headings of 'strategic approaches', 'curriculum interventions', 'year abroad' and 'internationalisation in the students' home learning environment', but these are not by any means intended to be exhaustive.

Strategic approaches

Some strategies can be utilised by HE institutions to support both home and international students to become more employable. These include:

- offering staff development in, for example, employability and career management skills, global and cross-cultural awareness and language training for all staff working with both home and international students;
- creating tailored work experience or work-related learning schemes for home and international students both at home and abroad;
- developing a more coordinated and collaborative approach to the sharing of information and good practice intra- and inter-institutionally (in the UK the latter could be coordinated through AGCAS and HECSU), e.g. labour market information on non-UK countries, employability strategies, what employers want in non-UK countries, and finding work overseas;

- a strategy to identify improvements in careers advisory services and employability in the curriculum for international and home students.

Curriculum interventions

The HE curriculum can be enhanced to more closely address employability, transferability of skills and international and cultural issues. Such interventions may include:

- tailored interventions for employability in the curriculum including employability and career management skills and international approaches to work-related learning;
- internationalisation of the curriculum to include references to other cultures' practices and international rather than simply local examples;
- greater awareness raising for both home and international students that the skills they are developing throughout their studies are transferable to employment contexts at home and globally;
- ensuring that personal and employability skills development forms part of the final degree classification or is listed in the transcript;
- adopting a content language integrated learning (CLIL) approach to enhance internationalisation.

Preparation for and reflection on the period abroad

If students of any nationality are to gain maximum benefit from spending a period of time studying or working in any other country, it is essential that they engage in a process of reflection prior to, during and after the experience. Activities to foster this process include:

- teaching students in advance the skills of reflection by offering a selection of tools and strategies such as journals, story-telling, dialogue and unsent letters;
- encouraging student interest in improving their language skills while abroad by making them aware of Stern's (1975) characteristics of the good language learner and using Oxford's Strategy Inventory for Language Learning (Oxford, 1990: Appendix B) as a basis for discussion on the types of strategies they might employ;
- setting up a buddying scheme by pairing each student planning to go abroad with one who is already in that student's destination country, so that they can maintain regular email contact and, when at home, gain a 'running commentary' of the issues faced by the student in the target country;
- inviting university alumni who spent a period abroad during their studies to share their experiences and discuss the skills and personal attributes

they developed during that experience and their relevance for the world of work;

- encouraging student reflection upon their activities, achievements and interests away from the academic environment, such as their hobbies, voluntary work and personal life, and document ways in which these activities have armed them with skills or experience which will contribute towards their preparation for the world of work.

Internationalisation in the students' home learning environment

Those students who are unable to spend time studying or working abroad should be given the opportunity to gain an internationalised university education at their home university, so that they can develop similar employability skills to those gained when studying abroad. Ways in which individual universities can foster this include:

- developing and implementing a university-wide internationalisation strategy aimed at fostering an ethos of internationalisation within the whole institution;
- internationalising learning, teaching and research through, for example, the internationalisation of the curriculum;
- devising innovative work-related activities such as collaborative projects, simulations, intercultural volunteering and CLIL teaching and learning strategies;
- developing staff capability for internationalisation by, for example, promoting their participation in international conferences and foreign language classes or encouraging them to further their intercultural competence;
- sharing good practice internationally though joint research opportunities and academic and non-academic staff international exchange;
- promoting the integration of home and international students studying at the institution.
  (see Leeds Metropolitan University (2003) Internationalisation Strategy)

Conclusion

In the twenty-first-century international labour market the development of employability skills and attributes through adopting international perspectives is essential to the enhancement of the employment prospects of students of any nationality. Employers in many countries world-wide share the same sorts of required graduate employability skills and attributes. Spending a period of time studying or working in another country permits students to develop these skills. In this case, it is important, however, that the students are made aware of their development of such skills and perspectives as part of their pre-travel preparation and post-travel reflection, so that they are better able to gain employment in the international marketplace. For those unable to spend a period of time abroad, similar employability skills can be developed in their home university through the firm embedding of employability and cross-cultural capability into the curriculum and the creation and implementation of a suitable internationalisation strategy.

Chapter 11

Internationalisation and engagement with the wider community

David Killick

Introduction

The community which surrounds the student, whether they are an international or a 'home' student studying in an international or an intercultural context, can provide a valuable resource for developing an understanding of aspects of the culture(s) of the host environment. The community can also provide a rich resource to help universities welcome and integrate their international students. If engagement is well thought through and carefully set up, there will be some reciprocal benefit in both resources and insights for the local community. Where community engagement is linked to an ethos of citizenship or 'service', benefits to the community will be more central to the project. Where an institution is seeking to 'internationalise' its entire student body, opportunities for intercultural interactions within the local community can provide a context for the development of personal awareness among the majority of non-mobile home students, and an important intervention within a strategy for 'internationalisation at home' (IaH) (Crowther *et al.*, 2000; Nilsson, 2003). Incorporating community engagement into outbound student mobility programmes can add significant opportunities for gaining a deeper understanding of the host culture. The integration of active learning and reflection in such programmes can be related to a range of learning theories, and argued to promote a number of generic 'transferable' skills (see Case studies 1 and 4),[1] enhanced notions of citizenship, and more transformational processes arising from raising to consciousness personal value systems, or establishing 'new resources of knowledge and authority' (Case study 2).

The focus of this chapter is limited to projects which engage individuals or small groups of students and members of the community. The rationales for community engagement are similarly limited in focus, but it is relevant to note that the projects take place within university contexts and, as such, may (or may not) reflect a broader institutional conceptualisation of the social and philosophical relationship between 'the' university and its community, and that this may be embedded in a social and/or an education vision (Sunderland *et al.*, 2004). That said, the reciprocal nature of the broader institutional relationship with its community, in which there 'is a commitment to sharing and reciprocity . . . partnerships, two way streets defined by mutual respect among the partners for what each brings to the table' (Kellogg Commission, 1999: vii), could equally fittingly be ascribed to the best levels of individual engagement.

Institutional rationales are themselves dependent upon broader conceptualisations of the purpose and nature of education in general, and Higher Education in particular, and upon their relationship to national objectives – whether social or economic. The most recent significant general review of HE in the UK was undertaken by Lord Dearing (Dearing, 1997); while individual academics or a university more broadly may contest some of Dearing's conclusions, community engagement can be seen to contribute to the first and the fourth of his basic aims of a university:

1   to develop individuals' potential to be well equipped for work and to contribute to society;
2   to increase knowledge and understanding – for their own sake and for the economy;
3   to serve the needs of the economy at all levels;
4   to shape a democratic, civilised and inclusive society.

In the world of the globalising twenty-first century, we must look for inclusivity beyond the 'local' society towards a notion of 'global citizenship'.

Similarly, engagement can be seen to provide the context for at least the fourth of Delors' 'pillars of learning' (Delors, 1996):

1   learning to do;
2   learning to know;
3   learning to be;
4   learning to live together.

Most relevantly, of course, this is learning to live together across cultural boundaries – whether national or local in nature.

As home student fee charging and competition for applicants mount, the pressures on universities to be more 'relevant', and to be so to more diverse students and *their communities*, can be seen as a more pragmatic driver for the introduction of projects in this area. At least one UK vice-chancellor has voiced this as a major focus into the future:

> In terms of *community* it presents a challenge to universities to be of and not just in the community; not simply to engage in 'knowledge-transfer' but to establish a dialogue across the boundary between the university and its community which is open-ended, fluid and experimental.

And: 'In terms of *citizenship*, it requires us to recognise civic duty and civic responsibility at a level deeper than mere political participation' (Watson, 2003: 16).

In the UK, the Russell Report (Russell, 2005), while not based on any specific concern for the international student or for the internationalisation of the home student, can provide an impetus for institutions to become more active in facilitating student volunteering work in which international and home students can participate, and for constructing volunteering opportunities which can help develop international and intercultural perspectives in participants.

While some of the above may seem somewhat tangential, an internationalisation agenda, like any other, can always be more effective when supported by and lending support to broader developments. This is not an issue to consider in any detail here, but the point should be made that, too often in Higher Education, internationalisation has been unhelpfully seen as separate from, an add-on to or even a contestant with the 'mainstream' activities of an institution.

I will outline the rationale, outcomes and processes for a number of different types of community engagement activity, illustrating these through case studies of successful programmes involving student volunteering, local family support projects, and a short intensive programme for home students on a 'study abroad' experience. I will refer to other work relating to programmes of 'service learning' (Annette, 2003; Tonkin, 2004) in the US and 'community-based' learning in the UK. Although these may not all have been originally established with regard to internationalisation objectives, their ethos, design and anticipated outcomes reflect closely their counterparts in international education. Involving students either through dedicated projects or through 'outreach' to encourage their participation in ongoing projects of this kind can make a valuable contribution to their 'international' development, as well as add an international/intercultural dimension to the project itself. While the focus of this chapter is primarily on the external community, much is also relevant to engagement with the internal community of the institution, specifically activities involving international and home students in some form of partnership activity. While the majority of projects mentioned here have been initiated by staff of the universities concerned, it should also be noted that a significant amount of valuable work in community engagement generally is being carried out through students' unions, although few seem to be specifically linked to international students or to developing international perspectives among home students (perhaps indicative of a limited perception of their role and of their membership).

Rationales and outcomes

The relationship between rationale and programme type is not a simple one, not least because the instigators of community engagement projects range from academic staff to student services (and students' unions), and may or may not be explicitly driven by the broader mission of the institution. For example, where a university feels that the local community is unsympathetic or even antagonistic towards its international student population, the primary rationale for establishing a project may be to challenge the perceptions which stimulate or sustain these attitudes. In this case, projects in which international students can showcase positive contributions will be a starting point for considering actions, for example, linking international students with local schools to provide culture days, translation services or individual learning support (e.g. the University of Nottingham Students' Union's Student Community Action 'Language Buddies' programme). The same type of project, however, could be stimulated by a completely different rationale, such as that of wishing to provide international students with insights into UK education systems, or as an experiential dimension for reflection based on the observation of children in learning, or simply as a mechanism for improving their feeling of 'belonging' through more meaningful contact with the local school community. Similarly, however, the first and last rationale could rather be the stimulus for establishing a family friendship scheme (Case study 3), on the basis that direct contact between individuals in the community and international students will personalise the 'other' and help both parties to re-evaluate their perceptions. A well-thought-through project may, of course, arise from several rationales and achieve several outcomes.

While the projects and case studies presented here differ considerably, each reflects a belief that students immersed in new cultural contexts can both contribute to and gain from meaningful contact with 'others' outside or inside their university, and supports the view that personal interaction and experiential learning provide valuable tools in the development of international and intercultural understanding, and can form the basis for transformational education.

As discussed elsewhere in this book, there are many models and rationales for internationalisation; establishing community engagement projects of any kind as a feature of an internationalisation strategy, however, seems to suggest that the institutions (or the individuals responsible for these projects at least) fall into what Leask labels the academic socio-culturalist camp, where 'all students, regardless of national or cultural background . . . [are] . . . contributors to and beneficiaries of the internationalisation agenda . . . [who need] . . . to develop international perspectives and will be able to assist others to do this in some way' (Leask, 2005a: 253).

While none of the projects refers explicitly to a general educational theory as its underpinning rationale, implicit reference to generalised perspectives on the learning process can be found in many. Educational theories of learning through engagement can be related to Dewey's view that our underlying values are formulated through our interactions in our social context (Dewey, 1916), and are also closely related to theories of supported experiential learning such as social constructivism (Vygotsky, 1962, 1978; Wertsch, 1985) or Lave's concept of situated learning (Lave, 1988) by effectively expanding the learning context beyond the classroom and enabling cultural 'experts' to interact in the (mutual) social construction of knowledge.

Transformational education (Mezirow, 1997, 2000) seeks to enable us to challenge our existing frames of reference, so as to become better able to act from positions based upon more developed and open beliefs. Such challenge is stimulated by new contexts and concepts, and the opportunity to reflect upon these and their relationship to our existing frameworks.

A related educational rationale for structured community engagement can be the direct feedback which exposure to 'real' informants and experiences can have on the relevance of the originating curriculum. One case study is very explicit about this (Case study 2), and goes further by emphasising the impact on the educator, who in this case at least was able to undergo transformation in her own appreciation of both her subject and the particular context for its exploration.

The process of moving from a closed to a more open and inclusive mindset resonates with more specific theories on the development of intercultural awareness and competences and cultural adaptation (moving along 'a continuum of increasing sophistication in dealing with cultural difference' (Bennett, 1993: 22)), familiar to intercultural trainers, and of interest to professionals in international student support, to those seeking to prepare students for international placements, study abroad programmes or exchanges and, indeed, to all those who share the view that the ability to work effectively within and across cultural boundaries is an essential graduate attribute for the post-modern world. The rationale for introducing international or intercultural community engagement can thus be rooted in a desire to facilitate the transition from the *ethnocentric* to the *ethnorelative* (Bennett, 1993), and can support any of these areas of interest. The literature on the development of intercultural competence abounds with references to the importance of self-discovery as the first step in being able to recognise the 'other', and as a process facilitated precisely through meaningful encounters with the 'other':

> The role and importance of self-reflection is crucial to the intercultural encounter as it provides a method for participants to move beyond the superficial exchange of information about the 'other'. It requires that individuals use the intercultural encounter specifically to learn something about themselves as well as learning about others.
>
> (Sen Gupta, 2003: 160)

This is a particularly relevant point to relate to 'internationalisation at home', since community engagement through inter*cultural* experience locally, either in the broader community or within the university community itself, can provide a context for 'real' intercultural contact as the basis for subsequent personal reflection and development.

Whether a project is established with reference to general educational theories, or the more specific theories relating to the development of intercultural competence, or simply because it feels instinctively appropriate, it is always necessary to bear in mind that 'mere contact does not always lead to mutual valuing of traditions' (Pritchard and Skinner, 2002: 234), and the 'development of intercultural competence relates to the quality of intercultural contacts rather than the quantity' (Otten, 2003: 13). In the pedagogy of intercultural education, to be positive and potentially transformational, that quality of contact must 'combine opportunities and provocations and support to look inside as well as outside' (Alred, 2003: 25). Unstructured contact with inadequate preparation, support and 'deconstruction' could have precisely the opposite effect.

Several universities operate international buddy or mentor schemes (Case study 4) (e.g. Exeter, Bath, London Metropolitan, Canberra) to help meet this need – a form of 'in-house' community engagement. In describing the outcome of one such scheme, Chamberlin-Quinlisk claims:

> First, assumptions are brought into question as students reflect on their apprehensions for participation and expectations for difference. Second, new perspectives are integrated into the students' ways of thinking as they examine their own prejudices and reposition themselves as members of an intercultural community.
>
> (Chamberlin-Quinlisk, 2005: 477)

It is unfortunate that the rationale behind many student 'buddy' schemes seems to be focused exclusively on the more immediate 'settling-in' needs of the international student rather than on the potential also to 'internationalise' the buddies. Even a project at the University of Ulster, which aims for 'both home and international students to become better citizens of the world' (Pritchard and Skinner, 2002: 346), may be seen to regard the reciprocal benefits to home students as a secondary consideration:

> They organised encounters that had the humanitarian purpose of helping the international students to settle more happily by mitigating culture shock and loneliness and perhaps giving them some insight into the factors preventing them from forming positive human relationships in a foreign culture. The project was also designed to facilitate valuing of cultural diversity among home students.
>
> (Pritchard and Skinner, 2002: 324)

The importance of reciprocity in community engagement is best illustrated through the concept of service learning. Service learning, deriving from President Clinton's National and Community Service Trust Act (1994), has been a highly successful innovation in the US and has had significant impacts on many campuses and their communities. Service learning programmes are extremely varied, but the concept is built around active citizenship or civil engagement, and emphasises the importance of a partnership approach to ensure any programme is of benefit to the community itself and is closely integrated into learning, providing an experiential dimension to support reflection and skills development relevant to the student.

> Service-learning combines service objectives with learning objectives with the intent that the activity change both the recipient and the provider of the service. This is accomplished by combining service tasks with structured opportunities that link the task to self-reflection, self-discovery, and the acquisition and comprehension of values, skills, and knowledge content.
>
> (National Clearing House)

> The focus of service learning programs is on both the learning that occurs within the individual and the service in the community.
>
> (Perkins and Miller, n.d.: 1)

Two of the case studies (Case studies 1 and 2) specifically relate themselves to the service learning construct, but evidence of a similar approach to the integration of learning and community engagement can also be seen in another case study (Case study 4), in particular through the joint development of each project with a community engagement partner of some kind (service learning expert, volunteering office, careers office). A search on most US university websites will now show a significant set of programmes based around service learning and volunteering within the local or the international community (e.g. University of Denver, California State University or, more specifically, Purdue University's index of their courses in service learning across many subject areas, and the *Michigan Journal of Community Service Learning*).

Echoing general education and intercultural learning theories already cited, service learning is most explicit not only in its requirements for reciprocal benefit, but also in the emphasis on integration with the curriculum, and opportunities for consolidation and reflection on the part of the student: 'The process of critical reflection is an essential element of service learning. It enhances student learning by connecting the service and the academic experiences. It links theory with practice, knowledge with action and campus with community' (University of Wisconsin, Community University Partnership).

One organiser of service learning opportunities in the UK, for example, builds reflection into its programmes as follows:

> Students reflect on their learning through exposure to several environments and activities. These include: on-going classroom study; case study reports; journals based on participation and observation in the work place, and a closing conference at which they present their work to peers and host employers.
>
> (Foundation for International Learning)

While the supporting pedagogy may not be evident in family friendship schemes (predominantly a US phenomenon, but gaining ground in the UK), consideration of mutual benefit is evident in many (Case study 3).

The Russell Commission sets out the objectives and benefits of youth volunteering, along with the expectation that 'all education institutions should have a volunteering ethos' (Russell, 2005: 14). Universities may find a more profound resonance with their institutional missions, their educational philosophies and their internationalisation strategies if they tie any volunteering activities more closely in with their curricula, as in the service learning model. This would seem to offer more appropriate educational value at HE level along with greater project sustainability. Several universities add motivation and sustainability through a volunteering award scheme (e.g. Middlesex University, University of London Birkbeck College).

Conclusion

Models for community engagement projects take many different forms, and may be underpinned by a range of rationales. For international students these may be rather specific, focused around building cultural knowledge, a sense of belonging, improved language skills, etc., or they may be more general, and applicable across the student body – gaining transferable skills, greater self-awareness, notions of citizenship, and so forth. Through international community engagement and locally based intercultural projects, all students may find a context in which to develop cross-cultural capability and a sense of global citizenship.

The integration of the curriculum with a community engagement project, if supported through opportunities for feedback, can provide curriculum enrichment and ground theory in experience.

Where an educational/intercultural learning objective underpins the establishment of a project, general theories of learning and methodologies associated with the development of intercultural competence are clearly of interest, and the need to provide space and the opportunity to prepare for and to reflect upon the experience should be an integrated part of the project itself.

Community engagement provides opportunities to bring together the university and its community, theoretical curricula and grounded experience, and individuals of different nationalities and cultures. Well-conceived projects should benefit all stakeholders and achieve a number of outcomes, but, as lead partner, the university must shoulder full responsibility and ensure any project is properly supported. Whether projects involve engagement with an international community, in a local intercultural context, or with peers from different cultures within the university, they can provide a context for the development of the perspectives and skills necessary for graduates in a globalising world.

Case study 1: 'Discover your City'

The potential for personal and academic gains made from 'service learning' have been demonstrated in many cases from the USA. The 'Discover your City' module on the Cert HE in International Foundation Studies (IFS) programme at Leeds Metropolitan University set out to enable integration, personal development and related reflection and learning through volunteering and community partnerships. At the beginning of the module, sixty learners join local community action groups with whom they maintain regular contact over one semester. During the module, learners are taken on a task-based discovery whereby they undergo various sub-tasks linked to the final outcome of a group-based project. These tasks develop language skills, cultural awareness, learner independence and study skills designed to help learners engage profitably on an undergraduate course, and include questionnaire design, concept design for the project and giving presentations.

Why volunteering?

Volunteering is developing as an important part of the student experience at the University. In addition to the Student Union organisation Community Action at Leeds Met, the University also has a Community Partnerships and Volunteering Office funded by the Active Community Fund, which gives invaluable support for the monitoring and overall success of the module, and offers a range of opportunities for staff and students. This project was developed and administered by the academic course leader in conjunction with this office to ensure both that the volunteering work is embedded within the curriculum and that it provides a genuine benefit to the community.

In addition to providing a 'real' context for English language practice, students also develop transferable employability skills in team working, communicating with others, planning work schedules and gaining understanding of how organisations work in another culture. Additionally, voluntary work can provide an excellent opportunity to experience aspects of the workplace and provide groundwork for making future study or career decisions.

The feedback

It can be difficult to provide a satisfactory experience for students of different backgrounds, countries and ages, but feedback on the first year of this programme was very encouraging. Around 67 per cent of questionnaire responders were positive about the experience overall, with most comments highlighting the value of meeting people and others noting the 'experience of communicating' and starting to 'feel inside the community'. It was also interesting to see that for many this was a completely new experience, and that it could leave participants eager to do more: 'We wanted to be involved more and we tried and the community responded well, but we didn't have time.'

As course leader and instigator of this project, I was heartened by the overwhelmingly positive nature of the feedback, while our experience and less positive feedback have provided a focus for improvements. Some of the comments relate to problems students had with the logistics of undertaking the volunteering. Students needed to negotiate the finer details with the voluntary groups and in some cases this proved to be very difficult. However, I was encouraged that the value of the volunteering itself wasn't undermined by these administrative frustrations, which in themselves provided valuable 'real world' experience for the students. Our impression is that the community projects themselves found the student volunteers made a very positive contribution, but this has not been formally researched.

Pitfalls

Three major areas of difficulty were: time commitment, working with vulnerable groups in the community, and student project groups. It was sometimes difficult for students to set up the initial meetings with the community organisations without significant coordination and support from the team involved. Some of the community projects required students to work with children or the elderly, so required detailed police checks. Local police stations run CRB checks, but with international students the process can take many weeks. Student group work can be problematic as there can often be differential levels of input. Therefore, clear work plans and careful monitoring of the groups are always needed.

The way forward

We intend to continue the programme with a more focused set of core options for the students, targeting those community action projects with the most appeal and easiest access. We also hope to add alternative initiatives which include a set of awareness-raising activities for Marie Curie Cancer Care and the Save the Children Fund.

Jo Appleton
Course Leader for International Foundation Studies and Enterprise
Teaching Fellow
Leslie Silver International Faculty
Leeds Metropolitan University
j.appleton@leedsmet.ac.uk

Case study 2: Service learning on a Greek island

The context

For nearly a decade, I have spent summers on the Cycladic island of Paros, teaching a course on contemporary Greece for American undergraduates, through the Greek institution known as College Year in Athens. Each summer, roughly fifteen to twenty students from several American universities and colleges have joined me in the port town of Paroikia for a course aimed at dispelling preconceptions, deconstructing Western fascination with classical antiquity, and leading students to understand the dynamics of Greek life on its own terms. Most students (from majors ranging from business to literature and, of course, anthropology) attended to fulfil a general education requirement.

The rationale

Although many of the students have expressed pleasant surprise when the course has also undermined their ethnocentrism and made them more thoughtful travellers, both they and I sensed something was missing. The students lived on Paros and did research projects in which they interviewed Parians, but their sense of connection to the island and its inhabitants was still superficial. On weekends, I generally had Paroikia to myself as students headed for the fashionable climes of Mykonos or Santorini.

For this reason I decided to add a service learning component to the course, substituting work with a local Parian organisation for the research project. Service learning, as it is understood at Indiana University, refers to a course-based, credit-bearing educational experience in which students participate in a community-based service activity, carefully reflecting on that activity to better understand course content and gain an enhanced sense of civic engagement (Bringle and Hatcher, 1995). Robert Bringle from my own university and later Nevin Brown from the International Partnership for Service-Learning and Leadership (Tonkin, 2004) were able to join me on Paros to assist in adding service learning to the course.

The project

In determining what students might do, we took our cue from Mayor Yannis Ragousis, for whom the island's future lay in the development of cultural rather than mass tourism. For monolingual American students, this provided ample opportunity to work with organisations intersecting with the English-speaking tourist trade. Separate service placements were developed for each student (or pair of students) and included working on the island's official website, dealing with the stray dog population engendered by tourism, assisting the local archaeological service, and volunteering with an organisation dedicated to eco-tourism. Ultimately, what students did, however, was less important than the spontaneous conversations and sense of engagement that emerged as they worked alongside Parians.

The impact

Developing a service learning component was not simply an addition to the course. It was, first of all, a transformation in student learning and engagement. Detailed course evaluations in 2004 and 2005 confirmed what I saw. Students no longer abandoned Paros on the weekends. They stayed to be with their Parian friends. They felt at home here and understood the island (and thereby small communities throughout Greece) on a level previous students had not. They felt they had a place on the island that was neither exploitative nor superficial. Rather than hide from the discomfort of not knowing Parians by retreating to the disconnected tourist world that operates as a parallel universe throughout Greece, students were now at ease in the places frequented by Parians. Service learning transformed student learning by changing their roles from tourist and observer to co-worker and participant, by speeding up the process of immersion (Lewis and Neisenbaum, 2005) and by imparting a deep appreciation for the assets of the local community. The findings revealed by the evaluations for my course resonate with the much broader study recently conducted by the Institute for the International Education of Students (IES), which has shown that the three factors most likely to enhance student learning in what Americans call study abroad are: living with host country nationals, taking courses directly in a host university, and engaging in service learning or internships (Dwyer, 2004).

The addition of service learning also transformed course content. New sources of knowledge and authority entered the course: the Parians with whom the students were working. Their views and voices appeared in the classroom both directly and indirectly as discussions were increasingly guided by student service experiences. This took the course in unexpected directions that required nimbleness on my part but ultimately reinforced (and substantiated) the value of dialogue in a postcolonial world. Service experiences also introduced new topics which enriched what students were learning and led me to dig more deeply into my own knowledge of modern Greece. Greek understandings of service, civic engagement, social justice and community relations became more prominent in the course, as did the global dimensions of citizenship and US–Greek and also tourist–local relations. Finally, I found myself turning abstract anthropological theories into practical guidelines for cross-cultural interaction, because such interaction was no longer simply contemplated, but quite real. Ultimately, as in all instances of transformative learning, this reverberated back to my understanding of the theories as well, confirming that service learning is not limited to students.

Susan Buck Sutton
Chancellor's Professor of Anthropology and Associate Dean of International Programs
Indiana University – Purdue University Indianapolis

Case study 3: International Friendship at Purdue

Overview

International Friendship at Purdue (IFP) has operated since it was established thirty-five years ago by a local women's organisation and was run by a local community centre until 1995 before transferring to its current location at Purdue University. It was created to ease the transition into American culture and the university setting for new international students and to provide the opportunity for local residents to open their homes and hearts to international students and experience a whole new world.

Participants are encouraged to visit their friendship volunteer once a month to share their culture. Friendship volunteers are encouraged to share their 'normal' American lives rather than trying to create 'special' events.

Of Purdue's international student population of around 5,000, about 100 to 150 international students are matched with a friendship volunteer each year.

Rationale

The University mission (Strategic Plan) includes: 'to serve the citizens of Indiana, the United States, and the world through *discovery* that expands the realm of knowledge, *learning* through dissemination and preservation of knowledge, and *engagement* through exchange of knowledge'.

The International Friendship programme enables citizens of Indiana and of the world to engage in the mutual exchange of knowledge. Our goal with this programme is engagement on two levels: the friendship volunteers will have a pathway to connect with the world and the international student will go beyond stereotypes of Americans to have a story of an American friendship they shared when they return home. The stated objectives are to:

- learn about different cultures by developing rich personal relationships;
- provide Purdue international students with an opportunity to see local family life first-hand and to participate more fully in community life;
- provide local residents and international students with an opportunity to gain new perspectives by exchanging ideas and customs.

Operation

We recruit friendship volunteers throughout the year, linking through established groups of people rather than individuals: religious, educational, corporate and community organisations. International students are recruited at the beginning of each semester. Volunteers and students are matched by our office.

To help prepare students and families to meet, both are required to attend orientation sessions. We believe this provides a common understanding of the objectives of linking, can offer 'protocols' to ease initial meetings, and gives some insights into cultural differences and intercultural communication through anecdotes and sharing experience.

Friendship volunteers are asked to contact the student first, and to meet within a month at a neutral location (not their home or the student's home). To encourage the first meeting, we organise a 'mixer' event: a reception in the autumn and a carry-in lunch in the spring.

Within four weeks, we contact the volunteers to help them with any difficulties in meeting their student. We also send a postcard each summer to them asking if they would like another international student (as their student may have graduated and moved on).

The programme requires two of us to run it, between our other duties. Additional resources are provided in the form of funds for applications, mailings, and refreshments for the autumn mixer event and an appreciation reception every April, and technical support to make and maintain a web-based database.

Personal perspectives and evaluation

Responses from participants to this programme range from the very practical gains of discovering new places, foods and cultural insights:

> My hosts introduced us to interesting places in the Lafayette area

and invited us to Thanksgiving dinner. They invited us to special events such as the play about Easter. We were able to have a good time going to the Battlefield Museum and the Wabash river walk. Without their help, we might not have known these places.

For me, being in the friendship programme was a great opportunity. I was introduced to a very great family. First they helped me to become familiar with the environment (like where to go shopping, restaurants and other daily facilities). Then we talked a lot with each other about each other's culture. They cooked their meal, and I cooked some Iranian food.

or the gaining of a sense of welcome:

The first time Huijun came to our house, she was so appreciative. She said she had dreamed about doing this, to have another family in America.

to more reflective commentary:

This programme is like a bridge between two nations and across the hearts of two cultures.

with appreciation also from family friends:

It started with Ali and then his buddies started coming . . . They play with our kids [three boys], and we watched the World Cup together, especially the German games. It is a breath of fresh air to have guys around who don't mind talking and sharing their thoughts. It is great.
(Lars Nielson, originally printed in *Journal and Courier*, Thursday, 1 August 2002, p. C3)

We look forward to continuing the programme as long as Purdue's goal is to engage the world coming to its doorstep. And we hope that everyone takes 'this opportunity to be a bridge that crosses the hearts of two cultures' (Michael A. Brzezinski, Ed.D., Director, Office of International Students and Scholars, Purdue University).

Marcus Hammack
Senior Immigration Counselor
International Friendship Coordinator
Office of International Students and Scholars
Purdue University
http://www.iss.purdue.edu/Programs/IFP/

Case study 4: Diablo Valley College and International Education Center Volunteer Program

Overview

Diablo Valley College (DVC) is a two-year institution offering a range of associate degrees and vocational programmes, with around 26,000 students. The International Education Center (IEC) set out to develop a programme that would address recurring comments on evaluations from international students, which indicated they wanted opportunities to engage in everyday conversation with native English speakers in relaxed, non-academic settings. The stated objective was to 'design and implement a volunteer component within our language program that will allow students to have unique language and cultural experiences with non-profit organizations and student mentors'. Through these opportunities, we were also contributing to the College president's aims to 'serve international students and to provide all students with an opportunity to increase their knowledge of other cultures and languages' and to 'continue to expand its efforts to integrate multi-cultural and international perspectives into its curriculum and programs'.

We strove to develop volunteering opportunities that would continue after the proposed programme dates. We realised that developing relationships with community organisations would take time and we wanted to ensure that the relationships were not cut short because the programme dates had finished.

Initially we chose five non-profit, community organisations to work with, and targeted a group of 100 Japanese students for our initial project. In the course of one year, we involved approximately 150 international students in volunteering in the programme. Volunteers helped in a number of ways, from providing help building houses to teaching language, cooking and sports.

Student mentors were recruited from the Career Center at Diablo Valley College, which operates an active service learning programme. This project provided opportunities for DVC students to volunteer while also serving as mentors for IEC student volunteers.

Implementation issues

There were two areas that made the project difficult to manage. The first is that three crucial members of our staff left, leading to some loss of momentum and expertise. There were also quite a few changes at the volunteer organisations. Because of these changes, we invested more time and resources in organising activities than planned. We should have been more vigilant about documenting the procedures and progress at every step to ensure a smoother transfer of information.

The second area was the decrease in public transportation routes in the area, imposed because of severe budget deficits in California. One of our initial strategies was to wean students from dependence on our providing transportation, but, depending on the location of the volunteer organisation, this became impossible in many cases. At the end of 2004, we were given access to Diablo Valley College vans at no charge, to help with the logistics of student transport.

Outcomes

All partners in the project gained benefits in different ways.

Students benefited from volunteering and working with and meeting community members, and by working with the mentors and having a link to Diablo Valley College. The most successful and rewarding aspects of the project came from watching the student volunteers as their self-confidence grew each week. They became more involved with preparing materials and more adventurous in speaking with community members. That confidence came through when the students gave presentations at the end of the sessions. After the first summer, some volunteers had the confidence and enthusiasm to continue with their organisations without IEC or mentor support. We also see the success of the programme now as increasingly students approach us about volunteering opportunities.

The mentors benefited mostly in their leadership roles. Many of them were the same age as the volunteers and the role of mentoring was new to them. Some struggled with the role at first, but through encouragement and occasional IEC intervention they grew into the roles.

IEC benefited in developing closer relationships with the Career Center. IEC and the College more generally also became better known in the community.

The volunteer organisations benefited by having wonderful volunteers at their sites. Not only did they provide practical help on a range of projects, but the volunteering organisations themselves gained cultural insights as they were able to interact with people from other countries in a natural setting.

Continuity

Volunteering has become an integral part of the programme at IEC. When hiring a new student services and activities coordinator this summer, duties included the volunteer project.

Owing to better communication and greater awareness between IEC and the Career Center at DVC, there is a constant flow of students who are interested in becoming mentors or getting involved with international students in other ways. Our conversation partner programme, which was sporadic and small prior to this project, is now flourishing.

Sally Conover
Director
International Education Center at Diablo Valley College
www.iec-dvc.org

Note

1 Square bracketed references refer to case studies within this chapter.

Chapter 12

Taking stock

An appraisal of the literature on internationalising HE learning

Glauco De Vita

Introduction

Although traditionally there has been a dearth of research on the UK learning experience of international (non-UK) students, during recent years we have witnessed growing interest towards cross-cultural issues in teaching and learning as evidenced by a non-negligible amount of published work, conferences and workshops focusing on this traditionally neglected but now topical area of study and debate.

As this literature grows, it appears opportune to engage in a sense-making, reflective exercise that entails taking stock of the main views and contributions that have prompted this important debate. The title of this chapter, therefore, reflects my attempt to begin this process by classifying, categorising, problematising and even critiquing the conceptualisations that have heretofore come to characterise the knowledge domain of this emerging field of research. Far from being a polished and exhaustive taxonomic framework, the critical synthesis proposed in this chapter reflects my intent to review and organise what I see as the most significant ideas and developments in the field so as to provide a functional map of 'what has gone before' in relation to three main themes: (i) the learning experience of international students; (ii) culturally inclusive teaching and assessment practices; and (iii) different conceptualisations of curriculum internationalisation. It is hoped that this map will itself provide a platform for further analysis and productive debate among teaching practitioners and scholars alike.

The learning experience of international students

When in the late 1990s I started to conduct scholarly inquiry into the learning experience of international students and culturally inclusive pedagogies, my initial impetus was driven by questions stemming from real challenges of the multicultural classroom which, surprisingly, had only received scant attention in relevant UK literature. I found the lack of systematic research on these issues particularly striking in that, by that time, British universities had already experienced a substantial expansion in non-UK student numbers[1] and, owing to pressures for greater accountability and appraisal, had become increasingly concerned with the quality of the teaching and learning experiences they provided to students. In spite of this climate, prior to 2003 hardly any contribution in the field of cross-cultural issues in teaching and learning came from the published work of UK academics.[2] Indeed, at the time I began to conduct research in this field, the community contributing to the development of this emerging debate was primarily populated by Australian scholars, who became my prime interlocutors.

It is worth stressing that UK education policy still largely ignores international students (the 2004 Higher Education Act, for example, makes no mention of them) and it was not until 2004 that the first report on *International Students in UK Universities and Colleges* (UKCOSA, 2004) was commissioned by the UK government. Although the report, which is based on a survey of nearly 5,000 international students, portrays a glowing picture of their experience (89 per cent are reported to be satisfied or very satisfied with their stay in the UK), this survey is, in itself, testament to the neglect towards the critical issue of a culturally inclusive pedagogy. Suffice to say that, out of the thirty-three questions and twenty-four sub-questions of the fourteen-page questionnaire, only one item of the instrument refers directly to the academic experience of international students in relation to their course of study. The majority of the items of the questionnaire were mainly concerned with uncovering the perceptions of international students in relation to much wider issues, including financial support, insurance, visa and resident permits, accommodation, career plans and, finally (item 33), travel arrangements since: 'STA TRAVEL, WHO ARE PROVIDING THE PRIZES FOR THE PRIZE DRAW, WOULD LIKE TO KNOW A BIT MORE ABOUT YOUR TRAVELS SINCE YOU CAME TO THE UK TO STUDY' [*sic*] (UKCOSA, 2004, Appendix B: Survey questions, p. 98).

Reservations over the representativeness of the sample of this survey should also be raised, given that, by UKCOSA's own admission, only 45 per cent of the respondents had English as a foreign language, and 72 per cent of the international students surveyed had already studied abroad in English-speaking countries (52 per cent in the UK, 14 per cent in the USA, 3 per cent in Australia and 3 per cent in Canada).

Evidently, there are still major gaps in the literature on the internationalisation of UK Higher Education, particularly with respect to the learning experience of international students. This sentiment is shared by Caruana and Hanstock (2003: 1), who recently commented, sarcastically, as follows: 'Internationalisation as a concept remains marginal and insignificant even in spite of such changes in the student population or is it so new as to constitute as yet, unexplored terrain?' In reality, especially if we go beyond the frontiers of UK-based literature, we find that this terrain is not totally unexplored.

Biggs's (1999) work offers a seminal roadmap to the pedagogic challenges encountered when teaching across cultures that is helpful for interpreting earlier contributions as well as subsequent research.

Drawing from the personal classroom account provided by Harris (1997), from research into lecturers' perceptions of international students (Samuelowicz, 1987; Chalmers and Volet, 1997) and from recommendations on how to handle international students (Ballard and Clanchy, 1997), Biggs (1999: 123–8) outlines what he describes as stereotypical misconceptions about the learning orientations and behaviours of international students:

- 'They rote learn and lack critical thinking skills.'
- 'They are passive, they won't talk in class.'
- 'They don't understand what plagiarism means.'
- 'They stick together . . . won't mix with locals.'
- 'They tend to look on lecturers as close to gods.'

I view Biggs's attempt to label these learning attitudes as inaccurate preconceptions as an attempt motivated by Biggs's laudable intention to pull the rug from under the feet of those teachers who, by viewing other academic cultural traditions as inferior products, use these generalisations as an excuse to perpetuate ineffective and ethnocentric teaching practices. As he puts it, 'The trouble with these misinformed stereotypes is that they exacerbate any teaching problems' (Biggs, 1999: 128).

However, the trouble with Biggs's own approach is that he tries to achieve commendable and much needed ends through his own inaccurate preconceptions in that there is nothing stereotypical about the real problems that international students, especially students from Confucian-heritage cultures (henceforth, CHC), appear to contend with when they make 'the transition from their first culture education to new constructs for learning, socialising, communicating and being' (Holmes, 2004: 294). Far from being false and pejorative portrayals by few commentators, these generalisations stem from a collective concept formation derived from genuine concerns that are widespread among teaching practitioners. It is not by denying their existence that we can have an impact. Indeed, international students are recurrently seen as viewing the lecturer and the textbook as the ultimate and unquestionable sources of knowledge, and lacking critical thinking and autonomous learning skills (see Robertson et al., 2000; Greenholz, 2003; Ottewill and MacFarlane, 2003), having inadequate language proficiency (Mullins et al., 1995; Ryan, 2000; Du-Babcock, 2002), being passive, silent and non-participative (Yanhong Li and Kaye, 1998; Ramsay et al., 1999), being unable to reference correctly and often found guilty of plagiarism (Watson, 1999; Carroll, 2002).

Biggs's point in relation to the 'rote learning' generalisation requires further qualification. He argued that Harris's (1997) comment that 'the educational systems of the Pacific Rim countries strongly promote surface and reproductive learning' misunderstands those Pacific Rim countries and fails to appreciate that rote learning is an essentially deep strategy in many tasks. Biggs (1999: 126) then tries to substantiate his argument as follows: 'CHC students are cleaning up the first class honours and gold medals in huge disproportion to locals in such subjects as architecture, business studies, engineering and science. Do they achieve this on the basis of rote learning?'

Dealing first with the issue of the relationship between memorisation, repetition and 'deep' learning, it must be said that it is a difficult relationship to unpack and, because of this, it has been subject to considerable debate. It is now generally recognised that repetition and memorising have a cultural dimension and can occur mechanically or precede understanding (Marton et al., 1993, 1997; On, 1996). After reviewing this literature, Dahlin and Watkins (1997) concluded that learning comes from an experience making a 'deep impression', and that this deep impression can emanate from an intense emotional experience, from processes of repetition or from deep learning approaches. However, the fact remains that educational systems of the Pacific Rim countries do promote reproductive pedagogies and, when these learning orientations and attendant behaviours are displayed in Western educational settings, they do create a mismatch of expectations and misunderstandings that lead to frustration among students and teachers alike.

Wu (2002) specifically addresses the question of how much English ideas about Chinese students and the learning orientations of their first schooling culture are stereotypes and how much they are a reality. Wu (2002) starts by depicting the Western impression of the Chinese student as one typically seen as polite, good at memorising, especially good at mathematics and accounting, but poor, and becoming rather nervous and baffled, when called upon to create something original. This impression is reinforced by the popular notion that typical Chinese schools spend a lot of time in rote learning. Against this backdrop, Wu (2002: 388) writes:

> It would be a pleasure to be able to point to some school or experience that would refute this popular picture as a misconception based on racist stereotypes. However, nothing in my own experience or observation permits me to do so.

Also Biggs's comment on the high performance of CHC students appears to be unconvincing. Whilst the high academic achievement of CHC students may well be a feature that applies to the Australian university system (see, for example, Dobson et al., 1998), the limited evidence pertaining to the performance of international students in the UK points to the opposite, suggesting the presence of unresolved pedagogic issues that preclude these students from the opportunity to achieve their full potential. Makepeace and Baxter (1990), for example, found that overseas-domiciled students in the

UK polytechnic sector (as it then was) generally did less well than their UK-domiciled counterparts. Using data from a large cohort enrolled on a first-year business studies programme in one institution, I (De Vita, 2002b) showed that international students achieved lower marks than UK students in all forms of assessment considered, the difference being statistically significant at the 95 per cent confidence level. These results are broadly consistent with my findings (De Vita, 2005a) which further demonstrated that, on average, the observed differential was particularly pronounced with respect to the academic achievements of UK students vis-à-vis students from China. Finally, using nation-wide HESA data for the 1995–2000 period, Morrison *et al.* (2005) showed that students domiciled in the European Union, Asia, Africa and the Middle East achieved fewer first or upper-second-class honours degrees than UK-domiciled students. These findings did not change after controlling for age, gender, discipline studied and prior qualifications.

What should then be concluded from all of the above? First, we should recognise once and for all that there are several unresolved pedagogic problems stemming from, or exacerbated by, cultural-diversity-related issues. These problems are very real, and include:

1   barriers to effective intercultural communication, such as cultural stereotyping, language fatigue (for both second-language speakers and listeners) and misunderstandings due to the unqualified use of colloquialisms, idiomatic expressions and analogies (see Ballard and Clanchy, 1997; Baldwin *et al.*, 1998; De Vita, 2000);
2   a cross-cultural awareness gap in approaches to essay writing, in terms of discourse structures, academic literacies and referencing practices (see Mullins *et al.*, 1995; Ledwith *et al.*, 1996; Bliss, 1999; Ryan, 2000; De Vita, 2000, 2005a);
3   a cultural clash of learning and teaching styles, exemplified by issues such as the reluctance by some international students to participate in class discussions and in other collaborative and student-centred activities (see Samuelowicz, 1987; Pratt, 1992; Ladd and Ruby, 1999; De Vita, 2001a, 2001b, 2002a, 2005b);
4   transitional difficulties in moving from dependence on rote learning to developing intellectual independence, critical thinking, the synoptic capacity and autonomous learning skills (see Pearson and Beasley, 2000; De Vita, 2005a).

It should be recognised that most of these pedagogic problems are not exclusive to international students. Two significant implications flow from this recognition. The first is that the persistence of these problems has as much to do with instructional methods as with the ways students from culturally diverse backgrounds go about learning. The second is that the onus primarily rests on teaching practitioners to make their teaching and assessment strategies culturally inclusive and, by doing so, enable better learning for all students.

Culturally inclusive teaching and assessment strategies

In examining different approaches to teaching in multicultural learning environments, the framework of reference that still commands benchmarking significance is, again, that provided by Biggs (1999), who formulated a typology of teaching responses when dealing with international students.

The first type of teaching response is characterised by awareness of different cultural learning behaviours co-existing in the multicultural classroom, but when difficulties are encountered they are interpreted as culturally induced deficiencies of the 'foreign' student. These students are then seen as in need of 'remediation' (Ryan and Hellmundt, 2003) and are often made to feel 'that the problem lay with them . . . rather than with the system' (Andrews et al., 1998: 169). Biggs (1999: 125) labels this approach 'the deficit model' to teaching international students and likens it to 'a view remarkably similar to that adopted by governments of countries receiving immigrants in the pre-multicultural days'.

The second type of response values cultural differences and different ways of knowing. It encourages expression of diverse cultural experiences, perspectives and background knowledge. Under this approach, pedagogic problems related to cultural-diversity issues are redefined as a matter of 'learning in context' (Volet and Renshaw, 1996), not as one of 'deficit'. As a result, the teacher's task is to explain what is required for the immediate context rather than imply it or, even worse, assume it as the tacit 'right way'. Significantly, this approach recognises that students from culturally diverse backgrounds learn differently and calls for the revision of one's teaching style and the adoption of strategies that ensure maximum engagement by all students. Biggs (1999), however, warns that adapting one's teaching to accommodate different learning styles may be difficult and unproductive. Moreover, he argues that this type of response may divert the teacher's attention from learning outcomes and tasks that specifically target intellectual and social development.

The third type of response places emphasis on cognitive outcomes to activate higher-level cognitive processes and skills that should be developed in all students. Biggs (1999) argues that, by focusing on what the student does rather than what the teacher does, we are able to gravitate towards a model of 'good teaching' that works across cultures. This type of response was further advocated by Watkins and Biggs (2001), who contended that there are some universal principles of good teaching that involve supporting students to engage with learning at an appropriate (higher) cognitive level.

I see the second and third type of responses sketched by Biggs as complementary rather than mutually exclusive, since facilitative, student-centred teaching practices conducive to the activation and development of higher-level cognitive processes are more effective if preceded or accompanied by a strategy that is didactically contextual, adaptive and culturally responsive. Hence, both are needed to move towards a culturally inclusive pedagogy. Several publications (including some of my own) have extended these two rudimentary blueprints of good teaching practice by providing them with theoretical support and by informing them with detailed practical content.

In an article specifically referring to the business studies context (De Vita, 2000), I made several suggestions for dealing with barriers to effective inter-cultural communication and active participation. The research emphasised the importance of supporting students to develop essay-writing skills by clarifying the local conventions for structuring and presenting material and by explaining rather than merely implying the criteria to be used for marking. Cortazzi and Jin (1997) also called for building bridges of 'mutual intercultural learning' by developing cultural synergies and harmony in the multicultural classroom through the mutual effort of teachers and students to connect with each other's cultures of communication and learning:

> discussions taking place in the multicultural classroom can provide the best lessons in cultural diversity and how to recognise, respect and turn the 'cultural baggage' that each student brings to the classroom into a positive experience for all (including the tutor). An opportunity, therefore, to learn from our differences, achieve cultural synergies and celebrate everyone.
>
> (De Vita, 2000: 174)

In my application of the Felder and Soloman's (1999) Index of Learning Styles (ILS) (De Vita, 2001a), I demonstrated how cultural conditioning leads to greater variation in learning style preferences and orientations in the multicultural classroom. In spite of Biggs's (1999) warning on the difficulties likely to be encountered when attempting to accommodate different learning styles, the paper proposed a theory-based conceptual framework of how variation in learning style preferences and orientations can profitably be used to develop a multi-style teaching approach to business management education. Such an approach not only can help students to respond more effectively to different learning stimuli and environments but, if followed up by a culminating curriculum designed to encourage students to take responsibility for their own learning and development, can act as a building block towards the formation of a more autonomous learner.

Whilst these examples illustrate significant progress within the blueprint of the 'learning in context' model of teaching across cultures, with a colleague I further promote the (complementary) idea of helping students construct understandings that are progressively more mature and critical:

> A corollary of this perspective is the pursuit of strategies aimed at

facilitating processes of self-enquiry, critical reflection, mutual dialogue and questioning. These strategies would lead to a more participative and student-centred approach, in which the lecturer becomes a facilitator and students become more responsible for their own learning and development.

(De Vita and Case, 2003: 393)

I also offer a specific template of how higher-level cognitive processes (critical reflection and evaluation) and self-regulated learning behaviours can be successfully activated in all students (De Vita, 2004). The template entails: (i) placing emphasis on ambitious cognitive outcomes (synoptic capacity); (ii) focusing on what students are doing rather than what the teacher is doing (non-taught module); and (iii) offering targeted support (ad hoc workshops and one-to-one tutorials to set proper expectations of the type of effort required and the standard to be reached).

Literature about developing culturally inclusive assessment is still very scarce (hence the need for this book) and has thus far been primarily concerned with highlighting the role of assessment in shaping different approaches to learning in different cultures (Baumgart and Halse, 1999; Chapter 5 of this volume), with stressing the importance of choosing culturally inclusive content for assessment (Manathunga and MacKinnon, 2001) and with exposing the dangerous implications of a dominant culture's assumptions about essay writing in general and literacy and discourse style in particular (MacKinnon and Manathunga, 2003). I have also addressed the more sensitive question of the extent to which conventional methods of assessment (multiple choice tests, coursework assignments and examinations) are culturally fair indicators of ability across diverse groups of students by subjecting these assessment methods to critical scrutiny for evidence of cultural bias (De Vita, 2002b). This study (the first of its kind, I believe) unveiled additional factors that are likely to affect the performance of students from different cultures in different ways. These include cultural predispositions for risk-taking behaviour and tolerance for ambiguity impacting upon multiple choice tests, and the time limits normally imposed on closed-book examinations. The study also showed that assessment by examination penalises international students (vis-à-vis home students) beyond differences in ability levels, as measured by multiple choice test and coursework assignment scores. These findings raise the additional question of how better to recognise international students' learning in ways that conventional methods of assessment fail to capture. This is essential if we are not to prejudice the progression of any particular groups of students by granting an innate competitive advantage to students from the 'host' culture (Haigh, 2002).

Although no single contribution setting out a grand alternative culturally inclusive assessment framework has yet emerged, scattered across the literature several suggestions on how to move towards more culturally inclusive approaches to assessment have been put forward. Building on the premise that, in assessment, especially in the multicultural classroom, one size does not fit all, it is self-evident that culturally responsive assessment must entail an expanded assessment portfolio which gives students the flexibility of choice of how and when to be assessed. Options may range from giving students the opportunity to demonstrate what they know, and their engagement with the subject through the oral medium (a heavily neglected form of assessment in UK Higher Education), to the choice of being assessed by means of a learning portfolio, which would better reflect the life space, cultural values and intellectual development of the individual learner. Moreover, as I have argued elsewhere (De Vita, 2004), tutors should take greater responsibility for the cultural discontinuities exemplified by transitional difficulties experienced by students when moving from reproductive pedagogies to deep learning approaches conducive to intellectual independence and the synoptic capacity. The research suggested that these difficulties cannot be overcome unless summative assessment practices of end products are preceded and supported by formative feedback-on-progress sessions on the processes by which those products are researched, constructed and presented.

Re-conceptualising curriculum internationalisation for promoting genuine internationalism and fostering intercultural learning

Although the internationalisation of the curriculum has now emerged as a research area in its own right, its development has a relatively short history. Teichler (1994: 41) commented on the genesis of this strand of literature as follows: 'while powerful models are indeed coming to be formulated, the present state of the field could be well likened to an academic specialism in the pre-paradigmatic phase of its evolution'. The development of the conceptualisations of curriculum internationalisation can be broadly categorised into three main approaches.

The first approach bears the mark of an exclusively commercial agenda based on competing for international (in the case of the UK, 'overseas', i.e. non-EU) fee-paying students, so as to expand Higher Education institutions' financial base (McNamara and Harris, 1997). According to Teichler (1996), this is the traditional British way of 'internationalisation through import'. The assumption underpinning this approach is that mass recruitment of international students will, by 'osmosis' (Martin, 2000), have a cascade effect on processes of curricular planning and implementation. In reality, the most significant consequences of this commercial orientation have been the legitimisation of a discourse that treats education as a marketable commodity (see, for example, Mazzarol and Soutar, 1999) and ever greater emphasis on 'the need to satisfy our customers' (Ackers, 1997: 180) by improving the 'awareness . . . and quality of the product' (ibid.: 189). Institutional efforts in these directions have, in turn, led to aggressive marketing activities that overstress the international and cosmopolitan flavour of university courses as their selling point (Fallon and Brown, 1999). As suggested by Bell (2004), because of this approach, internationalisation has come to mean 'education for profit'. Not surprisingly, this approach has not escaped criticism. Aulakh *et al.* (1997: 1), for example, commented on 'internationalisation through import' as follows:

> Internationalisation is not merely a matter of recruiting international students, though the presence of international students is an enormous resource for the university. The aim of internationalisation is to produce graduates capable of solving problems in a variety of locations with cultural and environmental sensitivity.

Sadly, despite its good intent, it is exactly this kind of criticism that has paved the way for the piecemeal approach to curriculum internationalisation, now commonly referred to as the 'infusion approach' (Tonkin and Edwards, 1981; Cogan, 1998). This approach is characterised by the attempt to infuse the curriculum 'with course content that reflects diverse perspectives . . . [and with] knowledge of differences in professional practices across cultures' (Whalley *et al.*, 1997: 10). The pervasiveness of this approach is evidenced by the fact that it has come to define what international curricula ought to be: 'Curricula with an international orientation in content, aimed at preparing students for performing (professionally and socially) in an international and multicultural context' (van der Wende 1999, cited in van der Wende, 2000: 27).

Implementation of these infused curricula (see de Wit, 1995) has led to the flourishing of courses in which traditional subject areas are broadened through international comparative methodologies (e.g. international accounting). It has also resulted in the increased provision of: (i) foreign-language modules; (ii) opportunities for exchange and study abroad programmes; (iii) internationally recognised professional qualifications; (iv) interdisciplinary programmes covering more than one country; and (v) programmes that assist in the development of cross-cultural communication skills.

Aside from very few exceptions (e.g. Leask, 2001) in which 'graduate qualities' for internationalisation have extended beyond the 'pragmatic' (Hayden and Thompson, 1995) confines of the mere acquisition of international content and skills, curriculum internationalisation strategies based upon the infusion approach have tended to overlook systematically the process of teaching and learning (Edwards *et al.*, 2003) and how to make this process culturally inclusive.

The third approach to curriculum internationalisation is still in its embryonic stage of development. It is rising from dissatisfaction with the infusion model, and from the concurrent desire to place culturally inclusive pedagogy at the core of an internationalised curriculum that, as suggested by Rizvi (2001: 5):

seeks to provide students with skills of inquiry and analysis rather than a set of facts about globalisation . . . [S]tudents need to develop questioning skills so that they are able to identify the sources of knowledge, assess claims of its validity and legitimacy, examine its local relevance and significance, determine its uses and applications and speculate about how it might be challenged and refuted. The ability to think reflectively and critically about knowledge creation and use requires a form of global imagination; the capacity to determine how knowledge is globally linked, no matter how locally specific its uses.

Significantly, this third holistic approach, the pursuit of which is described elsewhere in this volume, also recognises the need to move away from practices of curriculum internationalisation occurring solely in a few courses or as additives to existing programmes (see also Webb, 2005) towards culturally inclusive teaching and learning strategies that grant an equal opportunity of success to every student by providing equitably for the learning ambitions of all, irrespective of their cultural backgrounds (Haigh, 2002).

The significance of our contribution (De Vita and Case, 2003) ought to be framed within this 'next generation' approach to curriculum internationalisation. This paper offered a critique of both 'import' and 'infusion' models by exposing deficiencies and inconsistencies inherent in these approaches, and contributed to defining what a culturally inclusive curriculum should involve. Key principles proposed to inform its future development include:

- recognising that curriculum internationalisation is a profoundly complex task involving an individual and a university-wide process of continuous reflection, self-evaluation, review and improvement;
- valuing classroom diversity through open-ended forms of pedagogy that use students' experiences, ensure that cultural differences are heard and explored, and allow a conversation among different voices to discover cultural perspectives that are absent in traditional academic narratives;
- instigating a more participative and student-centred approach in which the lecturer becomes a facilitator and students become more responsible for their learning and development;
- creating a wider, more flexible and fair assessment system;
- developing a challenging hybrid culture where the multifarious cultural perspectives and experiences of those who make up the staff are themselves seen as the material which inspires the creation of new practices and change;
- fostering social inclusion, genuine internationalism and intercultural learning through authentic experiences of intercultural interaction.

The latter is perhaps the most underrated, neglected and yet critical element for a truly internationalised curriculum: first, because, as noted by Bretag

(2003), an important distinction needs to be made between the definition of the term 'internationalisation', literally signifying 'making international', and the much richer term 'internationalism', which refers to the advocacy of a community of interests among nations, a definition that suggests agency, cooperation and commitment; and, second, because there is a major difference between hosting a culturally diverse student population and having those students engaged in positive interaction. As pointed out by Wright and Lander (2003: 250), 'universities are deluding themselves if they believe that the presence of international students on campus contributes to the internationalisation of higher education'. In short, the rhetoric of education internationalisation hides the fact that intercultural interaction, in and outside the classroom, is not developing naturally, and is at best limited among students from culturally diverse backgrounds (De Vita, 2005b).

Evidence attesting to this problem is now ubiquitous (see Quintrell and Westwood, 1994; Volet and Ang, 1998; Thom, 2000; and Bargel 1998, cited in Otten, 2003) and demonstrates that the ideal of transforming a culturally diverse student population into a valued resource for activating processes of international connectivity, social cohesion and intercultural learning is still very much that, an ideal. This is obviously a direct consequence of the 'import' and 'infusion' approaches to curriculum internationalisation which have overlooked the genetic make-up of intercultural learning. Intercultural learning is not just about acquiring new international knowledge or merely 'rubbing shoulders' with fellow students from different cultural backgrounds; it involves 'the discovery and transcendence of difference through authentic experiences of cross-cultural interaction that involve real tasks, and emotional as well as intellectual participation' (De Vita and Case, 2003: 388).

Given the above, there seems to be a strong case for institutions and educators interested in genuine internationalisation to create curricular spaces that foster intercultural learning through multicultural group work. The potential of multicultural group work is reflected in several powerful outcomes associated with the creation of opportunities for authentic intercultural learning encounters. These include: (i) countering the predominantly ethnocentric approach to Higher Education found in most university systems (Furnham and Bochner, 1982); (ii) enhancing all students' understanding and appreciation of other cultures (Volet and Ang, 1998); (iii) challenging cultural stereotypes and sending an unambiguous message of equality to students (De Vita, 2000); (iv) promoting intercultural communication as a critical process of making meanings, of sharing meanings, and of building bridges across multiple realities and multiple truths (Fox, 1996; Hellmundt, 2003). These educational goals are not merely instrumental to the development of intercultural competencies dictated by changes in the demographic and cultural composition of our societies and the new requirements of the world of work; collectively, they form an agenda of social responsibility in fostering greater understanding, tolerance and respect among all people. They convey a message aimed at instigating a genuine process of cultural exchange intended to empower students to participate effectively in a better society, a society in which cultural, linguistic, ethnic and racial diversity are seen as a source of enrichment rather than as a problem, and inequality and discrimination are actively challenged (De Vita, 2005b).

Conclusions

The chapter began by providing a synthesis of the main pedagogic difficulties experienced by international students and their teachers in the multicultural classroom. Far from being false and stereotypical misconceptions, these difficulties exist and range from barriers to intercultural communication to cultural clashes of teaching and learning styles. It is argued that in UK Higher Education these difficulties are augmented by an assessment framework that is still too narrow and insufficiently flexible and that, by placing too much emphasis upon summative assessment of knowledge outcomes (rather than on formative processes of assessment), is not culturally responsive. Significantly, the problems affecting the learning and assessment of international students appear to compromise the performance, progression and achievement of such students.

Drawing from the contributions that have emerged from relevant literature and from the critical reflections of the author, the chapter has also traced avenues of how to move towards more culturally inclusive practices in teaching and assessment. The former entails two complementary teaching strategies: one didactically contextual, adaptive and culturally responsive; the

Commercial cascade effect or osmosis
as an agent of change

Infusion approach
generally overlooks teaching and learning but includes more language, more student exchange, internationally recognised qualifications, multi-country interdisciplinary programmes, cross-cultural communication skills

Culturally inclusive curriculum approach
real tasks, emotional and intellectual participation
the goal of genuine internationalism vs the internationalisation approach

Figure 12.1 A view of the evolution of the three approaches.

other facilitative, student-centred and conducive to the activation and development of higher-level cognitive processes and autonomous learning skills. With respect to assessment, the road to cultural inclusiveness starts from the recognition that in assessment, especially in the multicultural classroom, one size does not fit all. Since no single assessment method can be regarded as culturally inclusive per se, we should expand our assessment portfolios, allow more choice and place much greater emphasis on processes of formative assessment.

Finally, the chapter has offered a critical appraisal of current conceptualisations of the internationalisation of the curriculum and has outlined core principles to inform its future development for promoting genuine internationalism and for fostering intercultural learning.

Notes

1 Higher Education Statistics Agency (HESA) data show that, over the five-year period 1994 to 1999 alone, the international student population in UK Higher Education grew by 34 per cent. By 2004, international (non-UK-domiciled) students made up approximately 15 per cent of all students in UK Higher Education, bringing in over £1 billion in fee income annually (HESA, 1996, 2000, 2004).
2 The most notable exception is Harris (1997).

Part IV

European perspectives

Chapter 13

Approaches to services for international students[1]

Maria Kelo

Introduction

This chapter is based on a large-scale study on support for international degree-seeking students in Higher Education. The study, carried out by the Academic Cooperation Association (ACA) between October 2005 and October 2006, identified, described and analysed numerous examples of good practice in international student support in different countries, in terms of preparatory programmes prior to the undergraduate or postgraduate degree programme, as well as examples during the degree programmes in their different phases and aspects. Countries included in the study were Australia, Canada, Hungary, the Netherlands, Switzerland, the United Kingdom and to a lesser extent France. The chapter is based on information gathered from a selection of institutions in these counties, and explores the main motivations behind international student support, analyses the different approaches to services at institutional level, and describes briefly the main service items and organisational models of support for international degree students.

A changing European Higher Education scene

While the latest statistics show that almost half of all foreign students in European Higher Education are Europeans, and that geographical proximity has a strong impact on mobility flows, the number of students from other continents is steadily increasing and, especially, the number of Asian students has been growing in the last few years. In fact, Chinese students make up more than 6 per cent of all students in European Higher Education, thus representing the largest single country of origin of foreign students.[2] The increase in numbers of students from other continents is at least partly a product of the successful promotion of European universities in other parts of the world: while in many countries concerns for development cooperation through Higher Education continue to play a significant role, universities have started to show an interest in recruiting well-qualified students – or the 'best brains' – globally. To attract more international students to European

Higher Education, more than forty countries have joined the intergovern-mental Bologna process with the aim of achieving a higher degree of con-vergence between Higher Education degrees available across Europe. As a result of the structural reform of European degree programmes – from what was often a long first degree into a three- to four-year bachelors programme followed by a one- to two-year masters programme – international students are likely to start entering European Higher Education at a new point: directly for masters programmes. Students from other continents are likely to have different needs compared to home students or students from neighbour-ing countries, and within these the needs of postgraduate students are likely to differ from those of undergraduates. Universities have to be aware of and able to respond to the expectations of each of these student groups adequately if they wish to become – or remain – competitive.

In Continental Europe, the tendency for years has been to concentrate any practical support on international exchange students and those involved in organised student mobility, rather than on international degree students, or the so-called 'free movers' who transfer freely between nations while undertaking Higher Education programmes. In fact, in many countries support structures (such as special international welcome programmes, buddy schemes and language courses) are still offered exclusively or primarily for exchange students. However, with attention shifting from prioritising exchange students to attracting more and more international degree students, support will need in future to be developed accordingly, and extended to cater also for the latter. Few, if any, HEIs can afford to ignore the needs of inter-national degree students, and so need to invest in offering specific support for them, starting with essential basic services followed by more sophisticated services. Smaller or less well-known institutions especially may need to offer high-level services to assure their competitive advantage.

Approaches to services

At several institutions, services for students have become more and more a part of the package and are considered an essential element of the overall offer. However, not all institutions have reached this level of awareness and commitment to services, which are in many cases still seen as an add-on, to be addressed only to the minimum level and often ad hoc. The range, type and organisation of services for students in general and for international students in particular are both justified and influenced by a series of factors, related to both the institutional policy and a number of practical issues, including:

* whether the institution tries to attract a large number of students from a variety of countries, or the very best postgraduate students;
* whether it is a professionally oriented college or a research-intensive Ph.D.-awarding institution;

- whether it teaches in English or in another language; or
- whether it charges tuition fees or not.

The main questions institutions have to ask themselves when considering the approach to and organisation of student services are:

- What support do students in Higher Education need (regardless of nationality)?
- Do the needs of international students differ from those of home students and do they thus need special support and services compared to those available to all students?
- Who should take the responsibility for the organisation of such support and who should cover the costs so incurred?

Several assumptions can be made, all of which yield different overall pictures regarding the range of services that should be provided and the best way to organise them. The first assumption, rarely contested, is that students do need support, and that services beyond the purely administrative procedures (such as the registrations office, or student records) are important contributors to the overall student experience and an integral component of the institution's quality. The second point regards the specific needs of international students. Here the situation gets slightly more complicated. It may be assumed that international students have at least some different needs to home students, as they may face problems including those related to cultural differences, language difficulties or the demands of moving from one country to another and being far away from home. The question is, however, whether the differences are so great as to necessitate and justify particular attention: in other words, whether there should be specific services for international students or whether they should be mainstreamed. Regarding this, the following main attitudes may be identified:

- 'All students, whether home or international, need a lot of support.'
- 'International students have different needs and more (urgent) needs than national students, and thus need specific services.'[3]
- 'International students are not a homogeneous group: they need different levels of support depending on their cultural background, personal experience, language abilities, etc. The same applies to home students.'
- 'International students are the same as national students and separate services for them would only create a split university. There should be no "hand-holding" for any students, home or international.'

Which of these basic attitudes underlies the approach to service provision is again influenced by a number of factors: the institution's competitive position in the global Higher Education market, the institutional and national internationalisation and recruitment strategy, and the available financial and other resources, as well as the type (level, age and countries of origin) of international students, among others. Students may be perceived in significantly different ways, ranging from the perhaps extreme position (possibly a European perspective) of seeing students as customers to considering them as fortunate recipients of state-subsidised education and thus not entitled to expect or ask for anything more than they are already given.

Internal disagreements over the importance of services for international students within an institution can be frequently observed, most typically between student services staff or the international office, and academic staff or departments. Some argue that there should be no 'spoon-feeding' of students, whether international or home, as getting by on their own is an integral part of the student experience and prepares them for life in the 'real world'. Such opinions are contested by those believing in the importance of student support for a number of reasons, whether institutional or student-centred. The institutional management may be in favour of student support as part of the institutional policy or 'student-oriented approach' (who could afford to say they are openly against it?), but might not demonstrate that commitment in practice. Internal battles may make the provision of services less efficient, and more reliant on the good will of individuals, rather than an outcome of an overarching institutional policy.

A general 'service mentality', that is recognition of the importance of student support in general, and especially for international students, is more widely spread in some countries than in others. The overall approach to services within an institution seems to have a strong impact on the institution's sensitivity towards international students, and on the willingness to consider offering special services to them. Exceptional, innovative or particularly positive and well-functioning services for international students develop in many cases from strong emphasis on services for students in general. Indeed, at institutions with a strong 'service mentality', international degree students not only have full access to services available to home students, but the recognition of the importance of support leads to the development of specific services (or tailored programmes and activities within the existing ones) for international degree students. In contrast, where very little or no (and typically mainly administrative) support is on offer for the overall student body, similarly little in the way of specific services is likely to be available to international degree students. Out of good will, perhaps, these international students tend to be assimilated into the cohort of home degree students and thus left to manage on their own. Where little in the way of structured support is available for international students, in practice different offices deal with international students as best they can, or, if scarce services are available overall, those staff with more sensitivity take up service duties beyond their job description. Support for international students relies thus on the good will and interest of individual staff members. In such cases, a coherent institutional services strategy and an organised approach to their delivery would probably benefit substantially both the students and the institution.

Motivating international student support

Support for international students may be based on a number of expectations and aims and in many cases several of them are present at the same time. From the institutional point of view the most common motivating factors and aims cited for student support are the following:

- improving student retention, performance and success rate;
- a 'duty of care' and responsibility for the students' overall well-being;
- responding to the rising expectations of students, especially in programmes which charge (high) tuition fees;
- contributing to the internationalisation of the institution and most importantly to the international attractiveness of the institution.

The first one – improving student retention, performance and success rate – has been mentioned by many as the main motivation for the organisation of student support. In addition to academic support, which is designed specifically to improve student performance, other services are considered important contributors to this aim. The assumption is that 'a happy student performs better' and suggests that institutions concerned about student retention (and performance) should not concentrate exclusively on academically related support, but should adopt a more holistic approach addressing all areas of student life and experience.

Closely linked with a concern for student performance, a 'duty of care' is another key rationale in student support. Several of the visited institutions mention this as one of the main reasons for the provision of a number of their services. International students may be very young in age and away from home for the first time, and often it is perceived that institutional staff (lecturers or international office staff) need to act *in loco parentis* for the students, taking responsibility for their well-being and guidance. Indeed, responding to the needs of international students, even when not study-related, is considered at least in part the responsibility of the receiving institution.

Many European countries – and thus their institutions – are debating the introduction or raising of tuition fees for international students.[4] When Higher Education ceases to be free and becomes an investment, students' expectations are likely to rise, too: institutions need to consider what kind of value for money they are able to offer, and be able to demonstrate their quality, not only in terms of teaching and research, but also in terms of services they provide to their (international) students. Charging or increasing tuition fees may lead to a change in the attitude towards students, who start to be seen more as customers than recipients of (subsidised) education. Extensive facilities and services are often an important factor taken into consideration by students when choosing an institution, and therefore responding to those expectations (or failure to do so) may have a significant impact on the reputation and attractiveness of the institution.

Several of the motivational factors for the organisation of student support at the institutional level have an impact on, or make reference to, the institution's attractiveness for international students. This is one of the main rationales underlying service provision at the institutional level. The attractiveness of an institution is enhanced by better student performance and a lower drop-out rate, a caring attitude towards young international students, responsiveness to the perceived needs and expectations of students, and so on. A student who is satisfied with the overall experience gained at an institution is more likely to stay or return for further study, and to become an ambassador for the institution after graduation. Provision of support may be used by institutions to improve their competitive position in the Higher Education market, which may be especially important for less well-known or smaller institutions, or those that may not be able to compete solely on academic excellence. Services may be used to attract more students – whether fee payers or high achievers – or simply to increase the level of international-isation of the institution by facilitating the admission of students from a wide variety of countries.[5]

Indeed, the availability of specific services for international students may have a positive impact on the internationalisation of the institution, as dis-cussed extensively elsewhere in this volume. First of all, providing for the needs of international students may be instrumental in attracting students from a large variety of countries. In addition, some services are specifically designed to encourage and reward the international activity of both home and international students within an institution. Such activities include, for example, international awards, funds for international projects and travel, and programmes aiming at integrating international students with the local community. These services are considered very important, as simply having international students on campus does not necessarily and automatically make it truly international.

The various motivating factors for providing international student support are often interconnected and influence each other. However, institutions do not always have a thought-through services strategy or even simply a common approach to services and, if there is one, it is not necessarily linked to other institutional aims, such as, for example, the internationalisation strategy. The status quo is often arrived at through the uncoordinated indi-vidual initiatives of dedicated members of staff across the institution, and activities are frequently designed without overarching strategic aims in mind. In fact, services are sometimes seen as an optional extra, not inherently part of the university's core activities and not directly related to them. However, rather than considering services as separate from the teaching and learning mission of the institution, universities should start seeing all of their operations as a service to students: an encompassing student-mindedness, comprehensive of academic as well as other student life aspects, leads to a change in how services are perceived by the university management, administration, academics and even students, and is likely to lead to a more comprehensive approach to serving (international) students.

While various motivations may play a role in the design and delivery of student support from the institutional perspective, the students' needs should remain the main focal point, and services should be developed so as to meet those needs as fully as possible. In other words, available support should not be designed simply with financial concerns or the institution's competitiveness in mind. From the student perspective, the main aims of international student services are, firstly, enhancing the overall student experience, integration and academic performance and, secondly, levelling the disadvantages of international students vis-à-vis home students by addressing issues where they may face additional difficulties. However, international students are not a homogeneous whole and therefore cannot be treated as such. While all students are likely to require some basic services, such as adequate information, opportunities for language development, guidance on study methods, and support with practical arrangements, the extent of needs is likely to vary to a significant extent between students from different countries and cultural backgrounds. Indeed, students from neighbouring countries, for example within Europe, are likely to need less cultural adaptation than those arriving from further away. In addition, fewer services may be needed if students have for the most part already attended a preparatory programme or a language course prior to the start of the degree programme and, of course, if most international students are actually permanent local residents. Sensitivity towards individual students' needs and a personalised approach to support are fundamental in cases where great variations exist among international students or where a small number of individuals come from a different background compared to the main international student body.

From a narrow to a wider reading of 'essential services'

Institutions visited agreed largely that, for study success and integration, international students need to have adequate information at all stages from acceptance of the admissions offer to the period after graduation, to have access to an orientation programme during the first weeks after arrival, to receive support for practical issues such as applications for visas and in some cases finding accommodation, and to be introduced to the basic academic requirements. Beyond these formal aspects, further widely offered services include in-course language support, extensive study skills training, counselling and pastoral care, and social activities, as well as the organising and facilitating of work and training opportunities. These have become increasingly services that all expect to find, without which an institution may face a problem in terms of international competitiveness. Indeed, what is *essential* for study success and student satisfaction on the one hand, and the institutional attractiveness on the other hand, goes clearly beyond the simply administrative procedures. However, services considered essential by one institution may not be on another's agenda at all. Even the term 'services' has a different resonance and image in different countries.

Additional services, such as airport pick-up, international student lounges or one-to-one free language support, may be offered by institutions which want to make services their trade mark, for whatever reason. The value of such services is however relatively controversial, and investment in them more difficult to justify both at institutional and at national level. This resistance is partly explained by an improper understanding of 'essential' and 'additional' services, and is especially difficult to justify in cases where a restrictive notion of essential services prevails.

Increasingly, international student support is not only a question of addressing problems as they arise. Rather, ideally student services adopt a proactive attitude by taking concrete action in order to create specific schemes, workshops and programmes to provide opportunities for self-development, to improve the study success of all students of all abilities, and to take care of their general well-being by facilitating integration and cultural adjustment. When student support at an institution is highly developed, and therefore a lot of guidance, study support, language programmes and so on are available for home students, creating separate tools or programmes for international students may be less important. However, in systems where very little or no such support is available overall, international students are those who are likely to suffer most from their lack.

Organisational models: integrating or segregating international support

One of the main questions that universities need to address when considering services for international students, in addition to *why* they should offer services and *what* should be on offer, is *who* should be involved in their delivery and development. In most institutions several actors are likely to be involved with service provision (and design), and these include:

- the central-level office or offices (such as the international office or student support office);
- departments or faculties;
- students' unions or associations.

One of the most important decisions which has an impact on the organisation of services within a university is whether or not – and, eventually, to what extent – services for international students are delivered separately from those for home students. Some benefits associated with the separate treatment of international students include the following: first of all, it is argued that, if offered separately, the services for international students can be made more specific and tailored so as to correspond better to the needs and challenges these students face. Providing a wide range of services for international students in one place can lead also to a higher level of specialisation of staff, as well as a better visibility of international affairs within the institution. In parallel, there will be less need to have wide international awareness across the campus, or to take steps to ensure that staff in all service-related offices are internationally minded and knowledgeable about international students' needs. The international office is typically the first contact point for international students.

An integrated model, on the other hand, has the advantage of truly integrating international students with the locals, and thus helps to prevent the creation of a split university culture. This is considered one of the most important benefits of this model. Spreading international expertise across the campus may also raise the level of internationalisation of the university and create a wider awareness of and interest in international affairs. However, this is also a prerequisite for the integrated model to work: unless real international expertise can be found in all those offices which are to deliver support to both home and international students, the needs of the latter may risk not being adequately met.

The choice between the two main models depends on the institutional resources, internal organisation, international student numbers and other factors, but either of the two models may exist at an institution giving great attention to international students. However, whichever delivery model is chosen, institutions should make sure that international students know whom they can turn to with problems, and that support personnel have adequate international awareness and expertise to be able to address specific international student issues adequately. The key is to ensure proper communication channels and as extensive cooperation as possible between the different support units, and adequate training of staff on international student specific issues.

Conclusions

International students are likely to have different needs, more needs and more urgent needs than home students. Language difficulties, different learning and teaching methods (see Chapters 6 and 7), cultural shock, and the lack of a social network or family support may all have a strong impact on the experience and success of international students. Furthermore, international students face, in many cases, practical obstacles, such as those related to visas, work permits or health insurance schemes, which are not easily overcome without support from the host institution. The recognition of the different needs of international students is the first step in providing them with adequate support. However, when considering the appropriate institutional approach, the national context, such as legal requirements, institutional recruitment and internationalisation priorities, and the student numbers and countries of origin need to be taken into account. Various delivery models and specific programmes may work well in different situations and, while general recommendations can be made in relation to an approach to international student support, the practical arrangements may take different forms without this having a negative impact on support provision. Therefore, it is clear that in organising support for international students one size does *not* fit all: rather, each university has to consider carefully what best meets the needs of its international student body, as well as those of the institution.

Notes

1 The study on support for international students in higher education was carried out by the Academic Cooperation Association (ACA) in the period from October 2005 to October 2006. The study was financed by the DAAD – see Kelo (2006).
2 See Kelo *et al.* (2006). These data refer to thirty-two European countries: the twenty-five EU member states, as well as four EFTA countries (Iceland, Liechtenstein, Norway and Switzerland) and the then EU candidate countries Bulgaria, Romania and Turkey.
3 At some institutions a variation of this point is apparent, namely that international students should receive more and better services, *because they pay (higher) tuition fees.* This approach may be especially relevant in countries where home students pay significantly lower (or no) tuition fees compared to international students.
4 For institutions in the European Union member states, charging fees to students from other European countries is possible only if the same fee applies also to home students. Therefore in many countries where no or low fees are charged to home students, the higher international student fees apply only to students from countries outside the European Union. Fees at the masters level are usually less regulated by the home governments, and in most cases apply to all students, home and international, though the former may pay slightly less.
5 This is especially relevant in the context of university preparatory programmes.

Chapter 14

European and European Union dimensions to mobility[1]

Tim Birtwistle

Mobility requires much more than the physical movement of a body and mind for it to significantly add value in the context of Higher Education. The need for a knowledge-based economy in high-cost areas such as most of geographical Europe necessitates a common lexicon for Higher Education and developments that facilitate intellectual mobility in a wide variety of ways.

The terms 'Europe', 'the European Union' and indeed 'the United Kingdom' need some clarification, especially in the context of Higher Education. 'Europe' might be referred to as the 'wider Europe'; it is a concept loosely based around a geographical notion. The European Union (EU)[2] had twenty-five member states in 2006, which became twenty-seven in 2007, all located geographically in Europe. The United Kingdom (UK) of Great Britain and Northern Ireland is made up of England, Scotland, Wales and Northern Ireland, each with varying degrees of legislative competence and independence of action regarding Higher Education. The UK is a member of the EU and is crucially involved in matters of Higher Education in the wider Europe, through being one of the initial signatory states of the Bologna Process, and yet has a complex set of devolved rights within its own borders.

Much of Higher Education policy has traditionally been based around the idea of the autonomous nation state with its own historical traditions.[3] Each state has, largely, developed its own formula for what it perceives Higher Education to be. Because of this, in the Continent of Europe, neighbouring countries could have quite radically different norms with regard to Higher Education. These norms manifested themselves in a wide variety of ways, including marking conventions, for example marking scales that go (in terms of low to high) from 1 to 5, 5 to 1, 0 to 20, 0 to 13, 0 to 100, etc., or length of study for a particular academic title that in itself could not be easily translated into an equivalence from a neighbouring state, for example four years, five years, three years, seven years, and Magister, Doctor, Bachelor. There was an abundance of variety and no inconvenience to the vast majority of people, for they travelled little.

The majority of students and their professors happily remained in their locality. Within that locality the worth of a qualification or title was readily known and in any case this did not affect trade, commerce or the professions. People, in even the recent past, were predominantly static – no need to move, no desire to move and no means to move.

This has of course changed. After the Second World War, much changed in so many ways, and one change that did come about was the creation of what we now call the European Union (EU). The EU has competency for a great range of things that were previously the sole province of the nation state. One area that has been touched is Higher Education. Beyond the twenty-seven member states of the EU there is the land mass of Europe. Across this land mass is a growing realisation that, whilst individualism and what might be seen by others as idiosyncratic institutions are fine within the borders of the country, the creeping reality of globalisation is there. Others might want, or even demand, something different. The so-called 'Bologna Process' that will lead to the European Higher Education Area (EHEA) is a multi-government (more than forty-five signatory countries) series of agreements on policy development that has multiple objectives, but one major objective is mobility. This is the wider Europe, stretching from Azerbaijan to Iceland.

Although there is this apparent groundswell of demand for international recognition of study and qualifications and the ability to travel to other countries to study, the vast majority of people are static, for whatever reason. However, the static majority is exposed to international influences. At a micro level people now travel more than ever before. The phenomenon of the low-cost airline has enabled people to travel more frequently to more places, both long-haul and short-haul. The media enable people to see and hear the sights and sounds of other countries. Businesses are now owned by undertakings from other countries and managed by staff from other countries, and workers move between countries either for a single undertaking or between undertakings. The majority may be static but they have never been exposed to so many sights, sounds and ideas from around the globe. Can Higher Education be serving the best interests of its stakeholders if it does not prepare its students for the global reality?

What has the EU done in terms of recognition of global realities?

The role of 'Lisbon'

The role of 'Lisbon' in the future strategic development of the European Union is crucial, but 'Lisbon' has a variety of connotations attached to it. There is the rather narrow but important (from the point of view of mobility) Lisbon Recognition Convention,[4] which pre-dates the much broader and all-encompassing Lisbon Agenda[5] (covering many aspects of economic growth) originating from the spring 2000 European Council meeting.

The Convention is designed to streamline the legal framework at European level and to facilitate the recognition of academic qualifications, granted in one state, in another state, in terms of access to a Higher Education institution. It provides that requests should be assessed in a fair manner and within a reasonable time. The recognition can only be refused if the qualification is substantially different from that of the host country – and the onus is on the educational institution to prove that this is the case. The United Kingdom ratified the Convention on 23 May 2003 and it came into force on 1 July 2003.

The Lisbon Agenda is the way in which the EU has committed itself to follow a strategy for economic growth based on the concept of a knowledge-based economy. The original stated aim was that, by 2010, as a knowledge-based society, the EU would become the most competitive region in the world. These are the so-called 'Lisbon objectives'. Research has been added to the strategy, although there is now doubt being voiced as to whether or not all strategic objectives can be attained by 2010. As Commission President Barroso said (14 March 2005): 'the future has changed. It is time to rethink the Lisbon strategy . . . Creating . . . [a] "Europe of Opportunities" is what I think the Lisbon Agenda should be about.'[6]

A mid-term review of the Lisbon Agenda took place in March 2005. Much analysis has taken place about the speed of progress (or rather lack of it) and the causes of this. *The Lisbon Scorecard V: Can Europe Compete?*[7] is one analysis of the different speeds at which different member states are moving.

Europe will be full of 'opportunities', and 'knowledge' will enable citizens to benefit from the opportunities. The concepts are of course not only compatible, but also mutually supporting rather than mutually exclusive. 'Lisbon' remains crucial, albeit refocused, but a cornerstone of the future developments that will take place.

However, what must be remembered is that the Bologna Process (see p. 186) is not an EU initiative and that the EU was in fact a rather late entrant to the Process, albeit now a rather active one. Notwithstanding that, the Lisbon Agenda has been a force behind the Bologna Process.

EU mobility

In the EU context, mobility has a precise legal framework and is without doubt encouraged in all ways, that is, in terms of Treaty provisions, educational programmes, research programmes and, given the difficulties of arriving at an overall budget, finance. The Treaty provisions deal with free movement of persons and non-discrimination.

Article 12 EC prohibits any discrimination on grounds of nationality. The Treaty right to move and reside freely (Article 18(1)) makes the collection of data regarding the movement of those wishing to study difficult – hence the absence of any reliable data outside the Socrates Erasmus framework. Article 149(1) EC states that the Community shall contribute to the development of quality education by encouraging cooperation between member states while 'fully respecting the responsibility of the Member States for the content of teaching and the organisation of education systems and their cultural and linguistic diversity'.

Article 149(2) states that the Community will encourage 'mobility of students and teachers by encouraging, *inter alia*, the academic recognition of diplomas and periods of study'.

There is a variety of secondary legislative measures, in the form of directives that address detailed issues regarding residence. Directive 2004/38/EC[8] was to be transposed into the law of the member states (Article 40) by 30 April 2006. The directive contains some fundamental rights regarding mobility to study. These include citizenship, movement and residence for students as well as workers. There is a derogation, in certain circumstances, from granting financial assistance for studying.

Mobility outside EU programmes, such as Socrates Erasmus,[9] is protected as a Treaty right, but with the limiting factor that students must be 'to some extent integrated into the society' if they are to benefit from aspects of the host state's funding mechanisms. However, the EU educational programmes have had a significant influence on mobility.

In 1987 the European Commission began supporting the Erasmus mobility programme for European university students (named after the cosmopolitan scholar Erasmus). In the first year 3,000 students received grants. The Erasmus programme was later incorporated into the broader Socrates EU education programme that now involves thirty European countries. The main objective of Socrates is to build up a Europe of knowledge and to provide a framework to deal with the challenges of the twenty-first century: to promote life-long learning, encourage access to education for everybody, and help people acquire recognised qualifications and skills. Socrates seeks to promote language learning and to encourage mobility and innovation. In 2004, Erasmus celebrated the fact that 1 million students had enjoyed mobility within its framework. This is an achievement, but it is not the 10 per cent mobility that had been an original aim of the programme (with a much smaller number of member states).

An illustration of the levels of mobility is shown in Tables 14.1 and 14.2

Table 14.1 Levels of mobility

Country	1987/8	1992/3	1998/9	2003/4
UK	925	8,872	9,994	7,539
France	895	8,983	16,351	20,981
Italy	220	5,308	10,875	16,829
Spain	95	5,697	14,381	20,034
Netherlands	169	3,290	4,332	4,388

Table 14.2 Year of highest outward mobility

UK	France	Italy	Spain	Netherlands
1994/5	2003/4	2003/4	2003/4	1995/6

(from the Europa website[10]), but note that in 1987 there were eleven participating countries and in 2004 there were thirty-one.

Most countries have seen, as illustrated by France in Table 14.1, a steady increase in outward mobility. Given that reciprocity of numbers is an aim of the programme (and certainly of the governments funding Higher Education), greater outward numbers allow for greater inward numbers, which gives greater internationalisation, assuming that there are those willing to make that journey. The UK is not alone in seeing dropping numbers, as illustrated by the Netherlands in Table 14.2, but the stark volume of the decline from the UK is the most marked. Some countries have apparently achieved a steady state, for example Denmark (*circa* 1,700 students).

The UK suffers from the role of the English language in international trade and commerce: the lingua franca benefit/burden. The effect of this is that many students want to be inwardly mobile into the UK. The outward mobility from the UK continues to decline. Is this purely an effect of mother tongue? Whatever the reason, the effect is as shown in Table 14.3.

Reciprocity may be the aim but as can be seen it is not achieved. However, the level of imbalance is markedly different when comparing the UK with any other country. Naturally the overall programme figures do balance at 135,586 for 2003/4.

The EU programmes have had a significant impact on mobility and on the development of an attitude towards international education. Research, such as by Trends,[11] does show that the attitude of UK Higher Education towards international recruitment is largely based around fee income, whereas the attitude of the rest of the EU is to international cooperation, development and education rather than the balance sheet.

Table 14.3 Mobility from the UK

Country	Inward total	Outward total
UK	16,627	7,539
France	20,276	20,981
Italy	12,743	16,829
Spain	24,076	20,034
Netherlands	6,733	4,388

The Bologna Process

In 1988 the rectors of European universities present in Bologna for the 900th anniversary of the University signed the Magna Charta Universitatum.[12] Shortly afterwards the Sorbonne Declaration (25 May 1998) was signed by ministers of education from the UK, Italy, France and Germany in Paris[13] on the 'harmonisation of the architecture of the European Higher Education System'. The Sorbonne Declaration focused on:

- a progressive convergence of the overall framework of degrees and cycles in an open European area for Higher Education;
- a common degree-level system for undergraduates and graduates;
- the enhancing and facilitating of student and teacher mobility.

The Bologna Process was launched on 19 June 1999, when the declaration was signed on behalf of twenty-nine countries. To keep the momentum going, a series of summits (the ministerial element of the intergovernmental process) and conferences (the academic aspect of the process) have subsequently been held and are planned for the future. The summits are held under the presidency of a state, and many of the conferences are under the auspices of the European University Association, although the European Commission has become an active player.

There were six key themes of the Bologna Declaration:

- adoption of a system of easily readable and comparable degrees;
- adoption of a system essentially based on two main cycles;
- establishment of a system of credits;
- promotion of mobility;
- promotion of European cooperation in quality assurance;
- promotion of the necessary European dimensions in Higher Education.

A further three key themes were later added:

- life-long learning;
- Higher Education institutions and students;
- promoting the attractiveness of the European Higher Education Area.

Mobility is a recurrent, consistent and central theme to the Bologna Process.

The Process continues. The Trends IV report on the institutional progress made was published[14] in May 2005, the Tuning Project[15] is now in Stage 3, and the EU Commission document *From Berlin to Bergen: The EU Contribution* was published on 7 April 2005 confirming the objectives and commenting on progress to date.

Each signatory state (plus Scotland) is required to present a national report[16] to feed into the ministerial conferences (for example, Bergen 2005). Each report covers a range of areas including mobility. In fact it can be argued that most of the instruments and objectives of Bologna are totally meaningless without mobility. The concept of transparency is to facilitate mobility. The Lisbon Convention is of no consequence unless persons are mobile and seeking to study.

Bologna mobility

The Bologna Process is intergovernmental and stretches beyond the borders of the European Union to the wider Europe. Aspects of mobility must be looked at both in the context of the EU, for example in terms of funding, legal residence and mobility rights, etc., and in the context of the wider Europe, often with no legal rights to residence and mobility.

The statements on mobility within the framework of the Bologna Process are related to academic mobility at all three cycles. Given that the third cycle now often uses the term 'young researcher' and that there are calls from certain quarters to make doctoral candidates into employees rather than 'students', there is a mix between employment issues and academic issues.

The Bologna Declaration[17] stated:

> Promotion of mobility by overcoming obstacles to the effective exercise of free movement with particular attention to:
>
> • for students, access to study and training opportunities and to related services;
> • for teachers, researchers and administrative staff, recognition and valorisation of periods spent in a European context researching, teaching and training, without prejudicing their statutory rights.

Post-Berlin, the aim[18] was stated to be:

> *Promotion of mobility* – Mobility of students and academic and administrative staff is the basis for establishing a European Higher Education Area. Ministers emphasise its importance for academic and cultural as well as political, social and economic spheres. They note with satisfaction that since their last meeting, mobility figures have increased, thanks also to the substantial support of the European Union programmes, and agree to undertake the necessary steps to improve the quality and coverage of statistical data on student mobility.
>
> They reaffirm their intention to make every effort to remove all obstacles to mobility within the European Higher Education Area. With a view to promoting student mobility, Ministers will take the necessary steps to enable the portability of national loans and grants.

The volume of mobility by totally free movers (i.e. in no way connected with Erasmus) is not known, especially intra-Community mobility, as there is the legal right to residence and mobility.

The practicalities of mobility for citizens of the non-EU states remain the same. For those wishing to study in the United Kingdom there are the increased expense of visas, the much higher fee levels (than for EU citizens) and absolutely no access to loans and grants (or whatever system develops).

Instruments aiding student mobility

The value added to a person by mobility between states is much reduced if there is the legal ability to move but then access to education (or training) is restricted in some way. In academic terms, mobility means much more than just the physical act of moving; it also requires instruments that, if not ensuring, are at least aiding fair academic recognition of previous learning. A number of Bologna and EU instruments exist or are planned. The two main elements are:

1   *Diploma Supplement* (DS). As the ENIC-NARIC[19] website puts it:

   The Diploma Supplement is a project developed by the European Commission, the Council of Europe and the UNESCO-CEPES working group. Its purpose is to promote transparency and the recognition of higher education qualifications for academic and professional purposes. This project is a part of the Bologna Process.

   The mechanics of the DS are well documented and, post-Berlin, all graduating students must be given a DS free of charge (as from 2005). This has placed a technical and financial burden on universities. However, the DS is even wider than the Bologna signatory states, with it being a UNESCO-backed initiative.

2   *Europass.* Europass[20] brings together five documents in a new portfolio. It is forecast to be adopted by 3 million Europeans by 2010. The concept was adopted by the European Parliament and Council on 15 December 2004. Ján Figel, the European Commissioner for Education, Training, Culture and Multilingualism, said at the launch (February 2005): 'Europass is a direct service to citizens that will help them to make their qualifications and competences clearly understood throughout Europe. It will therefore facilitate their mobility for both occupational and life-long learning purposes.'

   The original five different documents have been amended to fit the new format, but cover skills, qualifications and experience. The new Europass consists of the Europass CV, Language Passport, Europass Mobility, Diploma Supplement and Certificate Supplement. It has been both criticised as being merely old wine in new bottles (the Observatory on

Borderless Education) and praised as being a direct help to those on the labour market (Eurofunding.com).

The Europass Mobility records any 'transnational mobility' undertaken by the holder of the pass, including academic, work or voluntary placements. The Mobility pass is to be completed by the home and host organisations involved and will replace the Europass-Training scheme, which has been in operation for five years and issued to about 100,000 people.

The Commission is committed to producing an evaluation report on the implementation of the Europass by 1 January 2008 and then every four years.

The other elements include a variety of information channels to try to assist persons who wish to be mobile either as students or as workers. There is the Portal on Learning Opportunities throughout the European space, known as PLOTEUS. This contains information about learning and training opportunities in member states and candidate countries, as well as EU exchange and grant programmes for students. Another is EURES[21] – the European Job Mobility Portal. This provides a way to find information on jobs and learning opportunities in Europe, including online information about free movement of workers' provisions and the country-specific details, as well as details on living and working, educational opportunities and a 'CV search' facility. Yet another is Euroguidance, the network of national resource centres for vocational guidance. It has its own website[22] and provides information on education and training opportunities in Europe, mainly for guidance practitioners.

There is also the major project generated by the Bologna Process to create a European qualifications framework (EQF). This is aimed at making the European Higher Education systems more transparent and compatible with each other. It will be an overarching framework giving a holistic sense to the national frameworks, which should describe qualifications in terms of workload, level, learning outcomes, competencies and profile. A qualifications framework based on credits needs a common understanding of credits and, ideally, a single credit system. The European Credit Transfer (and accumulation) System (ECTS) is viewed as the framework for this by many.

On what basis should the allocation of credits take place? The 'input' lobby remains strong – number of teaching hours is the crucial determinant in allocating credits. The 'outcomes' lobby has gained the ascendancy – the crucial elements are student workload and learning outcomes.

The 'new generation of EU programmes in education and training' (budget: €13.62 billion for 2007–13) is an integrated action programme. It covers life-long learning and comprises sectoral programmes on school education (Comenius), Higher Education (Erasmus), vocational training (Leonardo da Vinci) and adult education (Grundtvig), and is completed by transversal measures and an additional Jean Monnet programme focusing on European integration. There are specific mobility targets set for the new programmes. These are currently set at:[23]

- *for Comenius:* to involve at least one pupil in twenty in joint educational activities, for the period of the programme;
- *for Erasmus:* to contribute to the achievement by 2011 of 3 million individual participants in student mobility under the present programme and its predecessors;
- *for Leonardo da Vinci:* to increase placements in enterprises to 150,000 per year by the end of the programme;
- *for Grundtvig:* to support the mobility of 25,000 individuals involved in adult education per year, by 2013.

With the Bologna cycles of study there is increasing reference to 'horizontal mobility' and 'vertical mobility'. The former refers to the 'traditional' type of student exchange programme; the latter refers to students choosing to study at a different place for their second-cycle qualification (masters) than they did for their first-cycle qualification (bachelors).

Other objectives

The elements of Bologna that refer to the structure of programmes – cycles, credits, quality and hence 'a system of easily readable and comparable degrees' – can be dealt with together and are to some extent already subsumed in the notion of the qualifications framework (see p. 186).

Linked to mobility is the Recommendation of the Recognition of Joint Degrees as an amendment to the Lisbon Recognition Convention.[24] There remain structural problems for many universities, not in the concept of a joint degree but simply in the mechanics of how to award one. The QAA has produced a second edition of the Code of Practice for Collaborative Provision[25] which indicates that a level of caution and a tendency towards being risk-averse remains. This depends of course upon whether one views as 'risky' assessing in 'another language' and might also be viewed as being predicated on the view of 'unequal' partnerships rather than fundamentally based on equal partnerships. There are also various potential legal pitfalls regarding the award of such a degree.[26]

The degree of prescription might well militate against joint degrees and partnerships and therefore against participation in programmes such as Erasmus Mundus.

Prior to the 2005 Bergen Ministerial Bologna Conference, the UK's Position Paper[27] stated *inter alia* that 'the UK welcomes mobility'. But what will it do about actively promoting it? The UK is president of the Process through until the London conference in 2007.[28]

At the end of 2005, thirty-six of the forty-five signatory countries had adopted the Lisbon Recognition Convention. Mobility remains a key European objective, but it is recognised that funding is an issue, as are obstacles to mobility for non-EU citizens.

In which strategic direction does the future lie for universities? The trends in terms of student mobility are very variable with no clear pattern emerging, but what is clear is that business forces are taking advantage of a mobile business culture in terms of acquisitions as well as individual mobility. The number of 'undertakings' (the EU Treaty word that encompasses anything doing business, for example in Article 81 regarding, amongst other things, cartels) that are owned by a parent company that is not indigenous is remarkable: think of water, electricity, banks, insurance and motor manufacturing. The number of CEOs and other executives who are non-nationals is also high (and not only those employed by a parent company that is multicultural). The mobility of academics remains rather constant (although there is a lack of data and so this is an observed phenomenon); there will always be those who will follow research facilities and others who will seek a different cultural experience, whilst, just as with the students, the majority are indeed the static majority.

Can a university just ignore the meta-trends that Bologna identifies? I would propose that to do so is folly. Madame Reding stated that 'Bologna is not à la carte'; it is a total package that does embody a cultural and pedagogic shift in order to embed learning outcomes, credit accumulation and transfer, and qualifications frameworks at both national and supra-national levels, all wrapped around by the Lisbon Agenda and the identification of the need for a knowledge-based economy.

Stand still, and the likelihood is that a university will be marginalised, bypassed and eventually discarded because it will add no value to society. An awareness of all that is happening in the sphere of Higher Education around the world is not a marginal luxury pursuit; it is a core need to develop, refresh and provide a valuable intellectual service to the wider communities.

Notes

Original Bologna signatory states: Austria, Belgium (Flemish community), Belgium (French community), Bulgaria, the Czech Republic, Denmark, Estonia, Finland, France, Germany, Greece, Hungary, Iceland, Ireland, Italy, Latvia, Lithuania, Luxembourg, Malta, the Netherlands, Norway, Poland, Portugal, Romania, the Slovak Republic, Slovenia, Spain, Sweden, the Swiss Confederation and the United Kingdom.

1 Some of the sections of this chapter are based on a research report prepared for Eversheds LLP.
2 Note that the EU is made up of three pillars, and the European Community (EC) is one of these.
3 Van der Wende and Middlehurst (2003).

4 See http://www.cepes.ro/hed/recogn/lisbon/Default.htm.
5 See http://www.euractiv.com/Article?tcmuri=tcm:29–117510–16&type=
   LinksDossier.
6 The 2005 Robert Schumann Lecture for the Lisbon Council, Brussels, 14 March
   2005.
7 Murray and Wanlin (2005). Also see http://www.euractiv.com/Article?tcmuri=
   tcm:29–137075–16&type=News.
8 OJ 2004 L 229, p. 35; see also at: http://europa.eu.int/eur-lex/pri/en/oj/dat/2004/
   l_229/l_22920040629en00350048.pdf.
9 See   http://europa.eu.int/comm/education/programmes/socrates/erasmus/stat_en.
   html.
10 See   http://europa.eu.int/comm/education/programmes/socrates/erasmus/stat_en.
   html.
11 See http://www.eua.be/eua/en/policy_bologna_trends.jspx.
12 See http://www.magna-charta.org/magna.html.
13 See http://www.bologna-berlin2003.de/pdf/Sorbonne_declaration.pdf.
14 See http://www.eua.be/eua/en/policy_bologna_trends.jspx.
15 See http://europa.eu.int/comm/education/policies/educ/tuning/tuning_en.html.
16 For example, http://www.bologna-bergen2005.no/EN/national_impl/00_Nat-rep-
   05/National_Reports-Scotland_050124.pdf.
17 See at http://www.eua.be/eua/jsp/en/upload/OFFDOC_BP_bologna_declaration.
   1068714825768.pdf.
18 See at http://www.eua.be/eua/en/policy_bologna.jspx.
19 See http://www.enic-naric.net/instruments.asp?display=DS.
20 See http://europass.cedefop.eu.int/htm/index.htm.
21 See http://europa.eu.int/eures/.
22 See http://europass.cedefop.eu.int/europass/home/vernav/Information+and++
   Support /Euroguidance/navigate.action.
23 See http://europa.eu.int/comm/education/programmes/newprog/indexy_en.html.
24 See www.bologna-bergen2005.no/EN/Other/Lisbon_Recdoc/04069_
   Recommendation_joint_degrees.pdf.
25 See http://www.qaa.ac.uk/academicinfrastructure/codeOfPractice/section2/
   default.asp.
26 See the paper by Nick Saunders (Eversheds) presented in London at the joint
   seminar with the QAA, 20 June 2005.
27 Europe Unit UUK, 6 May 2005.
28 See www.eu2005.gov.uk.

Part V

Conclusions

Chapter 15

Contextualising international Higher Education

Elspeth Jones and Sally Brown

Working in universities around the world for short and extended periods, we have developed a view of what differentiates a university or college that is genuinely international from one which merely pays lip service to the approach. To provide a conclusion for the rest of this book, we have identified twenty key factors in internationalising Higher Education which, we argue, characterise institutions that welcome and celebrate international diversity, derived from collective experiences of our authors and others in organisations that take the issues seriously.

Designing a positive institutional approach

1 Vision

Higher Education institutions (HEIs) that successfully integrate international students within their communities need to have a clear articulation in the vision or mission of the institution, and this needs to be backed up by a supportive and enabling senior management. Without these, individuals striving to internationalise curriculum design and delivery approach in an unstructured way cannot hope to succeed other than in piecemeal initiatives.

2 Values

This needs to be underpinned by an institutional ethos which adopts a values-based or ethical approach rather than one simply founded on valuing the income which international students bring. The resulting culture of shared values, contacts and expertise, together with an understanding of the benefits for all of internationalisation, can offer a step change in the institution's approach to internationalisation and the results achieved. A collaboratively produced internationalisation strategy may offer evidence of this shared understanding of how internationalisation impacts on all aspects of university life.

3 Policies and strategies

To achieve a genuine culture shift within an HEI, there needs to be a mainstreamed whole-institution approach to internationalisation, involving the production of institutional policies and strategies which make explicit the relevance and importance of internationalisation. These are likely to include the university or college's corporate plan, together with nested strategies including learning and teaching, e-learning, research, retention and widening participation strategies with linked equality and diversity and sustainability policies.

4 Partnerships

Successful institutions are likely to have a number of strong international partnerships in order to facilitate staff secondments, student exchanges, international research, development and benchmarking opportunities.

5 Visible internationalisation

Universities and colleges that are aiming to be truly international will demonstrate regular recognition and celebration of international developments, positive partnership links that go beyond mere exchanges and visits, a programme of events that make explicit the HEI's international intents, and global perspectives made visible through the organisation's website, publicity materials and publications.

6 Management information

No organisation can achieve this without having effective management information to support internationalisation, including disaggregated data on students by nationality to enable analysis of source countries, success, career destinations and other indications of achievement. These are essential for planning and for targeting initiatives.

Supporting and encouraging staff

7 Breadth of activity

A whole-institution approach is required, including providing opportunities for both academic and support staff to engage in international research, knowledge exchange and capacity building, as well as a range of staff development opportunities (see 11 below). Restricting such activities to staff with 'international' as part of their job titles is restrictive and counter-productive.

8 International staff

Appointing diverse staff with varied international experience and bringing in regular international visiting lecturers are essential parts of a strategic approach to internationalising Higher Education. Equally important is enabling the institution's own staff of all categories to have international experiences as part of an institutional enrichment process, since broadening horizons makes for better-informed and more empathetic staff. International exchange programmes or visits to partner institutions are valuable for the majority of staff, and the resulting learning or benchmarking process can enhance practice in the home institution.

9 Enthusiasts

Not all staff will share equally the enthusiasm and the capability necessary for taking the international agenda forward, so it is crucial to identify, support and make good use of internationalisation champions across the institution. These might take the form of specially recruited staff, secondees, or staff selected to focus some of their energies on this area of the university's mission.

10 Support for international perspectives

Staff will not commit to any institutional initiative if they feel their efforts are ignored or not taken seriously. For this reason we regard valuing and rewarding international perspectives in learning, teaching, assessment and research as imperative. Whether this is linked to promotion and career progression, or whether it is celebrated by public recognition through internal awards, it is really important to value what staff do to promote international perspectives in all aspects of their work.

11 Staff development

Although staff are likely to have some personal inclinations and innate dispositions towards developing international perspectives, systematically providing staff development opportunities to support internationalisation will make a real impact on institutional change. This should be for both academic and support staff and it may include providing opportunities for language learning and cross-cultural capability awareness training, or learning to deal with students whose first language is not English. Perhaps most significantly, opportunities to research, observe and reflect on diverse and inclusive pedagogies can feed into good practice for working with both home and international students.

Supporting and engaging students

12 Communication

How a university or college presents itself to the world via its website and its publications will affect how prospective students see it. Therefore marketing to and communication with prospective and on-programme international students and with alumni need to be thought through very carefully, including the selection of inclusive (but not tokenistic) images, sensitive use of language and reference to the issues that might be anxiety points for prospective students, including accommodation, food and worship issues. All communications should be inclusive and should take account of international English rather than being culture-specific, and it is equally important for communications internal to the institution to adopt these guidelines.

13 Diversity

To avoid feelings of isolation and alienation, it is really helpful to have a critical mass of international students on campus across a range of courses and from diverse countries to support internationalisation. This needs to be coupled with actions to support effective integration within and across national and cultural boundaries, including welcome events for international students, buddying schemes, arranged opportunities for students to network within and beyond their national groups, and targeted social opportunities. It should also be linked to, and benefit from, the broader celebration of diversity across the institution, and to policies and practice which enhance the diversity of the home student population.

Improving the formal and extended curriculum

14 Internationalised curriculum

However welcome and supported students feel, they are unlikely to thrive educationally if they feel the curriculum marginalises them. Universities and colleges need to offer a flexible, integrated and discipline-focused internationalised curriculum, incorporating global perspectives, both for easier curriculum access for international students and to develop the international and intercultural perspectives of all students and staff.

15 Exchanges

Effective exchange programmes for students, academics and support staff have long been used in Higher Education to help broaden horizons. These, together with travel bursaries, encourage participation in activities designed to promote internationalisation, but they may need to be carefully focused to ensure the maximum benefit is achieved. For example, we would wish to see all staff undertaking international travel to reflect and report back on their experiences (see Chapter 3). An HEI might also wish to target an activity specifically, for example supporting staff to visit a nation or region from which considerable numbers of students are recruited. This could be done in order to explore the academic pedagogies of that area, so that unexpected assessment, learning and teaching surprises (see Chapter 5) can be antici-pated and avoided and, more significantly, so that our own pedagogies can be enriched.

16 Volunteering

One way to foster internationalisation is by offering a programme of opportunities for international volunteering by staff and students. Equally, 'service learning' can enable international students to engage with the local community in a way which benefits both the student and the local population (see Chapter 11). In the UK, volunteering for home students has been sup-ported financially in recent years by the funding councils, notably the Higher Education Funding Council for England, but these opportunities have spread in only a limited way to the international student body.

17 Internationalisation at home

It is certainly the case that more international students seek to study in the UK than UK students wish to study abroad. If all students are to benefit from the skills and experiences offered by an international experience, HEIs may seek to establish opportunities for internationalisation at home.

Internationalisation of the formal curriculum is the most significant vehicle for this, but extended curriculum opportunities can also contribute. These may include an international student buddies programme, tandem learning, clubs and societies appealing to home and international students, and international cultural events and competitions. There should also be close liaison with and support for students' unions and student societies which support integration.

Offering a range of appropriate support services

18 Services

Many of the factors that help students to feel at home (British Council, 2002) involve providing for the creature comforts of students, either studying away from home or learning in an environment that feels very distant from their home lives. A sensitive and positive institution will provide accommodation, food, worship and other facilities which recognise the needs of students from other cultures, with an awareness of the inherent dangers of ghettoisation to which 'special' services can lead.

19 Pastoral support

Individuals in transition may need additional support (Arthur, 1998) despite the fact that they may have been highly successful in their originating contexts, so it is important that institutions provide effective pastoral support programmes which recognise where needs differ and where extra support may be required. This could include, for example, specialist advisers on immigration issues, a formal pastoral support system and befriending opportunities where the support needs are social rather than practical.

20 Linguistic, cultural and academic support

An institution which provides a holistic approach will offer appropriate linguistic, cultural and academic support for staff and students, including: English language classes for non-native speakers; advice on UK academic cultural practice for students from outside the UK; cross-cultural communication skills for home students; and language, culture and cross-cultural capability development for those taking part in international visits.

Conclusions

No institution can claim to have a monopoly on solutions to the complex issues surrounding internationalising Higher Education. The university in which we both work, Leeds Metropolitan University, is striving to be a world-class regional university, with world-wide horizons, using all our talents to the full. In the spirit of sharing our endeavours to put this vision into practice, we conclude this book with the Leeds Met guidelines on cross-cultural capability (see Appendix), illustrating how we are working to achieve these ends in internationalising the curriculum. The authors would be delighted to receive comments on our approach and comparative examples of how other organisations are working towards similar aims.

World-wide horizons: cross-cultural capability and global perspectives – guidelines for curriculum review

David Killick

Table A.1 Related concepts

Diversity	Ethics	Race
Inclusivity	Justice	Gender
Multiculturalism	Equality	Disability
Widening participation	Sustainability	Socio-economic background
Internationalisation	Citizenship	Nationality
Anti-discriminatory practice	Responsibility	Ethnicity
		Sexuality
		Religion
		Age

Introduction

This document presents guidelines for curriculum review, as required in Aim 5 of the Leeds Metropolitan University Corporate Plan.[1] It has been refreshed in response to feedback and review work, to the new Education Strategy for Assessment, Learning and Teaching, and to broader developments within the University. In particular, the document makes more specific the linkages between cross-cultural capability and global perspectives, and indicates how these relate to internationalisation, diversity, widening participation and sustainability.

The document has three sections:

1   An introduction to cross-cultural capability and global perspectives, and their relevance as graduate attributes for the twenty-first century in a university seeking to achieve an ethos which is both international and multicultural.
2   Key questions for course review, supported by example responses.
3   Practical help for course review teams, which includes a pro forma for review, practical tips provided by Teacher Fellows from across the University, and related internet links.

This document and the review process it supports are intended to stimulate debate on the ethical and educational issues raised, as well as providing a practical stepping stone to facilitate the incorporation of cross-cultural capability and global perspectives across our assessment, learning and teaching practices. This in turn will support and be supported more broadly through non-academic practices, such as improving the sustainability of our facilities, applying ethical purchasing policies, widening participation, and engaging in support work with communities, both regional and international.

Curriculum review, the recruitment of students from diverse cultural backgrounds, both home and international, and increasing opportunities for international and intercultural experiences for students and staff are essential elements in providing the environment to support the development of worldwide horizons and promoting global citizenship.

Section one: cross-cultural capability and global perspectives

Cross-cultural capability

As a graduate attribute for effective and responsible engagement with a globalising world, cross-cultural capability can be seen as comprising three major elements:

1   Intercultural awareness and associated communication skills.
2   International and multicultural perspectives on one's discipline area.
3   Application in practice.

I Intercultural awareness and associated communication skills

Culture is interpreted here in its broadest sense, and from the standpoint that to be human is to be within and outside of a complex of cultures. The University itself is a multicultural environment, comprising individuals from over 100 national cultures, all world religions, a large number of ethnicities, all sexualities, several socio-economic groups, students with disabilities, speakers of many different first languages, and a wide range of ages (to name only a few). The world with which our graduates come into direct contact through their personal and professional lives is increasingly even more culturally diverse.

The awareness of self in relation to the 'other', the ability to communicate effectively across cultures, and the confidence to challenge one's own values and those of others responsibly and ethically are all aspects of what is meant by intercultural awareness and communication skills in a cross-cultural capability context. The focus on responsible and ethical responses is what may be seen to differentiate a cross-cultural capability approach.

2 International and multicultural perspectives on one's discipline area

Here we are concerned to ensure students' understanding of their subject area is representative of perspectives which derive from other cultures, philosophies, religions or nations. Graduates whose terms of reference are purely 'Western' or secular, for example, are not being well prepared to work with or to respond critically to others in their field.

As professionals in education, it is similarly incumbent upon us to understand the differing perspectives, needs, values and aspirations of our students as part of our own cross-cultural capability.

3 Application in practice

The ability to apply the awareness, skills and perspectives outlined above to our personal lives and professional practice.

Global perspectives

The inclusion of global perspectives provides an ethical underpinning for the development of cross-cultural capability, and a values-based ethos for its application. Through global perspectives we seek to demonstrate the relationships between local actions and global consequences, highlighting inequalities, helping us reflect upon major issues such as global warming, world trade, poverty, sustainable development and human migration, and promoting a response based on justice and equality not charity. As with cross-cultural capability, global perspectives in Higher Education build awareness of how these issues relate to a student's discipline, and to the ways in which that discipline may be applied. It is difficult to see how a university in the twenty-first century can ignore such dimensions to its curricula.

Links to related agendas in Higher Education

The University is adopting increasingly proactive approaches to a number of external and internal drivers, including: encouraging widening participation, embracing diversity, broadening internationalisation, taking positive steps to show that we are achieving and demonstrating equal treatment with regard to race, and seeking to ensure our own work contributes to a more sustainable future. Each of these agendas requires us to enable students and ourselves to engage critically with diversity, with local and global issues, and with a variety of perspectives on those issues, ensuring we are all equipped to make considered and informed responses to the differences that we encounter, whether individual, institutional or in the external environment. This applies to all students and staff, not least to the potentially interculturally naive 'traditional' white, middle-class, confident, educationally successful male.

Every student has needs. We have sought in the past to respond to the needs of a relatively homogeneous student population, though we have had to come to terms with issues of gender and race representation, for example. In these two areas we have sought to eliminate direct discrimination from our practices where it has been identified, but we also realise that sexual discrimination and racism can still be encountered. Our ethical and legal responsibilities to promote and evidence clear actions to promote better race relations could hardly be better served than through effective curricular and extra-curricular work to support our students in their ability to respond to the 'other'. Any reflection on the length of time the elimination of sexism or racism is taking is instructive in the light of these broader inclusivity agendas. Underpinning our response to the greatly expanded heterogeneity of our University with a critical appreciation of cultural diversity and global inequities can provide graduates with the opportunity to understand their own role and that of their chosen profession in promoting ethical responses to diversity both locally and internationally.

Higher Education faces the challenge of engaging with sustainability, both in its own working practices and within the curriculum. Work by the Higher Education Academy, supported by HEFCE, to identify and support good practice in the integration of sustainable development in the curriculum should impact across the University. As with intercultural communication, the need for sustainability can be argued as a business case on purely economic grounds. However, a much deeper dimension can be found within global perspectives. Through engaging students with global perspectives within their curriculum, and thereby enabling them to incorporate informed considerations of social, environmental and economic impacts in the application of their curriculum, we are providing a context in which an ethical basis for seeking greater sustainability may inform our graduates. Additionally, though, we need to look beyond the immediate curriculum to the broader student experience as facilitated through membership of the university community. For sustainability this may include, for example, the heating of the immediate environment, the impact of travel to and from classes, impacts of field trips or placements on local environments, and so forth.

Cross-cultural capability, global perspectives and the university environment

Our institutional culture must be one which welcomes diversity as a significant dimension of a twenty-first-century education. It is important to recognise that a cross-cultural capability agenda is not simply about *accommodating* differences in our student body. It is about the even more complex task of *challenging* all students and staff to be capable of recognising, of making informed responses towards, and of living and working comfortably with the diversity they encounter now and in the future. Students who are not challenged to recognise and evaluate their own values, beliefs and behaviours and those of their discipline and its application are unlikely to be able to recognise or lay claim to world-wide horizons.

Insofar as life experience impacts on the ways in which we do our jobs, the increased diversity among our staff and students should have a positive impact in reducing our insularity and lack of confidence and competence when faced with an 'other', as should increasing opportunities for international experience through, for example, off-shore teaching and staff and student exchanges, and opportunities for local engagement through volunteering and civic duties. In this, though, it is important that we take note of the fact that contact, even sustained contact, with 'others' is not in itself any guarantee that we will do anything other than maintain or even reinforce our own insularity and incapability. An informed, engaged and reflective approach across the curriculum and the broader student experience is required if these opportunities are to be transformative.

Leeds Met has a growing Global Perspectives Network which has undertaken innovative developments in stand-alone modules in global perspectives, flexibly designed to integrate into any discipline area, and which is linking with organisations like the Development Education Association[2] to integrate global perspectives across UK Higher Education. Additionally, through initiatives ranging from Leeds Met Africa[3] to the support for the Sanjay Nagar Leprosy Rehabilitation Centre in India, the University is demonstrating through actions its support for justice, sustainability, knowledge transfer, access to education, and poverty reduction.

There are many examples of other work within the University which support and are supported by cross-cultural capability and global perspectives. An indicative (and by no means definitive) list would include:

- establishing a School of Applied Global Ethics;
- promoting local and international volunteering;
- appointing International Teacher Fellows;
- appointing professors of ethics;
- promoting international student mobility;
- gaining Fairtrade status;
- gaining a Green Gown award;
- publishing a daily International Reflection on the website;
- institutional membership of the Development Educational Association;
- a Forum for the Future gap analysis on sustainable literacy in the School of the Built Environment;
- pioneering work in ethical tourism research;
- partnering health worker training programmes in Zambia;
- academic staff in Carnegie Faculty serving as trustees on the World Studies Trust.

Curriculum review for cross-cultural capability and global perspectives, then, is not taking place in isolation, but is just one facet of our work to ensure that an international, multicultural ethos pervades the University, promoting world-wide horizons and global citizenship.

Section two: guidelines for curriculum review

The curriculum review process should critically examine how the student, through participation on the course and as a member of the university community, is enabled:

- to develop the awareness, knowledge and skills to operate in multicultural contexts and across cultural boundaries;
- to develop the awareness, knowledge and skills to operate in a global context;
- to develop values commensurate with those of responsible global citizenship.

'Awareness' and 'values', of course, are invisible and so immeasurable; we may be able to describe them as objectives or learning outcomes, but we cannot assess them. This poses a great problem for the approach we have developed to our course and module descriptions. Equally, values are not discrete, package-able bites. This poses a problem for the approach we have developed for chunking courses into modules and credit points. Rather than narrowly setting learning outcomes or trying to assess cross-cultural capability and global perspectives, therefore, we are seeking to arrive at an ethos across the institution and its programmes, and to support and evidence that ethos through practices, strategies, policies and actions. This, of course, requires us to continuously unearth and critically examine the values and ethics which underpin the way we work. Curriculum review, therefore, is not a one-off process, and for this reason the Assessment, Learning and Teaching Strategy[4] makes cross-cultural capability an explicit element within programme approval and re-approval.

In designing, implementing and reviewing courses and their components we need to examine both the knowledge and the experience within (and surrounding) the course, with a view to what is *likely* to promote and enable the development of the values of cross-cultural capability and global perspectives and, conversely, what has the potential to leave contrary values unchallenged or even supported.

It is unlikely that any real transformation will occur without encountering and engaging with difference in ways which are intellectually and affectively challenging both to ourselves and to our students. For this reason, the key questions in Table A.2 refer not only to integrating global and intercultural perspectives and knowledge, but also to the broader student experience, both directly on the course and less directly through wider opportunities, encouraged or facilitated through participation in the course and membership of a culturally diverse university, whose staff and students themselves present a significant resource for intercultural encounters and perspectives.

Table A.2 Key questions

Key question	Examples
Knowledge	
How does the course seek to incorporate the knowledge and understanding brought to it by students from diverse backgrounds?	– Students are required/encouraged to share and critique personal knowledge through tutorials/ seminars/presentations. – Students produce display artefacts for Faculty spaces which relate aspects of their own cultural heritage.
How are students given the opportunity to analyse and recognise their own tacit knowledge and the influence of their experiences and cultural identity?	– Students are required to work in groups on tasks requiring a variety of personal perspectives. – Students are partnered with students in two universities outside the UK for email discussions on comparative issues within the subject.
How does the course make students aware of the global impacts of professions related to the subject area?	– Explicit reference is made to the Millennium Goals, with students being required to undertake a major study into the impacts which applications of the subject could have on poverty reduction. – Students are presented with case studies from majority world contexts as the basis for personal reflection and a group assignment. – Students are required to incorporate an analysis of the environmental impacts of products and actions associated with their subject in assignments at Levels 2 and 3.
What level of use does the course make of materials from outside the 'traditional' canon?	– Reading lists include literature which is 'non-Western'; politically influenced; written from a feminist perspective; etc. – Students are required to locate and incorporate alternative sources in their assessed coursework.

(Continued overleaf)

Table A.2 continued

Key question	Examples
How does the course enable other knowledge/perspectives to be recognised and valued?	– Assessment criteria include the potential for alternative perspectives/sources. – Students are required to critique a predominant perspective from another/other perspective(s). – Students are required to debate a series of issues within the subject from perspectives taken from other cultures.
How does the course enable students to develop wider perspectives and respond positively to difference?	– Students can elect to take language modules within their core curriculum. – The course actively encourages students to participate in international exchange programmes. – The course requires students to consider how at least one key aspect of their subject relates to issues of disability. – The course incorporates intercultural contact across its student body to promote internationalisation at home (for example, through setting up international tandem learning sets).
How are students given the opportunity to study particular issues of diversity and equal opportunity within their mainstream study?	– Value statements derived from various world religions and political philosophies (including the 'raced' and 'gendered' and 'sexualised' philosophies) are presented and discussed.
In what ways are students helped to examine their own values, compare them with the values of others, and engage in respectful debate where differences occur?	– Alternative ethics and value systems are closely related to practical issues which arise in various parts of the course curriculum.
In what ways does the course enable students to confront hostile discrimination?	– Learning outcomes include the ability to value and debate diverse perspectives coherently and critically.
In what ways does the course seek to link issues of cross-cultural capability, diversity and global responsibility to employability?	– A Global Perspectives module is available as an elective on the programme of study. – Students are guided to include evidence of intercultural learning and international experience within their progress files. – Students submit case studies illustrating the benefits and impacts of including sustainability as a consideration in making business decisions.

Experience at course level

How does the course respond positively to and encourage different learning cultures/needs?	– There is a wide range of learning strategies employed on the course – independent learning, group work, individual work, learning by heart, etc.

– An early component of the course includes working with students to identify their individual learning styles and needs; results are fed back into module/course review and development.

– Specific required learning strategies are explicitly developed, with help and guidance overtly built in.

– Key concepts/knowledge/skills are supported by learning materials in a variety of formats – audio/written/large text/etc.

– Case studies and illustrative examples encompass a range of experiences likely to be of direct relevance to the widest diversity of students.

How does the course encourage students to be curious beyond their own cultural boundaries?

– Students are required to engage with other students beyond their peers through activities such as international student mentoring, interdisciplinary learning sets, etc.

– The School has a dynamic display of materials illustrating how the subject area is interpreted in a range of global contexts.

– Students are encouraged to engage in off-campus learning (for example, on international student exchange, on community projects, in work-based learning activities).

– Students take part in cultural simulation exercises to gain experiential perspectives as the basis for reflections on how different ethnicities may respond to issues within the discipline.

– The course delivery requires students to interact in positive ways with all students in the cohort.

(Continued overleaf)

Table A.2 ontinued

Key question	Examples
How does the course encourage different approaches to teaching?	– Staff have undertaken/regularly undertake development to consider alternative approaches. – Staff have engaged in experiential learning related to cross-cultural capability (for example, to issues relating to disability, gender, sexuality and class). – School policy encourages academic staff to consider the environmental impacts of how the course is delivered. – Staff have engaged in training on non-discriminatory practice which is related to their classroom teaching. – International staff exchanges are encouraged – and the experience disseminated. – The course utilises guest lecturers from a range of cultural backgrounds, such as sexual orientation, degree of physical ability and class experience. – There is a programme of peer observation. – There is a programme of team teaching. – Module evaluation specifically explores student experience of/response to teaching methodology encountered, and to their learning about cross-cultural and anti-discriminatory issues. – There is a positive approach to staff recruitment and deployment which facilitates diversity.
How does the assessment of the course respond to different success criteria?	– Assessment tasks enable/encourage students to present assessed work in a variety of formats. – Learning outcomes/assessment criteria are varied across the course (for example, 'critical reflection' may be being assessed in several modules while 'ability to summarise information from a variety of sources' is absent). – The focus and content of assessment tasks value and recognise the achievements of other cultures, races and religions. – Assessment criteria are focused only on what is central to the module; students are not penalised for peripheral 'presentation' skills.

– The course team has specifically evaluated the assessment mechanisms in consultation with a disability specialist.
– Assessment criteria reward intercultural perspectives.
– Assessment is used diagnostically to discover the strengths and weaknesses of students and to provide appropriate support to improve student performance.
– Accurate explicit briefs are provided for all assessment tasks (whether exams or coursework) in appropriate media and using clear, unambiguous and well-defined language.

Where assessment involves work placements, what attempts are made to monitor and eliminate discrimination that might arise in the workplace?	– Students are provided with guidance and procedures to deal with situations if they arise. – Employers and students agree a learning contract before the placement. – Placements are monitored and a database maintained.
Do the organisation and scheduling of assessment take into account diversity and difference?	– The following issues are considered by course teams when scheduling assessment: religious observation, childcare provision, non-teaching assistance/signers/amanuenses, use of language, assessment venue, technical support.

Experience beyond course level

How does a student on this course benefit from/contribute to the broader social context?	– Students are encouraged to join voluntary societies, charities, and so forth (for example, credits are available for such off-campus activities). – Students undertake a local environment improvement project which is credited through an assessed report. – The course brings in external perspectives through local specialist 'informants' (e.g. disability experts, cultural representatives, etc.). – Students are required to demonstrate an understanding of how aspects of the subject impact upon a group/context other than their own. – The course actively seeks to recruit students from diverse cultural and socio-economic backgrounds. – Student final-year projects involve research and development work in not-for-profit organisations.

(Continued overleaf)

Table A.2 continued

Key question	Examples
How does a student on this course benefit from/contribute to the broader learning support facilities and opportunities?	– Resources have been reviewed to ensure they do not cater only/predominantly for particular students. – Module evaluation disaggregates responses to learning support facilities and opportunities by student 'type'. – Students are encouraged to undertake additional language learning courses; these are made explicit in personal development portfolios.
How does a student on this course benefit from/contribute to the broader educational culture?	– Faculty policy requires student representation at course, faculty and University committees to be representative of the diversity of the student body. – Alternative feedback/participation mechanisms are in place and have lines of communication into the decision-making processes (for example, student focus groups are set up, and research projects into the student experience are encouraged and responded to). – Within the course we specifically explore aspects of the institutional educational culture. – Within the course we allow any student to make a case for submitting assessed work which may appear to be outside 'normal' practice. – Student performance/attrition rates and so forth are monitored by nationality, ethnicity and disability.
How is a student from this course prepared to interact with/benefit from/ contribute to diversity in the world beyond the University?	– Students cannot complete the course without having engaged in some significant form of cross-cultural learning experience and acquiring a thorough understanding of the various sources of unfair discrimination. – The course has made students capable of analysing their own values and ethics, understanding those of others, and debating issues that arise effectively and peacefully.

Section three: help for course teams

Tips from the Teacher Fellows Network

Language

- *Be sensitive to the use of language in the field of disability.* Look on the web at a guide to appropriate and inappropriate language, e.g. use 'blind people' or 'people with visual impairments', not 'the blind', etc.
- *Take care of mass stereotyping in your own use of language* – and challenge students when they use expressions like 'Asians are . . .', 'In Africa . . .', 'The third world . . .', 'Poor people . . .'.
- *The use of the word Gypsy is not always derogatory.* In Romania the Cigan population are generally comfortable with calling themselves Cigan (the Romanian word for Gypsy). It would be patronising to call a Romanian Gypsy anything else.
- *Take care when using race as an adjective.* For example, I once heard someone complain that a 'Pakistani shopkeeper' had been selling cigarettes to underage children. The shopkeeper's actions were clearly wrong, but his race was completely irrelevant.
- *Ensure a comprehensive range of language dictionaries.*
- *Speak and write clearly in good plain English.*
- *Ensure that all printed and online Library guides and publications avoid jargon and conform to Plain English Campaign recommendations.* Consider applying for the Crystal Mark awarded by the Plain English Campaign.
- *Display Welcome signs in different languages in the libraries during induction weeks.*
- *Subtitle Library induction videos.*

Splitting up or pairing students

- *Match up home and international students* when you ask them to 'get into pairs to discuss something'.
- *Pair diverse students as 'critical friends'.* They can read each other's assignment work, comment critically and learn from each other's work.
- *Institute a 'buddy system'*, using home 2nd years with new international 1st years.
- *Think carefully before forcing very small minority groups to split up, at least initially.* If your class contains (for example) only two female students, or only two Chinese students, it may be a good idea to allow them to work in the same team at the beginning of the course.
- *During group work exercises, engineer the groups to contribute to cross-cultural capability.* Experience suggests that, left to their own devices, students will form groups only with their friends, thus remaining in their

'comfort zone'. Requiring students to work in other groups is likely to broaden their experience. Recognise, however, that 'contact, even sustained contact, with "others" is not in itself any guarantee that we will do anything other than maintain or even reinforce our own insularity and incapability'.

Culture awareness

- *Culture shock awareness.* Try placing UK staff and students in simulated situations so they begin to understand this concept.
- *Food.* Have food fairs associated with the national days of different countries.
- *All students should do a mini-project on a (hypothetical) visit to another country*: done by searching the web. It could be planning a holiday, gap year, volunteering, conservation, etc.
- *Not all Europeans are wealthy.* It is wrong to assume that all the world's poor countries are in the Southern hemisphere. Some of the most disadvantaged people in the world live in Eastern Europe, especially in Romania and Moldova.
- *Children have different cultures as well.* It is wrong to assume that children's tastes, needs and interests are the same throughout the world.
- *Treat children with the same respect as adults.* Too often we forget that children's culture is as important to them as an adult's culture is to the adult. They will be just as offended to have their tastes ridiculed as an adult would.
- *Do not assume familiarity with British bureaucracy just because your students are resident in Britain.* If you use examples referring to National Insurance numbers (or the NHS or the Inland Revenue), make sure you explain what a National Insurance number (etc.) is.
- *The implication seems to be that 'cross-culture' is the same as 'international/ overseas'. But we have a multitude of cultures indigenous to the UK and we should be encouraging cross-over between them.* There is particular urgency for us to find ways of helping white (and some black) British people to understand Islamic culture in the UK, in the Middle East, in Indonesia, in Turkey – in fact, its various forms all over the globe. Our British Muslim students and staff are a major resource here, and we should be actively engaging everyone to join in a series of Islamic dialogues.
- *Encourage an international experience for all students by promoting and displaying international materials* – for example, the Library collection of world film and literature.
- *Ensure access to international newspapers and other news sources online and/or in print.*

Assessment

- *Encourage assessment criteria to reward intercultural perspectives.* Many module assessments could have some weighted component that relates to this. The students are then 'forced' to think about and address the issues.
- *Incorporate CCC into project work.* Almost all project work will involve ethical and CCC issues. Encourage students to consider these, and allow for such in assessment criteria.
- *Ask yourself 'Am I excluding/offending/disadvantaging anyone in my practice?'* It might be wise, for example, to evaluate your assessment mechanisms with a disability specialist. Teaching examples centred on (say) cricket should be complemented with other examples that cater for people from cultural backgrounds that don't include cricket.
- *Seek feedback through Library surveys/focus groups.*
- *Focus on content not form* – for example, 'coherence' is often interpreted to mean 'linear structure and argument', but not all cultures consider that this kind of structure produces a coherent piece of work. Does an alternative structure to the presentation of ideas necessarily mean the learning outcomes for a specific module have not been achieved?

Teaching methods

- *In class get them to use examples from their own experience.* When talking about health services don't just focus on the NHS but ask for opinions from a wider range of global health care services.
- *Use CCC in counter-arguments.* The lecturer I remember most from my (distant) undergraduate days could come up with an instant counter-argument to any point anyone ever made – a very effective way of encouraging critical thinking. Try to base such counter-arguments on CCC issues.
- *In design projects, encourage students to ask 'Who am I excluding?'* Even the most apparently innocuous design may inadvertently exclude; for example, a computer system using text excludes people who cannot read. Even if the design is not excluding anybody, it's good to get students to consider the question.
- *Hold extra information skills sessions including during vacations.*
- *Ask learning advisers and other fund holders to liaise with academic staff in purchasing books and other Library materials*, with an international, or non-UK-centric perspective where possible and appropriate.

E-learning

- *Use e-learning to actively build bridges and introduce collaboration with students in other countries.*

- *Start podcasting* (http://www.ipodder.org/whatIsPodcasting, and http://www.podcastingnews.com/forum/link_18.htm) so that students can download materials appropriate to greater cultural awareness (different themes at regular times).

Staff development

- *Encourage (and pay for) staff to obtain a qualification* in Teaching English as a Foreign Language so they understand the difficulties students have in not having English as a first language, and so they are exposed to non-UK culture.
- *Support some staff to do overseas volunteer work.*
- *Organise a plain English course for Library staff.*
- *Keep up to date with initiatives and good practice in other universities.*
- *Share international perspectives* – staff returning from overseas visits lead a seminar each semester.
- *Raise cross-cultural capability and global perspectives in your appraisal and staff development meeting.*

Related links

Internal

The Global Perspectives Network at Leeds Met: www.leedsmet.ac.uk/gpn
Leeds Met – Sustainable Tourism: http://www.leedsmet.ac.uk/lsif/the/sustainability.htm
Leeds Met Strategy Documents: http://www.leedsmet.ac.uk/staff/documents.htm

UK sites

Department for International Development (DfID): http://www.dfid.gov.uk/
Royal Geographical Society – DFID Project on Global Perspectives in Higher Education (project reports, case studies and links): http://www.rgs.org/OurWork/Research+and+Higher+Education/GeographyInHEProjects/The+global+perspectives+of+British+students.htm
Development Education Association (DEA): http://www.dea.org.uk/
Council for International Education (UKCOSA): http://www.ukcosa.org.uk/
World Studies Trust – Global Teacher Project: http://www.globalteacher.org.uk/index.htm
Higher Education Academy (HEA): http://www.heacademy.ac.uk/
HEA subject centres involved in work on global perspectives:

- Philosophical and Religious Studies Subject Centre – Supporting Cultural

and Religious Diversity Interim Report: http://www.prs-ltsn.ac.uk/
diversity/interim_report.html
- Business, Management, Accountancy and Finance Subject Centre: http://
  www.business.heacademy.ac.uk/
- Economics Network: http://www.economics.heacademy.ac.uk/
- Geography, Earth and Environmental Sciences Subject Centre: http://
  www.gees.ac.uk/
- Hospitality, Leisure, Sport and Tourism Network: http://www.
  hlst.heacademy.ac.uk/
- Languages, Linguistics and Area Studies Subject Centre: http://www.
  llas.ac.uk/
- Sociology, Anthropology, Politics Subject Network: http://www.c-sap.
  bham.ac.uk/

HE Academy – sustainable development: http://www.heacademy.ac.uk/
sustainability.htm
Forum for the Future: http://www.forumforthefuture.org.uk
HEFCE – sustainable development in HE: http://www.hefce.ac.uk/pubs/
hefce/2005/05_28
HEFCE – equality and diversity monitoring: http://www.hefce.ac.uk/pubs/
hefce/2004/04_14/
HEFCE – successful student diversity case studies: http://www.hefce.ac.uk/
pubs/hefce/2002/02_48.htm
HEA – widening participation: http://www.heacademy.ac.uk/199.htm
Commission for Racial Equality – re Race Relations (Amendment) Act:
http://www.cre.gov.uk/legal/rra.html
UK Socrates: Erasmus Council: http://www.erasmus.ac.uk/

International sites

UNESCO – Decade of Education for Sustainable Development: http://
portal.unesco.org/education/en/ev.php-
URL_ID=27234&URL_DO=DO_TOPIC&URL_SECTION=201.html
United Nations – Millennium Goals: http://www.un.org/millenniumgoals/
American Council on Education: http://www.acenet.edu/AM/Template.cfm
?Section=International&Template=/CM/HTMLDisplay.cfm&Content
ID=9578
Association of International Educators (NAFSA): http://www.nafsa.org/
National Service Learning (integrating volunteering and curriculum – USA):
http://www.servicelearning.org/
Campus Compact (integrating volunteering and curriculum – USA): http://
www.compact.org/
Council of Europe – European Year of Citizenship through Education initia-
tive: http://www.coe.int/T/E/Com/Files/Themes/ECD/

European Commission – Socrates programmes: http://europa.eu.int/comm/education/programmes/socrates/socrates_en.html
European Association for International Education: http://www.eaie.nl/
Australian Government Research Database (International Education): http://aei.dest.gov.au/AEI/PublicationsAndResearch/ResearchDatabase/Default

Curriculum review report form

Please utilise the key questions form in Table A.3 as the basis for your review. Courses (or programmes or schemes) are encouraged to respond as appropriate for their own subject areas, student populations and professional contexts. The table is a guide, not a tick list, and consideration of the key questions should be approached as a developmental process rather than simply an audit of existing practice.

Please email completed reports to: d.killick@leedsmet.ac.uk.

Table A.3 Curriculum review report form

Title of provision:

School:

Person responsible for the report:

Date of review completion:

Key question	*Examples*
Knowledge	
How does the course seek to incorporate the knowledge and understanding brought to it by students from diverse backgrounds?	
How are students given the opportunity to analyse and recognise their own tacit knowledge and the influence of their experiences and cultural identity?	
How does the course make students aware of the global impacts of professions related to the subject area?	
What level of use does the course make of materials from outside the 'traditional' canon?	
How does the course enable other knowledge/perspectives to be recognised and valued?	
How does the course enable students to develop wider perspectives and respond positively to difference?	
How are students given the opportunity to study particular issues of diversity and equal opportunity within their mainstream study?	

In what ways are students helped to examine their
own values, compare them with the values of
others, and engage in respectful debate where
differences occur?

In what ways does the course enable students to
confront hostile discrimination?
In what ways does the course seek to link issues of
cross-cultural capability, diversity and global
responsibility to employability?

Experience at course level

How does the course respond positively to and
encourage different learning cultures/needs?

How does the course encourage students to be
curious beyond their own cultural boundaries?

How does the course encourage different
approaches to teaching?

How does the assessment of the course respond
to different success criteria?

Where assessment involves work placements, what
attempts are made to monitor and eliminate
discrimination that might arise in the workplace?

Does the organisation and scheduling of
assessment take into account diversity and
difference?

Experience beyond course level

How does a student on this course benefit from/
contribute to the broader social context?

How does a student on this course benefit from/
contribute to the broader learning support
facilities and opportunities?

How does a student on this course benefit from/
contribute to the broader educational culture?

How is a student from this course prepared to
interact with/benefit from/contribute to diversity
in the world beyond the University?

This document was authored by David Killick with the advice and support
of colleagues across the University. Particular thanks to Max Farrar, Alison
Jones, Elspeth Jones and Sheila Scraton for their extensive input to the first
version, dated 2003.

Notes

1 http://www.leedsmet.ac.uk/about/keydocuments/corp_plan_2004–08.pdf

2 http://www.dea.org.uk/
3 http://www.leedsmet.ac.uk/internat/region/africa/leedsmetafrica.htm
4 http://www.leedsmet.ac.uk/about/keydocuments/
   Version32AssesmentTeachingLearningStrategy1.pdf

Bibliography

Abu-Arab, A. (2005) 'Language and academic skills advising in the era of internationalisation: a multiliteracies perspective', LAS 2005: Critiquing and reflecting, Monash University.

Ackers, J. (1997) 'Evaluating UK courses: the perspective of the overseas student', in D. McNamara and R. Harris (eds), *Overseas Students in Higher Education: Issues in Teaching and Learning*, pp. 187–200, London: Routledge.

Alred, G. (2003) 'Becoming a "better stranger": a therapeutic perspective on intercultural experience and/as education', in G. Alred, M. Byram and M. Fleming, *Intercultural Experience and Education*, Clevedon: Multilingual Matters.

Alred, G., Byram, M. and Fleming, M. (2003) *Intercultural Experience and Education*, Clevedon: Multilingual Matters.

Andrews, T., Dekkers, J. and Solas, J. (1998) 'What really counts? A report on a pilot investigation identifying the significance of learning style and cultural background for overseas students in flexible learning environments', in *Proceedings of the 3rd International Conference on Open Learning*, pp. 167–72, Brisbane: Queensland Open Learning Network.

Angelo, T. (1999) 'Doing assessment as if learning matters most', *AAHE Bulletin*, May.

Angelo, T. A. and Cross, K. P. (1993) *Classroom Assessment Techniques: A Handbook for College Teachers*, Jossey-Bass, Hoboken, NJ.

Annette, J. (2003) 'Community and citizenship education', in A. Lockyer, B. Crick and J. Annette (eds), *Education for Democratic Citizenship*, Aldershot: Ashgate Publishing.

Arthur, N. (1998) 'Managing cross-cultural transitions', in L. Donaldson, B. Hiebert, M. Pyryt and N. Arthur, *Making Transitions Work: Navigating the Changes*, Calgary: Detselig Enterprises.

Association of Graduate Careers Advisory Services (AGCAS) (2005) *Going Global: A Staff Guide to Enhancing International Students' Employability*, Sheffield: AGCAS.

Association of Graduate Recruiters (AGR) (1995) *Skills for Graduates in the 21st Century*, Cambridge: AGR.

Aulakh, G., Brady, P., Dunwoodie, K., Perry, J., Roff, G. and Steward, M. (1997) *Internationalising the Curriculum across RMIT University*, Melbourne: RMIT. Available online at: http://www.rmit.edu.au/browse/Our%20Organisation%2FInternational%2FInformation%20and%20Services%2FPolicies%20and%20

Activities%2FInternationalising%20RMIT%E2%80%99s%20teaching%20and%20
learning%2FInternationalising%20the%20University:%20implications%20for%20
teaching%20and%20learning%2FCSDF%20Project%20Full%20Report:%20
Internationalising%20the%20University/.

Baldwin, G., Jones, R. and Prince, N. (1998) *Report on Survey of International Students at the University of Melbourne*, Melbourne: Centre for Study of Higher Education, RMIT.

Ballard, B. and Clanchy, J. (1997) *Teaching International Students: A Brief Guide for Lecturers and Supervisors*, Deakin, ACT: IDP Education Australia.

Barnett, R. (2000) *Realizing the University in an Age of Supercomplexity*, Ballmoor, UK: Society for Research into Higher Education and Open University Press.

Baumgart, N. and Halse, C. (1999) 'Approaches to learning across cultures: the role of assessment', *Assessment in Education*, 6(3), pp. 321–39.

Bell, M. (2004) 'Internationalising the higher education curriculum: do academics agree?', University of Wollongong, Australia. Available online at: http://hersda 2004.curtin.edu.my/Contributions/RPapers/P036-jt.pdf.

Bennett, M. (1993) 'Towards ethnorelativism: a developmental model of intercultural sensitivity', in M. Paige (ed.), *Education for the Intercultural Experience*, Yarmouth, MA: Intercultural Press.

Biggs, J. B. (1996) 'Western misperceptions of the Confucian-heritage learning culture', in D. Watkins and J. Biggs (eds), *The Chinese Learner: Cultural, Psychological, and Contextual Influences*, pp. 45–68, Hong Kong: Centre for Comparative Research in Education/Camberwell, Victoria: Australian Council for Educational Research.

Biggs, J. B. (1998) 'Learning from the Confucian heritage: so size doesn't matter', *International Journal of Educational Research*, 29, pp. 723–38.

Biggs, J. (1999) 'Teaching international students', in J. Biggs (ed.), *Teaching for Quality Learning at University*, pp. 121–40, Buckingham: Society for Research into Higher Education and Open University Press.

Biggs, J. B. and Watkins, D. A. (2001) 'Insights into the Chinese learner', in D. Watkins and J. Biggs (eds), *Teaching the Chinese Learner*, pp. 277–300, Hong Kong: Comparative Education Research Centre.

Bliss, A. (1999) 'Diversity and language: ESL students in the university classroom'. Available online at: http://www.Colorado.EDU/ftep/support/diversity/div02.html.

Boud, D. (1995) 'Assessment and learning: contradictory or complementary?', in P. Knight (ed.), *Assessment for Learning in Higher Education*, pp. 35–48, London: Kogan Page.

Boud, D., Keogh, R. and Walker, D. (eds) (1985) *Reflection: Turning Experience into Learning*, London: Routledge.

Bowden, J., Hart, G. and Trigwell, K. (2000a) 'Generic capabilities of ATN university graduates', Draft report, RMIT University, Queensland University of Technology, University of Technology Sydney, University of South Australia, Curtin University.

Bowden, J., King, B., Trigwell, K. and Watts, O. (2000b) *Generic Capabilities of ATN University Graduates*, Melbourne: RMIT University, Queensland University of Technology, University of South Australia, Curtin University, University of Technology Sydney. Available online at: http://www.clt.uts.edu.au/ATN.grad. cap.project.index.html.

Bremer, L. and van der Wende, M. (1995) (eds), *Internationalising the Curriculum in Higher Education: Experiences in the Netherlands*, The Hague: Netherlands Organisation for International Co-operation in Higher Education.

Bretag, T. (2003) 'Reconceptualising the internationalisation of higher education', Invited keynote address to the National Union of Students National Conference: The Hidden Agenda, Adelaide University, South Australia, July.

Bringle, R. G. and Hatcher, J. A. (1995) 'A service-learning curriculum for faculty', *Michigan Journal of Community Service Learning*, 2, pp. 112–22.

British Council (2002) *Feeling at Home: A Guide to Issues of Cultural Awareness for Those Working with International Students*, 2nd edn, London: British Council.

Brown, G., Bull, J. and Pendlebury, M. (1997) *Assessing Student Learning in Higher Education*, London: Routledge.

Brown, S. and Knight, P. (1994) *Assessing Learners in Higher Education*, London: Kogan Page.

California State University Service Learning. Available online at: http://www.csulb.edu/divisions/aa/personnel/cce/.

Callan, H. (2000) 'Higher education internationalization strategies: of marginal significance or all pervasive?', *Higher Education in Europe*, 25(1), pp. 15–24, UNESCO.

Carroll, J. (2002) *A Handbook for Deterring Plagiarism in Higher Education*, Oxford: Oxford Centre for Staff and Learning Development.

Carroll, J. (2005) 'Strategies for becoming more explicit', in J. Carroll and J. Ryan (eds), *Teaching International Students: Improving Learning for All*, pp. 26–34, London: Routledge.

Carroll, J. and Ryan, J. (2005) *Teaching International Students: Improving Learning for All*, London: Routledge.

Caruana, V. and Hanstock, J. (2003) 'Internationalising the curriculum: from policy to practice', Conference proceedings of Education in a Changing Environment, pp. 1–11, University of Salford, Salford, UK.

Centro Europeo para el Desarrollo de la Formación Profesional (n.d.) 'Iniciativas nacionales para promover el aprendizaje a lo largo de la vida en Europa'. Available online at: http://www.eurydice.org/ressources/eurydice/pdf/0_integral/026ES.pdf#search=%22iniciativas%20nacionales%20para%20promover%20el%20aprendizaje%20a%20lo%20largo%20de%20la%20Vida%20en%20europa%22

Chalmers, D. and Volet, S. (1997) 'Common misconceptions about students from South-East Asia studying in Australia', *Higher Education Research and Development*, 16(1), pp. 87–98.

Chamberlin-Quinlisk, C. R. (2005) 'Across continents or across the street: using local resources to cultivate intercultural awareness', *Intercultural Education*, 16(5), pp. 469–79.

Chang, L. (2004) 'Chinese job search mismatch', *Wall Street Journal*, 22 June 2004, p. A17.

CHEERS (n.d.) 'Careers after higher education: a European research study'. Available online at: http://www.uni-kassel.de/wz1/TSEREGS/sume.htm.

China Education News (2004) 'Master's degree holders facing embarrassing situation in employment', 19 December 2004.

Cogan, J. J. (1998) 'Internationalisation through networking and curricular infusion', in J. A. Metstenhauser and B. J. Ellingboe (eds), *Reforming the Higher Education Curriculum*, pp. 106–17, Phoenix, AZ: Oryx Press.

Coleman, J. (2004) 'Residence abroad'. Available online at: http://www.lang.ltsn. ac.uk/resources/goodpractice.aspx?resourceid=2157.

Connor, S. (1989) *The Post Modern Culture*, Oxford: Blackwell.

Cortazzi, M. and Jin, L. (1997) 'Communication for learning across cultures', in N. McNamara and R. Harris (eds), *Overseas Students in Higher Education: Issues in Teaching and Learning*, London: Routledge.

Cowan, J. (2006) *On Becoming an Innovative University Teacher: Reflection in Action*, Maidenhead: Open University Press.

Crowther, P., Joris, M., Otten, M., Nilsson, B., Teekens, H. and Wachter, B. (2000) 'Internationalisation at home: a position paper', European Association for International Education. Available online at: http://www.nuffic.nl/pdf/netwerk/ IAH-Booklet.pdf (accessed July 2006).

Curry, P., Sherry, R. and Tunney, O. (2003) 'What transferable skills do employers look for in third-level graduates?' Available online at: http://www.skillsproject.ie/ downloads/pdfs/Employer%20Survey%20Report.pdf.

Dachi, H. and Garrett, R. (2002) *Child Labour and its Impact on Children's Access to and Participation in Primary Education*, London: Department for International Development.

Dahlin, B. and Watkins, D. (1997) 'The role of repetition in the process of memorising and understanding', Paper presented at the Biennial Conference of the European Association for Research on Learning and Instruction, Athens, August.

Dawe, G., Jucker, R. and Martin, S. (2005) *Sustainable Development in Higher Education: Current Practice and Future Developments*, London: HEA.

Deardorff, D. K. and Hunter, W. (2006) 'Educating global-ready graduates', NAFSA, *International Educator*, 15(3).

Dearing, R. (1997) *Higher Education in the Learning Society*, London: HMSO.

Delors, J. (Chair) (1996) *Learning: The Treasure Within*, Report of the International Commission on Education for the Twenty-first Century, Paris: UNESCO.

Department of the Environment, Department for Education and Employment, and Welsh Office (1993) *Environmental Responsibility: An Agenda for Further and Higher Education* (the Toyne Report), London: HMSO.

De Vita, G. (2000) 'Inclusive approaches to effective communication and active participation in the multicultural classroom: an international business and management context', *Active Learning in Higher Education*, 1(2), pp. 168–80.

De Vita, G. (2001a) 'Learning styles, culture and inclusive instruction in the multicultural classroom: a business and management perspective', *Innovations in Education and Teaching International*, 38(2), pp. 68–78.

De Vita, G. (2001b) 'The use of group work in large and diverse business management classes: some critical issues', *International Journal of Management Education*, 1(3), pp. 27–35.

De Vita, G. (2002a) 'Does multicultural group work really pull UK students' average down?', *Assessment and Evaluation in Higher Education*, 27(2), pp. 153–61.

De Vita, G. (2002b) 'Cultural equivalence in the assessment of home and international business management students: a UK exploratory study', *Studies in Higher Education*, 27(2), pp. 221–31.

De Vita, G. (2004) 'Integration and independent learning in a business synoptic module for international credit entry students', *Teaching in Higher Education*, 9(1), pp. 69–81.

De Vita, G. (2005a) 'Tracking the academic progression of home and international business management students: an exploratory study', *Brookes e-Journal of Learning and Teaching*, 1(3), September.

De Vita, G. (2005b) 'Fostering intercultural learning through multicultural group-work', in J. Carroll and J. Ryan (eds), *Teaching International Students: Improving Learning for All*, pp. 75–83, London: Routledge.

De Vita, G. and Case, P. (2003) 'Rethinking the internationalisation agenda in UK higher education', *Journal of Further and Higher Education*, 27(4), pp. 383–98.

Dewey, J. (1916) *Democracy and Education: An Introduction to the Philosophy of Education*, New York: Free Press.

DfES (2004) *Putting the World into World-Class Education*, London: HMSO.

DFID (1999a) *Building Support for Development*. Available online from: www.dfid. gov.uk/pubs/files/buildingsupportdevelopment.pdf (accessed 25 October 2006).

DFID (1999) *Helping not Hurting Children*, London: DFID.

Dobson, I. R., Sharma, R. and Calderon, A. J. (1998) 'The comparative performance of overseas and Australian undergraduates', in D. Davies and A. Olsen (eds), *Outcomes of International Education: Research Findings*, pp. 3–18, Canberra: IDP Education Australia.

Du-Babcock, B. (2002) 'Teaching a large class in Hong Kong', *Business Communication Quarterly*, 65(1), pp. 80–8.

Dunn, L., Morgan, C., O'Reilly, M. and Parry, S. (2004) *The Student Assessment Handbook: New Directions in Traditional and Online Assessment*, London: Routledge.

Dwyer, M. (2004) 'The internship effect', *International Educator*, 13, pp. 18–20.

Economist (2005) 'China's people problem'. Available online at: http://www.economist. com/printedition/PrinterFriendly.cfm?story_id=3868539.

Edwards, V. and Ran, A. (2006) 'Meeting the needs of Chinese students in UK universities'. Available online at: http://www.ncll.org.uk/10_about/50_research/ 10_research_projects/MeetingTheNeeds.pdf (accessed October 2006).

Edwards, R., Crosling, G., Petrovic-Lazarovic, S. and O'Neil, P. (2003) 'Internationalisation of business education: meaning and implementation', *Higher Education Research and Development*, 22(2), pp. 184–92.

Fallon, G. and Brown, R. B. (1999) 'What about the workers? Academic staff opinions about working with non-UK postgraduate students in higher education', *Journal of Further and Higher Education*, 23(1), pp. 41–52.

Farrar, Max (2005) 'Leeds foot-soldiers and the London bombs', *openDemocracy*, 22 July 2005. Available online at: www.opendemocracy.net/articles/View.jsp?id=2696.

Farrar, Max (2006) 'When alienation turns to nihilism: the dilemmas posed for diversity post 7/7', *Conversations in Religion and Theology*, 4(1), May, pp. 98–123.

Felder, R. M. and Soloman, B. A. (1999) 'Index of learning styles'. Available at www2.ncsu.edu/unity/lockers/users/f/felder/public/ILSdir/ILS-a.htm.

Financial Times (2005a) 'Graduates may fail Chinese economy'. Available online at: http://www.mckinsey.com/aboutus/mckinseynews/pressarchive/pdf/RP2105_ Graduates.pdf.

Financial Times (2005b) 'The Achilles' heel of Chinese business'. Available online at: http://www.mckinsey.com/aboutus/mckinseynews/pressarchive/pdf/RP2105_ Achilles.pdf.

Fisher, S. and Hicks, D. (1985) *World Studies 8–13: A Teacher's Handbook*, Edinburgh: Oliver and Boyd.

Foundation for International Learning. Available online at: http://www.fie.org.uk.

Fox, C. (1996) 'Listening to the other: mapping intercultural communication in postcolonial educational consultancies', in R. Paulston (ed.), *Social Cartography: Mapping Ways of Seeing Social and Educational Change*, London: Garland Publishing.

Fryer, B. (2005) 'Universities and citizenship: the forgotten dimension?', in S. Robinson and C. Katulushi (eds), *Values in Higher Education*, Glamorgan: Aureus.

Furnham, A. and Bochner, S. (1982) *Culture Shock: Psychological Reactions to Unfamiliar Environments*, London: Methuen.

Gao, L. B. and Watkins, D. (2002) 'Conceptions of teaching held by school science teachers in PR China: identification and cross-cultural comparisons', *International Journal of Science Education*, 24(1), pp. 61–79.

Global Perspectives in Higher Education. Available online at: http://www.rgs.org/OurWork/Research+and+Higher+Education/GeographyInHEProjects/The+global+perspectives+of+British+students.htm (accessed November 2006).

Greenholz, J. (2003) 'Socratic teachers and Confucian learners: examining the benefits and pitfalls of a year abroad', *Language and Intercultural Communication*, 3(2), pp. 122–30.

Haigh, M. J. (2002) 'Internationalisation of the curriculum: designing inclusive education for a small world', *Journal of Geography in Higher Education*, 26(1), pp. 49–66, Carfax Publishing.

Halpin, E., Trevorrow, P., Webb, D. and Wright, S. (eds) (2006) *Cyberwar, Netwar and the Revolution in Military Affairs*, Basingstoke: Palgrave.

Handa, N. and Power, C. (2005) 'Land and discover! A case study investigating the cultural context of plagiarism', *Journal of University Teaching and Learning Practice*, 2(3b). Available online at: http://jutlp.uow.edu.au/ (accessed May 2006).

Harris, R. (1997) 'Overseas students in the United Kingdom university system', in D. McNamara and R. Harris (eds), *Overseas Students in Higher Education: Issues in Teaching and Learning*, pp. 30–45, London: Routledge.

Harvey, L. and Green, D. (1994) *Employer Satisfaction*, Birmingham: Quality in Higher Education Project, University of Central England.

Harvey, L. and Knight, P. (2003) *Briefings on Employability 5*, York: Enhancing Student Employability Co-ordination Team/LTSN Generic Centre.

Harvey, L., Moon, S. and Geall, V. with Bower, R. (1997) *Graduates' Work: Organisational Change and Students Attributes*, Birmingham: CRQ, AGR (supported by DSEE and CIHE).

Hawkridge, D. (2005) 'Enhancing students' employability: the national scene in business, management and accountancy', Paper prepared for the Higher Education Academy by the Subject Centre for Business, Management and Accountancy (BEST), York.

Hayden, M. and Thompson, J. (1995) 'International schools and international education: a relationship reviewed', *Oxford Review of Education*, 21(3), pp. 327–45.

Hedge, T. (2000) *Teaching and Learning in the Language Classroom*, Oxford: Oxford University Press.

HEFCE (2003) 'International strategy for HEFCE'. Available online at: http://www.hefce.ac.uk/partners/world/strategy (accessed October 2006).

HEFCE (2005) 'Sustainable development in higher education: consultation on a support strategy and action plan'. Available online at: www.hefce.ac.uk/pubs/hefce/2005/05/05_28/05_28.doc (accessed 25 October 2006).

Hellmundt, S. C. (2003) 'Theory and practice: strategies to promote intercultural communication among international and local students', Unpublished manuscript.

Hicks, D. (2003) 'Thirty years of global education: a reminder of key principles and ingredients', *Educational Review*, 55(3), London: Carfax.

Higher Education Academy (HEA) (2006) *Sustainable Development in Higher Education: Current Practice and Future Developments – A Progress Report for Senior Managers*, London: HEA.

Higher Education Academy/ESECT (n.d.) 'Employability'. Available online at: http://www.heacademy.ac.uk/869.htm.

'Higher education and graduate employment in Europe' (2000) Final report. Available online at: http://improving-ser.jrc.it/default/show.gx?Object.object_id=TSER----0000000000000A74&_app.page=show-TSR.html.

Higher Education Careers Services Unit (HECSU) (2005) 'Careers advisory services and international students'. Available online at: http://www.hecsu.ac.uk/cms/ShowPage/Home_page/Research_reports/CASIS/p!ebfdekm.

Higher Education Partnership for Sustainability. Available online at: www.heps.org.uk.

Higher Education Statistics Agency (HESA) (1996) *Students in Higher Education Institutions 1994/1995*, Cheltenham: HESA.

Higher Education Statistics Agency (2000) *Students in Higher Education Institutions 1998/1999*, Cheltenham: HESA.

Higher Education Statistics Agency (2004) *Students in Higher Education Institutions 2002/2003*, Cheltenham: HESA.

Hofstede, G. (1991) *Cultures and Organizations: Intercultural Cooperation and Its Importance for Survival: Software of the Mind*, London: Harper Collins.

Hofstede, G. (2001) *Culture's Consequences: Comparing Values, Behaviors, Institutions, and Organisations across Nations*, Thousand Oaks, CA: Sage Publications.

Hofstede, G. (2005) *Cultures and Organizations: Software of the Mind*, New York: McGraw-Hill.

Holmes, A. and Brown, S. (2000) 'The themed approach to audit', in A. Holmes and S. Brown (eds), *Internal Audit in Higher Education*, London: Kogan Page.

Holmes, P. (2004) 'Negotiating differences in learning and intercultural communication', *Business Communication Quarterly*, 67(3), pp. 294–307.

Jiménez, A. J., Sánchez, C. J. and Montero, G. R. (2003) *Educación Superior y Empleo: la Situación de los Jóvenes Titulados en España*, Granada: Universidad de Granada.

Kellogg Commission on the Future of State and Land Grant Universities (1999) *Returning to our Roots: The Engaged Institution Third Report*, Washington, DC: National Association of State Universities and Land Grant Colleges.

Kelo, M. (2006) *Support for International Students in Higher Education: Practice and Principles*, Bonn: Lemmens Verlags- & Mediengesellschaft.

Kelo, M., Teichler, U. and Wächter, B. (eds) (2006) *EURODATA: Student Mobility in European Higher Education,* Bonn: Lemmens Verlags- & Mediengesellschaft.

Kezar, A. and Eckel, P. D. (2002) 'The effect of *institucional cultura* on change strategies in higher education: universal principles or culturally responsive concepts?', *Journal of Higher Education*, 73(4), pp. 435–60, Ohio State University. Available online at: http://muse.jhu.edu/journals/journal_higher-education/ (accessed October 2006).

Kielland, A. (2006) *Children at Work: Child Labor Practices in Africa*, New York: Lynne Rienner.

Knight, J. (1994) *Internationalization: Elements and Checkpoints*, CBIE Research No. 7, Ottawa: Canada Bureau for International Education.

Knight J. (2004) 'Internationalization remodeled: definitions, approaches, and rationales', *Journal of Studies in International Education*, 8(1), pp. 5–31, Association for Studies in International Education.

Knight, J. and de Wit, H. (1995) 'Strategies for internationalisation of higher education: historical and conceptual perspectives', in H. de Wit (ed.), *Strategies for Internationalisation of Higher Education*, Amsterdam: EAIE.

Knight, J. and de Wit, H. (1997) *Internationalisation of Higher Education in Asia Pacific Countries*, Amsterdam: European Association for International Education.

Knight, P. (ed.) (1995) *Assessment for Learning in Higher Education*, pp. 35–48, London: Kogan Page.

Kung, H. (1991) *Global Responsibility*, London: SCM.

Kung, H. and Schmidt, H. (eds) (1998) *Global Ethic and Global Responsibilities*, London: SCM.

Ladd, P. and Ruby, R. (1999) 'Learning styles and adjustment issues of international students', *Journal of Education for Business*, 74(6), pp. 363–7.

Lave, J. (1988) *Cognition in Practice: Mind, Mathematics, and Culture in Everyday Life*, Cambridge: Cambridge University Press.

Leask, B. (2001) 'Bridging the gap: internationalizing university curricula', *Journal of Studies in International Education*, 5(2), pp. 100–15, Association for Studies in International Education.

Leask, B. (2003) 'Beyond the numbers: levels and layers of internationalisation to utilise and support growth and diversity', Conference paper: IDP AIEC Conference, October.

Leask, B. (2005a) 'Competing rationales for and discourses of internationalisation: implications for academic staff development', Higher Education Research and Development Society (HERDSA), University of South Australia.

Leask, B. (2005b) 'Internationalisation of the curriculum: teaching and learning', in J. Carroll and J. Ryan (2005) *Teaching International Students: Improving Learning for All*, London: Routledge.

Leask, B., Hicks, M., Kohler, M. and King, B. (2005) 'AVCC offshore quality project: a professional development framework for academic staff teaching Australian programs offshore', University of South Australia, Adelaide. Available online at: http://aei.dest.gov.au/AEI/GovernmentActivities/QAAustralianEducationAnd TrainingSystem/USA_1.htm.

Ledwith, S., Lee, A., Manfredi, S. and Wildish, C. (1996) *Multiculturalism: Student Group Work and Assessment*, Oxford: Oxford Brookes University.

Lee, S. (2003) 'Inaugural lecture'. Available online at: http://www.lmu.ac.uk/the_news/docs/proflee_inaugural.pdf (accessed November 2006).

Lee, W. O. (1996) 'The cultural context of Chinese learners: conceptions of learning in the Confucian tradition', in D. Watkins and J. Biggs (eds), *The Chinese Learner*, pp. 45–67, Hong Kong: Comparative Education Research Centre.

Leeds Metropolitan University (2003) 'Internationalisation Strategy'. Available online at: http://www.leedsmet.ac.uk/internat/faculty/docs/Internationalisation%20Final. doc (accessed October 2006).

Leeds Metropolitan University (2004) 'Corporate Plan'. Available online at: http:// www.leedsmet.ac.uk/about/keydocuments/corp_plan_2004–08.pdf   (accessed October 2006).

Leeds Metropolitan University (2005) 'Assessment, Learning and Teaching Strategy'. Available online at: http://www.leedsmet.ac.uk/about/keydocuments/Version32 AssesmentTeachingLearningStrategy1.pdf (accessed October 2006).

Leeds Metropolitan University, 'International Reflections'. Available online at: http:// www.leedsmet.ac.uk/internat/reflects/index.htm.

Lester, K. (2003) *Are Your Students Employable? Employability Issues for Student Unions and Development Workers*, York: Learning and Teaching Support Network.

Lewis, T. L. and Neisenbaum, R. A. (2005) 'The benefits of short-term study abroad', *Chronicle of Higher Education*, 51(39), p. 20. Available online at: http://chronicle. com/.

Lightbown, P. M. and Spada, N. (2006) *How Languages are Learned*, 3rd edn, Oxford: Oxford University Press.

Lo Bianco, J., Liddicoat, A. J. and Crozet, C. (1999) 'Intercultural competence: from language policy to language eduaction', in C. Crozet, A. J. Liddicoat and J. Lo Bianco, *Striving for the Third Place: Intercultural Competence through Language Education*, Canberra: Language Australia.

Lockyer, A., Crick, B. and Annette, J. (eds) (2003) *Education for Democratic Citizenship*, Aldershot: Ashgate Publishing.

London Metropolitan University peer support scheme. Available online at: http:// www.londonmet.ac.uk/depts/bssm/current-students/peer_support.cfm.

McKenzie, A., Bourne, D., Evans, S., Brown, M., Shiel, C., Bunney, A., Collins, G., Wade, R., Parker, J. and Annette, J. (2003) *Global Perspectives in Higher Education*, London: DEA. Available online at: http://www.dea.org.uk/downloads/p_gp-in-he.pdf (accessed July 2006).

MacKinnon, D. and Manathunga, C. (2003) 'Going global with assessment: what to do when the dominant culture's literacy drives assessment', *Higher Education Research and Development*, 22(2), pp. 131–44.

McNamara, D. and Harris, R. (eds) (1997) *Overseas Students in Higher Education: Issues in Teaching and Learning*, London: Routledge.

McTaggart, R. (2003) 'Internationalisation of the curriculum', James Cook University. Available online at: http://www.jcu.edu.au/office/tld/teachingsupport/documents/ International_CurriculumAB.pdf#search=%22mctaggart%20%22 internationalisation%20of%20the%20curriculum%22%22 (accessed September 2006).

Makepeace, E. and Baxter, A. (1990) 'Overseas students and examination of failure: a national study', *Journal of International Education*, 1(1), pp. 36–48.

Manathunga, C. and MacKinnon, D. (2001) 'Socially and culturally responsive assessment: preparing students for the new economy', in F. Beven, C. Kanes and D. Roebuck (eds), *Knowledge Demands for the Economy*, Proceedings of the 9th Annual International Conference on Post-Compulsory Education and Training, pp. 32–9, Brisbane: Australian Academic Press.

Markham, I. (2007) *Do Morals Matter? A Guide to Contemporary Religious Ethics*, Oxford: Blackwell.

Martin, K. (2000) 'Internationalisation: what does it mean for the curriculum?' Available online at: http://www.csd.uwa.edu.au/newsletter/issue0500.

Martin, S. and Jucker, R. (2005) 'Educating earth literate leaders', *Journal of Geography in Higher Education*, 29(1), March, pp. 19–29.

Marton, F., Dall'Alba, G. and Tse, K. L. (1993) 'The paradox of the Chinese learner', Occasional Paper 93/1, Educational Research and Development Unit, Royal Melbourne Institute of Technology, Victoria.

Marton, F., Dall'Alba, G. and Tang, C. (1997) 'Discontinuities and continuities in the experience of learning: an interview study of high school students in Hong Kong', *Learning and Instruction*, 7(1), pp. 21–48.

Marton, F., Wen, Q. and Won, K. C. (2005) 'Read a hundred times and meaning will appear: changes in Chinese university students' views of the temporal structure of learning', *Higher Education*, 49, pp. 291–318.

Mazzarol, T. and Soutar, G. N. (1999) 'Sustainable competitive advantage for educational institutions: a suggested model', *International Journal of Education Management*, 13(6), pp. 287–300.

Meadows, D. (1999) 'Indicators and information systems for sustainable development', in D. Sattherthwaite, *The Earthscan Reader in Sustainable Cities*, London: Earthscan.

Mezirow, J. (1991) *Transformative Dimensions of Adult Learning*, San Francisco, CA: Jossey-Bass.

Mezirow, J. (1997) 'Transformative learning: theory to practice', in P. Cranton (ed.), *New Directions in Adult and Continuing Education*, No. 74: *Transformative Learning in Action: Insights from Practice*, San Francisco, CA: Jossey-Bass.

Mezirow, J. (2000) *Learning as Transformation: Critical Perspectives on a Theory in Progress*, San Francisco, CA: Jossey-Bass.

Michigan Journal of Community Service Learning. Available online at: http://www.umich.edu/~mjcsl/.

Michigan State University (n.d.) 'Recommendations of the Boldness by Design Internationalization Taskforce'. Available online at: http://strategicpositioning. msu.edu/documents/BbdImperative3_000.pdf#search=%22 internationalization%20student%20integration%20university%2   (accessed September 2006).

Middlesex University volunteering awards. Available online at: http://www.mdx. ac.uk/24–72/volunteering/awards.htm.

Mora, J. G. (2001) 'Lifelong learning policies in Spanish universities', *European Journal of Education*, 36(3), pp. 317–27.

Mora, J. G., García-Montalvo, J. and García-Aracil, A. (2000) 'Higher education and graduate employment in Spain', *European Journal of Education*, 35(2), pp. 229–37.

Morrison, J., Merrick, B., Higgs, S. and Le Metais, J. (2005) 'Researching the performance of international students in the UK', *Studies in Higher Education*, 30(3), pp. 327–37.

Mullins, G., Quintrell, N. and Hancock, L. (1995) 'The experience of international students at three Australian universities', *Higher Education Research and Development*, 14(2), pp. 201–31.

Murphy, D. and Mathew, D., 'Nike and global labour practices: a case study prepared for the New Academy of Business Innovation Network for Socially Responsible

Business'. Available online at: http://www.new-academy.ac.uk/publications/keypublications /documents/nikereport.pdf.

Murray, A. and Wanlin, A. (2005) *The Lisbon Scorecard V: Can Europe Compete?*, London: CER.

National Service Learning Clearing House. Available online at: http://www.servicelearning.org/.

NCIHE (National Committee of Inquiry into Higher Education) (1997) *Higher Education in the Learning Society* (the Dearing Report), London: HMSO. Also available online at: http://www.leeds.ac.uk/educol/ncihe/ (accessed November 2006).

Newman, J. H. (1852) *The Idea of a University*. Available online at: http://www.newmanreader.org/works/idea/index.html (accessed November 2006).

Nilsson, B. (2000) 'Internationalising the curriculum', in P. Crowther, M. Joris, M. Otten, B. Nilsson, H. Teekens and B. Wächter, *Internationalisation at Home: A Position Paper*, European Association for International Education. Available online at: http://www.nuffic.nl/pdf/netwerk/IAH-Booklet.pdf.

Nilsson, B. (2003) 'Internationalisation at home from a Swedish perspective: the case of Malmö', *Journal of Studies in International Education*, 7(1), pp. 27–40.

Nunan, D. (1999) *Second Language Teaching and Learning*, Boston, MA: Heinle and Heinle.

Nunan, D. (2000) *Language Teaching Methodology*, Harlow: Pearson Education.

On, L. W. (1996) 'The cultural context for Chinese learners: conceptions of learning in the Confucian tradition', in D. A. Watkins and J. Biggs (eds), *The Chinese Learner: Cultural, Psychological and Contextual Influences*, pp. 29–41, Hong Kong: Comparative Education Research Centre.

O'Neill, O. (2002) *A Question of Trust: The BBC Reith Lectures*, Cambridge: Cambridge University Press.

Otten, M. (2003) 'Intercultural learning and diversity in higher education', *Journal of Studies in International Education*, 7(1), pp. 12–26.

Ottewill, R. and MacFarlane, B. (2003) 'Pedagogic challenges facing business and management educators', *International Journal of Management Education*, 3(3), pp. 33–41.

Oxfam (2000) *A Curriculum for Global Citizenship*, Oxford: Oxfam.

Oxford, R. L. (1990) *Language Learning Strategies: What Every Teacher Should Know*, New York: Newbury House Publishers.

Paige, M. (ed.) (1993) *Education for the Intercultural Experience*, Yarmouth, MA: Intercultural Press.

Paige, M. (2003) 'The American case: the University of Minnesota', *Journal of Studies in International Education*, 7(1), pp. 52–63, Association for Studies in International Education.

Parkin, S., Johnston, A., Buckland, H., Brookes, F. and White, E. (2004) 'Learning and skills for sustainable development: developing a sustainability literate society'. Available online at: http://www.forumforthefuture.org.uk/docs/publications/256/curriculum.pdf (accessed 25 October 2006).

Pearson, C. A. L. and Beasley, C. J. (2000) 'An evaluation of an integrative framework of student characteristics and learning approaches'. Available online at: www.qut.edu.au/daa/asdu/fye/abtracts/PearsonandBeasleyAbstract.htm.

Perkins, D. F. and Miller, M. (n.d.) 'Why community service and service-learning?

Providing rationale and research'. Previously available online at: http://www.lions-quest.org/content/Resources/ServiceLearningArticles/slarticle2.htm.

Pratt, D. D. (1992) 'Conceptions of teaching', *Adult Quarterly*, 42, pp. 203–20.

Pratt, D. D., Kelly, M. and Wong, W. S. S. (1999) 'Chinese conceptions of "effective teaching" in Hong Kong: towards culturally sensitive evaluation of teaching', *International Journal of Lifelong Education*, 18(4), pp. 241–58.

Pritchard, R. M. O. and Skinner, B. (2002) 'Cross-cultural partnerships between home and international students', *Journal of Studies in International Education*, 6, pp. 323–52.

Purdue University, 'Index of courses in service learning'. Available online at: http://www.krannert.purdue.edu/centers/citizen%5Fed/Survey/course%20index.html.

Quality Assurance Agency (n.d.) 'Guidelines for HE progress files'. Available online at: http://www.qaa.ac.uk/academicinfrastructure/progressFiles/guidelines/progfile2001.asp#pdp.

Quintrell, N. and Westwood, M. (1994) 'The influence of a peer-pairing program on international students' first year experience and use of student services', *Higher Education Research and Development*, 13(1), pp. 49–57.

Race, P. (2006) 'Issues, challenges and reflections', Chapter 7 in *The Lecturer's Toolkit*, 3rd edn, London: Routledge.

Ramsay, S., Barker, M. and Jones, E. (1999) 'Academic adjustment and learning processes: a comparison of international and local students in first year study at university', *Higher Education Research and Development*, 18(1), pp. 129–44.

Rao, P. K. (2000) *Sustainable Development: Economics and Policy*, Oxford: Blackwell.

Rizvi, F. (2000) 'Internationalisation of curriculum', Royal Melbourne Institute of Technology. Available online at: http://www.pvci.rmit.edu.au/ioc/back/icpfr.pdf#search=%22rizvi%20%22internationalisation%20of%20curriculum%22%22 (accessed September 2006).

Rizvi, F. (2001) 'Internationalisation of curriculum', RMIT University, Melbourne (mimeo).

Robertson, M., Line, M., Jones, S. and Thomas, S. (2000) 'International students, environments and perceptions: a case study using the Delphi technique', *Higher Education Research and Development*, 19(1), pp. 89–102.

Robinson, S. and Katulushi, C. (eds) (2005) *Values in Higher Education*, Glamorgan: Aureus.

Russell, I. M. (2005) *A National Framework for Youth Action and Engagement: Executive Summary to the Russell Commission*, London: HMSO. Available online at: www.russellcommission.org.

Ryan, J. (2000) *A Guide to Teaching International Students*, p. 43, Oxford: Oxford Centre for Staff and Learning Development.

Ryan, J. and Hellmundt, S. (2003) 'Excellence through diversity: internationalisation of curriculum and pedagogy', Conference proceedings of the 17th IDP Australian International Education Conference: Managing Growth and Diversity, Melbourne.

Ryan, J. and Carroll, J. (2005) 'Canaries in the coalmine: international students in Western universities', in J. Carroll and J. Ryan (eds), *Teaching International Students*, pp. 3–10, London: Routledge.

Ryan, J. and Louie, K. (2005) 'Dichotomy or complexity: problematising concepts of scholarship and learning', in M. Mason (ed.), *Proceedings of the Critical Thinking and Learning Conference: Values, Concepts and Issues*, 34th Annual Conference of the Philosophy of Education Society of Australia, 24–27 November, pp. 401–11, Hong Kong: Philosophy of Education Society of Australia. Available online at: http://www.pesa.org.au/html/documents/2005-papers/Paper-40__Janette_Ryan_and_ Kam_Louie.doc (accessed September 2006).

Ryan, Y. (2004) 'Teaching and learning in the global era', in R. King (2004) *The University in the Global Age: Universities in the 21st Century*, p. 167, Basingstoke: Palgrave Macmillan.

Sakurako, M. (2000) 'Addressing the mental health concerns of international students', *Journal of Counseling and Development*, 78(2), pp. 137–44.

Samuelowicz, K. (1987) 'Learning problems of overseas students: two sides of a story', *HERDSA*, 6(2), pp. 121–33.

Schon, D. A. (1991) *The Reflective Practitioner: How Professionals Think in Action*, New York: Arena.

Scott, W. and Gough, S. (2003) *Sustainable Development and Learning: Framing the Issues*, London: RoutledgeFalmer.

Sen Gupta, A. (2003) 'Changing the focus: a discussion of the dynamics of the intercultural experience', in G. Alred, M. Byram and M. Fleming, *Intercultural Experience and Education*, Clevedon: Multilingual Matters.

Shah, S., Pell, K. and Brooke, P. (2004) 'Beyond first destinations: graduate employ-ability survey', *Active Learning in Higher Education*, 5(1), pp. 9–26.

Spencer Stuart (2004) 'Succeeding in China: best practices in overcoming the war for talent'. Available online at: http://content.spencerstuart.com/sswebsite/pdf/lib/ Succeeding_in_China.pdf.

Sterling, S. (2001) *Sustainable Education: Re-visioning Learning and Change*, Schumacher Briefing No. 6, Dartington: Schumacher Society/Green Books.

Sterling, S. (2004) 'Higher education, sustainabilty and the role of systemic learning', in P. B. Corcoran and E. J. Wals (eds), *Higher Education and the Challenge of Sustainability*, Amsterdam: Kluwer.

Stern, H. H. (1975) 'What can we learn from the good language learner?', *Canadian Modern Language Review*, 31, pp. 304–18.

Sunderland, N., Muirhead, B., Parsons, R. and Holtom, D. (2004) 'The Australian Consortium on Higher Education, Community Engagement and Social Responsi-bility: foundation paper'. Available online at: http://eprint.uq.edu.au/archive/ 00001255/01/foundation%20paper.pdf.

Survey Monkey. Available online at: http://www.surveymonkey.com/ (accessed October 2006).

Tang, C. and Biggs, J. B. (1996) 'How Hong Kong students cope with assessment', in D. Watkins and J. Biggs (eds), *The Chinese Learner*, pp. 159–82, Hong Kong: Comparative Education Research Centre.

Taylor, J. (2004) 'Toward a strategy for internationalisation: lessons and practice from four universities', *Journal of Studies in International Education*, 8(2), pp. 149–71, Association for Studies in International Education.

Teichler, U. (1994) 'Research on academic mobility and international cooperation in higher education: an agenda for the future', in P. Blumental, C. Goodwin, A. Smith and U. Teichler (eds), *Academic Mobility in a Changing World: Regional and Global Trends*, pp. 41–67, London: Jessica Kingsley Publishers.

Teichler, U. (1996) *The British Involvement into European Higher Education Programmes*, London: Society for Research in Higher Education.

Thom, V. (2000) 'Promoting intercultural learning and social inclusion for international students', in B. Hudson and M. J. Todd (eds), *Internationalising the Curriculum in Higher Education: Reflecting on Practice*, pp. 50–7, Sheffield: Sheffield Hallam University Press.

Tomlinson, B. (ed.) (1998) *Materials Development for Language Teaching*, Cambridge: Cambridge University Press.

Tonkin, H. (ed.) (2004) *Service-Learning across Cultures: Promise and Achievement*, New York: International Partnership for Service-Learning and Leadership.

Tonkin, H. and Edwards, J. (1981) *The World in the Curriculum: Curricular Strategies for the Twenty-first Century*, New Rochelle, NY: Council on Learning.

Truscot, B. (1951) *The Red Brick University*, 2nd edn, Harmondsworth: Penguin.

UKCOSA (2004) *International Students in UK Universities and Colleges: Broadening Horizons*, Report of the UKCOSA survey, London: UKCOSA, The Council for International Education.

University of Bath buddy scheme. Available online at: http://www.bath.ac.uk/international/pre-arrival/mentor/index.html.

University of Canberra buddy scheme. Available online at: http://www.canberra.edu.au/int-future-students/support-services/host-program.

University of Denver Center for Community Engagement and Service Learning. Available online at: http://www.du.edu/engage/index.htm.

University of Denver International Service Learning. Available online at: http://www.du.edu/intl/isl/.

University of Exeter buddy scheme. Available online at: http://www.offices.ex.ac.uk/ises/welcome_week_Sem2_2005_buddy.shtml.

University of London Birkbeck College volunteering certificate. Available online at: http://www.bbk.ac.uk/study/ce/subjects/volunteering/volunteercd.

University of Nottingham Students' Union Student Community Action. Available online at: http://www.students-union.nottingham.ac.uk/activities/activities_sca.php.

University of Saskatchewan (2003), *Globalism and the University of Saskatchewan: The Foundational Document for International Activities at the University of Saskatchewan*. Available online at: http://www.usask.ca/research/files/details.php?id=107.

University of Wisconsin, Community University Partnership. Available online at: http://www.uwplatt.edu/cup/.

Volet, S. and Renshaw, P. (1996) 'Chinese students at an Australian university: adaptability and continuity', in D. A. Watkins and J. Biggs (eds), *The Chinese Learner*, pp. 205–20, Hong Kong: University of Hong Kong Comparative Education Research Centre.

Volet, S. E. and Ang, G. (1998) 'Culturally mixed groups on international campuses: an opportunity for inter-cultural learning', *Higher Education Research and Development*, 17(1), pp. 5–23.

Vygotsky, L. S. (1962) *Thought and Language*, Cambridge, MA: MIT Press.

Vygotsky, L. S. (1978) *Mind in Society*, Cambridge, MA: Harvard University Press.

Watkins, D. and Biggs, J. (2001) *Teaching the Chinese Learner: Psychological and Pedagogical Perspectives*, Hong Kong: Comparative Education Research Centre.

Watson, D. I. (1999) ' "Loss of face" in Australian classrooms', *Teaching in Higher Education*, 4(3), pp. 355–62.

Watson, D. (2003) 'Universities and civic engagement: a critique and a prospectus', Keynote address for the 2nd biennial 'Inside-out' conference on the civic role of universities, Charting Uncertainty: Capital, Community and Citizenship. Available online at: http://www.brighton.ac.uk/cupp/word%20files/engage_dw.doc.

WCED (1987) *Our Common Future* (the Brundtland Report), Oxford: Oxford University Press.

Webb, G (2005) 'Internationalisation of curriculum: an institutional approach', in J. Carroll and J. Ryan, *Teaching International Students: Improving Learning for All*, London: Routledge.

Wende, M. C. van der (2000) 'Internationalising the curriculum: new perspectives and challenges', in B. Hudson and M. J. Todd (eds), *Internationalising the Curriculum in Higher Education: Reflecting on Practice*, pp. 25–38, Sheffield: Sheffield Hallam University Press.

Wende, M. van der and Middlehurst, R. (2003) *Cross-Border Post-Secondary Education in Europe*, Paris: OECD/CERI. Available online at: http://www.flyspesialisten.no/vfs_trd/ufd/3-OECD-Europe.pdf.

Wertsch, J. V. (1985) *Culture, Communication, and Cognition: Vygotskian Perspectives*, Cambridge: Cambridge University Press.

Whalley, T., Langley, L., Villarreal, L. and College, D. (1997) *Best Practice Guidelines for Internationalizing the Curriculum*, British Columbia: Ministry of Education, Skills and Training and Centre for Curriculum, Transfer and Technology. Available online at: http://www.jcu.edu.au/office/tld/teachingsupport/documents/Whalley-Best-Practice.pdf (accessed July 2006).

Wit, H. de (1995) *Strategies for Internationalisation of Higher Education: A Comparative Study of Australia, Canada, Europe and the United States of America*, Amsterdam: EAIE.

Wright, S. and Lander, D. (2003) 'Collaborative group interactions of students from two ethnic backgrounds', *Higher Education Research and Development*, 22(3), pp. 237–52.

Wu, S. (2002) 'Filling the pot or lighting the fire? Cultural variations in conceptions of pedagogy', *Teaching in Higher Education*, 7(4), pp. 387–95.

Yanhong Li, R. and Kaye, M. (1998) 'Understanding overseas students' concerns and problems', *Journal of Higher Education Policy and Management*, 20(1), pp. 41–50.

Yorke, M. and Knight, P. (2004a) *Embedding Employability in the Curriculum*, York: Learning and Teaching Support Network.

Yorke, M. and Knight, P. (2004b) *Employability: Judging and Communicating Achievements*, York: Learning and Teaching Support Network.

Index